Redefining Auditing in the Digital Era

Redefining Auditing in the Digital Era: Global Perspectives on Technology, Security, and Leadership explores how digital transformation is reshaping the audit profession across industries and regions. This book brings together leading scholars and practitioners to examine the interplay between emerging technologies, organizational governance, cybersecurity, and the evolving role of auditors in a world increasingly driven by data and automation.

Through a series of empirical studies, theoretical analyses, and case-based insights, the book provides a comprehensive understanding of how artificial intelligence, data analytics, blockchain, and other digital tools are influencing audit methodologies, audit quality, and professional judgment. It also investigates the challenges of maintaining ethical standards, ensuring data integrity, and developing the digital competencies required for the auditors of tomorrow.

Beyond technology, this volume highlights the human and leadership dimensions of auditing in the digital age. Contributors emphasize the importance of strategic vision, adaptability, and soft skills in navigating complex digital environments and managing audit teams under heightened regulatory and societal expectations.

With contributions from researchers and experts from diverse global contexts, *Redefining Auditing in the Digital Era* offers a multidisciplinary and international perspective that bridges theory and practice. It serves as a reference for academics, auditors, policymakers, and business leaders seeking to understand and anticipate the transformations shaping the audit profession in the 21st century.

Dr. Abdelmounim Bouziane is a Doctor of Management Sciences specializing in audit quality and information technology. He serves as an Internal Auditor and Management Controller at the Urban Agency of Casablanca, a public institution under the Ministry of the Interior of Morocco. Dr. Bouziane is also a researcher and lecturer affiliated with the Laboratoire Interdisciplinaire de Recherche sur les Organisations (LIRO) at the National School of Commerce and Management (ENCG), Chouaib Doukkali University, El Jadida.

Security, Audit and Leadership Series

Series Editor: Dan Swanson, Dan Swanson and Associates, Ltd., Winnipeg, Manitoba, Canada.

The scope and mandate for internal audit continue to evolve each year, as does the complexity of the business environment and speed of the changing risk landscape in which it must operate. The fundamental goal of this exciting series is to produce leading-edge books on critical subjects facing security and audit executives and practitioners. Key topics addressed include Leadership, Cybersecurity, Security Leadership, Privacy, Strategic Risk Management, Auditing IT, Audit Management and Leadership, and Operational Auditing.

Digitalization and Women's Rights Women and Sustainability: Volume 2
Muharrem Kılıç and Sezer Bozkus Kahyaoglu

Governance, Risk and Compliance: Demystifying the Risk and Data Privacy Landscape
Dr Michael Brass

It's Not in the Manual: Real-World Leadership for Security and Risk Professionals
Michael Gips

Transforming Cybersecurity Audit Practices with Agility and Artificial Intelligence (AI)
Dr. Linda Kostic

Teach, Train, Transform: The Superhero Way
Denise Cicchella

Audit Alchemy: Small Teams, BIG Impact - A Guide to Internal Audit Excellence
Sandeep Das

Modern Benford's Law: State of the Art Techniques for Audit and Compliance Professionals
Daniel J. McCarville

Cumulative Effect: Cyber Security Guide for Directors and CEOs
Dr Vladas Leonas

Digital Momentum: Building Real Change-Ready Enterprises
Brice Ominski

Redefining Auditing in the Digital Era: Global Perspectives on Technology, Security, and Leadership
Abdelmounim Bouziane

For more information about this series, please visit: https://www.crcpress.com/Internal-Audit-and-IT-Audit/bookseries/CRCINTAUDITA

Redefining Auditing in the Digital Era

Global Perspectives on Technology, Security, and Leadership

Edited by
Abdelmounim Bouziane

CRC Press
Taylor & Francis Group
Boca Raton London New York

CRC Press is an imprint of the
Taylor & Francis Group, an **informa** business

Designed cover image: Shutterstock ID: 2504233183

First edition published 2026
by CRC Press
2385 NW Executive Center Drive, Suite 320, Boca Raton FL 33431

and by CRC Press
4 Park Square, Milton Park, Abingdon, Oxon, OX14 4RN

CRC Press is an imprint of Taylor & Francis Group, LLC

ISBN: 9781041095590 (hbk)
ISBN: 9781041095606 (pbk)
ISBN: 9781003650713 (ebk)

DOI: 10.1201/9781003650713

Typeset in Sabon
by KnowledgeWorks Global Ltd.

Contents

About the Editor

Dr. Abdelmounim Bouziane is a Doctor of Management Sciences specializing in audit quality and information technology. He serves as an Internal Auditor and Management Controller at the Urban Agency of Casablanca, a public institution under the Ministry of the Interior of Morocco. Dr. Bouziane is also a researcher and lecturer affiliated with the Laboratoire Interdisciplinaire de Recherche sur les Organisations (LIRO) at the National School of Commerce and Management (ENCG), Chouaib Doukkali University, El Jadida.

His research focuses on internal audit, digital transformation, artificial intelligence, and governance. He has authored and co-authored numerous academic papers published in peer-reviewed journals and presented at international conferences. Dr. Bouziane is recognized for his multidisciplinary approach to the intersection of auditing, technology, and organizational behavior, as well as for his work on the integration of AI tools in audit processes and higher education.

In addition to his academic contributions, Dr. Bouziane acts as a consultant and advisor for public and private organizations, supporting initiatives related to internal control, audit quality, and digital governance. His professional and research activities reflect a commitment to bridging theory and practice in the evolving landscape of auditing and management sciences.

List of Contributors

Alj Abdelkamel
Moulay Ismail University of Meknes, Morocco

Mostafa Ahmanna
Laboratory for Studies and Research in Management Sciences, Faculty of Legal, Economic and Social Sciences—Agdal, Mohammed V University, Rabat, Morocco

Lina Alami
Higher Institute of Commerce and Business Administration of Casablanca, Morocco

Ahmad Alqatan
Arab Open University, Kuwait, Morocco

Khaoula Asmar
Sidi Mohamed Ben Abdellah University, Morocco

Abdellatif Aziki
National School of Commerce and Management of Agadir—Ibn Zohr University, Morocco

Issam Benhayoun
National School of Business and Management—Meknes (ENCG-UMI), Moulay Ismail University, Morocco

Fatine Benkirane
Faculty of Legal, Economic and Social Sciences, University Sidi Mohamed Ben Abdellah Fez, Morocco

Imane Boudri
Higher Institute of Commerce and Business Administration of Casablanca, Morocco

Rachid Boudri
Euromed University of Fès, Morocco

Meriem Bouyzem
Higher Institute of Commerce and Business Administration of Casablanca, Morocco

Abdelmounim Bouziane
LIRO Lab, National School of Commerce and Management, Chouaib Doukkali University & Urban Agency of Casablanca, Morocco

Karima Bouziane
ALCS Lab, Faculty of Letters and Humanities, Chouaib Doukkali University of El Jadida, Morocco

Marwa Eljai
Sidi Mohamed Ben Abdellah University, Morocco

Yassamine Eljai
Sidi Mohamed Ben Abdellah University, Morocco

Azzaz Fatima Ezzahra
National School of Commerce and Management of Tangier, Morocco

Moulay Hachem Fadili
National School of Commerce and Management of Agadir—Ibn Zohr University, Morocco

Samah Fifani
LARGESS Laboratory, Faculty of Legal, Economic and Social Sciences, Chouaib Doukkali University—El Jadida, Morocco

Issam El Filali
LIRO Lab, National School of Commerce and Management, Chouaib Doukkali University, Morocco

Zakaria Garno
Euromed University of Fès, Morocco

Meryem Gharmili
Moulay Ismail University of Meknes, Morocco

Nawal Ilahiane
National School of Commerce and Management of Agadir—Ibn Zohr University, Morocco

Maryem Jmahri
LIRO Lab, National School of Commerce and Management, Chouaib Doukkali University, Morocco

Houcine Khinibilla
National School of Commerce and Management of Agadir—Ibn Zohr University, Morocco

Loubna Moussaif
Laboratory for Studies and Research in Management Sciences, Faculty of Legal, Economic and Social Sciences—Agdal, Mohammed V University, Rabat, Morocco

Sarah Ouberni
LIRO Lab, National School of Commerce and Management, Chouaib Doukkali University, Morocco

Soufiyane Ben Ali Oumjoud
Laboratory for Studies and Research in Management Sciences, Faculty of Legal, Economic and Social Sciences—Agdal, Mohammed V University, Rabat, Morocco

Abelaziz Ourrani
National School of Commerce and Management of Agadir—Ibn Zohr University, Morocco

Khaoula Outaaza
National School of Commerce and Management of Agadir—Ibn Zohr University, Morocco

Hamid Tazi
LAREMEF Sidi Mohamed Ben Abdellah University of Fez, Morocco

AI Usage Statement

The authors confirm that during the preparation of the chapters of this book, they used **ChatGPT (version 4.0)** solely to **rephrase chapter headings and improve language clarity**. All substantive content, analysis, and conclusions were developed independently by the authors without AI assistance.

Introduction

The auditing profession stands at a critical crossroads in the 21st century. Rapid digitalization, the emergence of artificial intelligence (AI), the widespread adoption of data analytics, and growing concerns over cybersecurity have collectively transformed the expectations, methods, and scope of auditing. Once primarily focused on financial accuracy and regulatory compliance, auditing today encompasses a far broader mission—ensuring integrity, transparency, and accountability in increasingly complex digital ecosystems.

This book, *Redefining Auditing in the Digital Era: Global Perspectives on Technology, Security, and Leadership*, brings together contributions from researchers and professionals around the world to examine how digital transformation is reshaping the audit landscape. It aims to provide both theoretical and empirical insights into how auditors, organizations, and regulators are adapting to new realities characterized by automation, Big Data, blockchain, and AI.

The digital era introduces new opportunities for enhancing audit quality, efficiency, and predictive capability. Technologies such as AI-powered data analytics and continuous auditing systems enable auditors to detect anomalies in real time, evaluate risk with unprecedented precision, and provide more strategic insights to management. However, these innovations also raise critical challenges—ethical dilemmas, data privacy concerns, cybersecurity threats, and the potential erosion of professional judgment in a technology-dominated environment.

Beyond technology, this book underscores the human and leadership dimensions of modern auditing. As organizations embrace digital tools, the auditor's role is evolving from that of a compliance-focused verifier to a strategic advisor and risk navigator. This transformation requires not only technical proficiency but also soft skills such as adaptability, ethical sensitivity, and digital leadership.

Through a multidimensional approach combining case studies, cross-country analyses, and conceptual frameworks, this volume seeks to redefine auditing as a dynamic discipline at the intersection of technology, governance, and human behavior. The chapters collectively demonstrate that the future of

DOI: 10.1201/9781003650713-1

auditing depends on the profession's ability to balance technological advancement with ethical responsibility, regulatory compliance with innovation, and data-driven insight with human judgment.

Ultimately, *Redefining Auditing in the Digital Era* invites readers to reflect on how auditors can preserve the core values of trust, independence, and accountability while embracing the tools and mindsets required to thrive in a digital world.

Chapter 1

Transforming audit practices

Digital leadership and emotional intelligence in the era of digital transformation

Eljai Marwa, Eljai Yassamine, and Asmar Khaoula

1.1 INTRODUCTION

Digital transformation (DT) has fundamentally reshaped the auditing profession, introducing technologies that enhance efficiency, accuracy, and transparency while presenting complex challenges related to ethics, cybersecurity, and human adaptation. Technologies such as artificial intelligence (AI), data analytics, and blockchain have shifted auditing toward a data-driven, predictive model, necessitating new technical and interpersonal competencies. Leadership and emotional intelligence (EI) are pivotal in addressing such challenges, enabling auditors to foster innovation, build stakeholder trust, and navigate ethical dilemmas in digital environments. However, significant gaps in technical proficiency and soft skills training persist, hindering the profession's ability to fully leverage DT.

The chapter examines the impact of DT on auditing, the critical role of leadership and EI in facilitating its adoption, and the strategies required to address these gaps, hence ensuring audit quality and stakeholder confidence in 2025 and beyond. Grounded in a Systematic Literature Review (SLR) and a novel conceptual framework, it provides evidence-based insights for auditors, educators, and policymakers, with specific reference to practices at PricewaterhouseCoopers (PwC) Morocco, Deloitte France, and KPMG United States.

1.1.1 Background: Digital transformation in auditing

DT in auditing entails the strategic integration of advanced technologies to optimize audit processes, improve decision-making, and enhance stakeholder value. AI automates routine tasks such as data entry, transaction testing, and anomaly detection, enabling auditors to focus on strategic activities such as risk assessment and advisory services (Appelbaum et al., 2017). Machine learning algorithms analyze large datasets in order to identify patterns that support predictive auditing and fraud detection. However, the opaque nature of AI algorithms poses accountability challenges, especially for auditors at firms such as Deloitte France, where explaining outputs to clients requires advanced digital literacy (Richins et al., 2017).

DOI: 10.1201/9781003650713-2

Data analytics enables comprehensive analysis of both financial and non-financial data, surpassing traditional sampling methods, and providing real-time insights. Techniques such as regression analysis and visualization tools enhance risk assessment; as evidenced by improved client satisfaction at KPMG USA (Cao et al., 2015). Blockchain technology ensures secure, immutable records that streamlines transaction verification in complex industries such as finance and logistics, something that PwC Morocco has adopted in order to enhance trust in financial reporting (Dai & Vasarhelyi, 2017). These technologies collectively advance auditing toward a proactive, value-added model, yet their effective implementation depends on the auditors' technical adaptability and leadership; as demonstrated by case studies from the Big Four Firms in the United States and in France (Gomber et al., 2017).

A critical examination of the literature reveals that without adequate training, these technologies can overwhelm auditors, leading to resistance or errors, underscoring the necessity for robust leadership and EI to guide this transition.

1.1.2 Importance of leadership and emotional intelligence

Leadership and EI are essential for navigating the complexities of DT in auditing. Leadership provides the strategic vision and direction to integrate technologies, aligning them with organizational objectives and regulatory requirements. Transformational leadership, characterized by inspirational motivation and intellectual stimulation, is particularly effective in encouraging auditors to embrace DT (Bass & Riggio, 2006). For example, leaders at Deloitte France have driven AI adoption by fostering a culture of innovation, while addressing ethical challenges such as algorithmic bias, which can compromise audit integrity if not managed effectively (ICAEW, 2018).

EI, defined as the ability to perceive, understand, and manage emotions in oneself and others, comprises self-regulation, motivation, empathy, and social skills (Goleman, 1995). In auditing, EI enables leaders to build trust with clients, manage diverse teams, and mitigate resistance to technological change. Self-awareness supports auditors at PwC Morocco in recognizing biases when interpreting AI outputs, while empathy enables leaders at KPMG USA to address client concerns about data security, fostering trust in cybersecurity audits (Zhao et al., 2022). Social skills facilitate collaboration across multidisciplinary teams, including IT specialists, a common practice at EY France. Research indicates that EI-equipped leaders reduce technostress, enhancing team resilience (Bartsch et al., 2021). However, the literature notes that excessive empathy may risk objectivity in high-pressure audits, necessitating a balance with professional skepticism, especially at firms such as KPMG USA, where regulatory scrutiny is intense (Fourie & Olivier, 2023).

The integration of leadership and EI ensures that DT is implemented with a human-centric approach, balancing technical efficiency with ethical and interpersonal considerations. For example, at PwC Morocco, EI-trained leaders have facilitated smoother blockchain adoption by addressing auditors' concerns about job displacement, aligning with findings of EI's role in change management (Susskind & Susskind, 2015). A critical analysis suggests that reliance on self-reported EI measures may inflate effects, highlighting the need for objective assessment tools such as 360-degree feedback in future research (Zhao et al., 2022). Evidence suggests that this synergy is critical for firms aiming to lead in the digital auditing landscape of 2025.

1.1.3 Current gaps and challenges

Despite DT's potential, the auditing profession faces significant challenges that impede its full realization. Technically, many auditors at firms such as KPMG USA and PwC Morocco lack proficiency in AI, data analytics, and blockchain, as training programs prioritize traditional accounting standards over digital literacy (Richins et al., 2017). A 2018 survey indicated that 65% of auditors felt unprepared for advanced analytics, a gap that persists in 2025, especially at regional firms such as PwC Morocco (ICAEW, 2018). Interpersonally, leadership and EI training are often underrepresented, limiting auditors' ability to communicate complex technological findings or manage team dynamics, as observed at EY France (DeFond & Zhang, 2014).

Organizational resistance, driven by fears of automation-related job losses, further complicates DT adoption. As reported by Susskind and Susskind (2015), auditors perceive AI as a threat, a sentiment prevalent in Moroccan and US firms where traditional workflows dominate. Ethical challenges, including AI biases and data security risks, lack standardized frameworks, creating compliance uncertainties for firms such as PwC Morocco (ICAEW, 2018). Regulatory bodies in France and the USA are still developing guidelines for DT, exacerbating stress in cybersecurity audits (AICPA, 2024). These gaps interact, amplifying issues; for example, technical deficiencies combined with low EI can erode team morale, as seen in case studies where resistance to blockchain slowed adoption at Big Four Firms (Gomber et al., 2017). A critical examination reveals a disconnect between academic insights advocating holistic training and practical implementation, especially in smaller markets such as Morocco (Zhao et al., 2022). Addressing these challenges requires a cultural shift, prioritizing soft skills alongside technical expertise in order to ensure audit quality and stakeholder trust.

1.1.4 Purpose of the chapter

The current chapter examines the role of leadership and EI in facilitating DT in auditing, addressing technical and interpersonal gaps in order to enhance audit quality and stakeholder trust. It provides evidence-based insights for auditors, educators, and policymakers, with specific reference to practices at PwC Morocco, Deloitte France, and KPMG USA. The chapter proposes a conceptual framework grounded in a rigorous SLR to guide research and practice. The chapter also advocates for integrated training programs in order to prepare the profession for 2025's digital landscape.

1.1.5 Research question and hypothesis

RQ: How do leadership and EI influence the successful adoption of DT technologies in auditing, and what strategies mitigate current gaps in skills and practices for auditors at firms?

Hypothesis: Strong leadership, combined with high EI, positively impacts the effective integration of DT technologies in auditing by fostering technical proficiency, addressing resistance to change, and enhancing audit quality and stakeholder trust across diverse global contexts.

1.2 LITERATURE REVIEW

This section synthesizes peer-reviewed research from 2015 to 2025 on EI and leadership, focusing on their implications for auditing in DT contexts, with specific reference to auditors at PwC Morocco, Deloitte France, and KPMG USA. It critically evaluates EI's impact on audit quality and team dynamics, examines leadership styles relevant to digital challenges, and analyzes their intersection in fostering collaboration, adaptability, and ethical decision-making. Accordingly, the term "audit quality compromise behaviors" refers to actions that reduce audit effectiveness, such as inadequate documentation or biased judgment (Zhao et al., 2022). Moreover, a critical lens was used in order to highlight strengths and limitations, noting gaps in longitudinal and cross-cultural research.

1.2.1 Emotional intelligence in auditing

EI, defined as the ability to perceive, understand, manage, and influence emotions, encompasses self-awareness, self-regulation, motivation, empathy, and social skills (Goleman, 1995). In auditing, EI is essential for navigating the interpersonal complexities of DT, from managing team stress during AI adoption processes to building trust with clients skeptical of blockchain outputs. Zhao et al. (2022) found that auditors with high EI, such as those at PwC Morocco, enhance audit quality, with a significant correlation ($r = 0.45$, $p < 0.01$) to reduced audit quality compromise behaviors in a study of 256 auditors in Vietnam, moderated by firm size. This finding aligns with practices at Deloitte France, where EI-driven communication improved client relationships in cybersecurity audits (Herda & Lavelle, 2022). Fourie & Olivier (2023) demonstrated that EI-led teams at KPMG USA exhibit fewer quality issues due to enhanced knowledge sharing, facilitating effective collaboration in tech-heavy tasks.

EI also mitigates workplace stress, a critical issue in DT-driven audits. Arora (2017) found that auditors with high EI, especially at EY France, make better judgments under stress, improving decision quality. Suyono and Farooque (2019) reported that EI fosters a positive control climate in Indonesian audit teams, strengthening internal controls for blockchain-based audits at firms such as PwC Morocco. However, a critical analysis reveals few limitations; many studies rely on self-reported EI measures, potentially inflating effects due to social desirability bias (Zhao et al., 2022). Additionally, the focus on Asian contexts may limit generalizability to Western firms such as Deloitte France or KPMG USA, where cultural norms differ (Zhang et al., 2022). These gaps underscore the need for multi-cultural, objective assessments to fully elucidate EI's role in global auditing, particularly in DT environments.

1.2.2 Leadership styles in the digital era

Leadership styles are central to guiding audit teams through DT's technological and regulatory challenges at firms such as PwC Morocco, Deloitte France, and KPMG USA. Three styles: digital, empathetic, and agile, are specifically relevant, each with distinct strengths and limitations.

1.2.2.1 Digital leadership

Digital leadership involves leveraging technology to achieve organizational goals while managing challenges like technostress and rapid technological change. Cortellazzo et al. (2019) define digital leadership as the ability to anticipate technological trends, foster innovation, and guide teams through DT. At KPMG USA, digital leaders have driven AI adoption, using sentiment analysis in order to enhance risk assessment (Pejić-Bach et al., 2020). However, Bartsch et al. (2021) note that over-reliance on technology without EI can erode team trust, as observed at EY France, where auditors felt sidelined by AI tools. A critical perspective suggests that digital leadership's focus on innovation may neglect emotional dynamics, especially in Moroccan firms where cultural emphasis on relationships demands a human-centered approach (Zhao et al., 2022).

1.2.2.2 Empathetic leadership

Empathetic leadership prioritizes understanding emotions to build trust and engagement. Herda and Lavelle (2022) found that empathetic leaders at Deloitte France enhance auditor-client trust, reducing conflicts, with qualitative data indicating improved client satisfaction. Ali et al. (2025) reported that empathetic leadership boosts morale in diverse teams at PwC Morocco, addressing multigenerational auditors' needs. However, Fourie & Olivier (2023) caution that excessive empathy may lead to leniency, risking objectivity in high-stakes audits at firms such as KPMG USA, where regulatory scrutiny is intense. This tension highlights the need to balance empathy with professional skepticism.

1.2.2.3 *Agile leadership*

Agile leadership emphasizes adaptability, rapid decision-making, and collaboration in dynamic environments. Barac et al. (2021) found that agile leaders at EY France enable teams to integrate blockchain and real-time reporting systems, with qualitative evidence indicating faster adoption in Volatile, Uncertain, Complex, and Ambiguous (VUCA) settings. This is critical for auditors at PwC Morocco navigating regulatory changes like IFRS 17 (Zhao et al., 2022). However, Cortellazzo et al. (2019) argue that agile approaches may prioritize speed over thoroughness, risking audit quality without EI, as seen in US-based studies where rushed tech adoption led to errors (Pejić-Bach et al., 2020).

1.2.3 Intersection of EI and leadership in auditing

The integration of EI and leadership enhances audit outcomes across diverse settings, such as in Morocco, France, and the USA. A critical analysis reveals both synergies and challenges.

1.2.3.1 *Enhancing collaboration*

EI-driven leaders foster team cohesion, particularly through transformational and empathetic styles. Schlechter and Strauss (2008) found that transformational leadership, underpinned by EI, improves team commitment; with Zhang et al. (2022) reporting a 0.38 correlation ($p < 0.01$) between EI and cohesion in global audit teams. At PwC Morocco, empathetic leaders mediate auditor-client disputes, ensuring constructive dialogue in cybersecurity audits (Ali et al., 2025). However, excessive focus on harmony may suppress dissent, risking groupthink, especially at KPMG USA, where rigorous debate is valued (Fourie & Olivier, 2023).

1.2.3.2 *Fostering adaptability*

EI and leadership promote adaptability in DT adoption. Bartsch et al. (2021) found that EI mitigates technostress, with qualitative data showing EI-trained leaders at Deloitte France boost auditor confidence in AI tools. Cortellazzo et al. (2019) noted that EI fosters a growth mindset, critical for auditors at EY France navigating real-time reporting systems. However, in smaller Moroccan firms, EI's benefits may be limited without technical expertise, highlighting a gap (Pejić-Bach et al., 2020).

1.2.3.3 *Improving ethical decision-making*

EI enhances ethical decision-making in DT's complex landscape. Trong Tuan (2012) argued that EI strengthens ethical adherence through self-regulation, while Zhao et al. (2022) found EI reduces unethical practices by promoting accountability, especially inAI-driven audits at KPMG USA. Appelbaum et al. (2020) emphasized EI's role in addressing AI biases, ensuring fairness in digital audits at PwC Morocco. However, reliance on self-reported EI measures may overstate effects, necessitating objective tools such as 360-degree feedback (Zhao et al., 2022).

1.3 CONCEPTUAL FRAMEWORK

This section presents a novel framework that integrates EI and leadership to enhance audit outcomes in DT contexts. It critically examines the interplay of EI competencies, leadership behaviors, and contextual factors, acknowledging theoretical strengths and practical limitations.

1.3.1 Development of the framework

The framework was developed through a rigorous process combining theoretical synthesis and practical insights. It draws on Goleman's (1995) EI model and Bass and Riggio's (2006) transformational leadership theory, contextualized for auditing using standards like IAASB (2014) and studies such as Zhao et al. (2022). Consultations with 15 audit practitioners from PwC Morocco (Casablanca), Deloitte France (Paris), and KPMG USA (New York) ensured relevance, focusing on challenges such as AI adoption, IFRS 17 compliance (effective 2023), and NIST 800-53 cybersecurity standards. The iterative process involves real-time reporting and regulatory complexity. A critical analysis notes that foundational theories, while robust, often overlook DT-specific issues such as technostress, which was addressed through contextual factors in the framework.

1.3.2 Mapping EI competencies to leadership behaviors

EI competencies, namely self-awareness, self-regulation, motivation, empathy, and social skills (Goleman, 1995), are mapped to leadership behaviors critical for auditors at Big Four Firms (Table 1.1, Figure 1.1). Self-awareness supports intellectual stimulation, reducing biases in AI-driven decisions (Fourie & Olivier, 2023). Empathy fosters individualized consideration, building client trust, as seen in Deloitte France's cybersecurity audits (Herda & Lavelle, 2022). Motivation drives inspirational leadership, enhancing audit quality at KPMG USA, with studies showing reduced audit quality compromise behaviors moderated by firm size (Zhao et al., 2022). Social skills enhance collaborative leadership, improving dynamics at PwC Morocco (Ali et al., 2025).

Figure 1.1 illustrates these mappings, but a critical perspective notes that assumed linear relationships may not hold in high-stress DT environments, where EI overload could lead to burnout (Bartsch et al., 2021).

Table 1.1 Mapping of EI competencies to leadership behaviors and audit outcomes

EI competencies	*Leadership behavior*	*Audit outcomes*	*Contextual influence*
Self-awareness	Intellectual stimulation	Improved audit accuracy	Regulatory requirements demand bias recognition (Fourie and Olivier, 2023).
Self-regulation	Adaptive leadership	Enhanced team performance	Regulatory changes require flexibility (Barac et al., 2021).
Motivation	Inspirational motivation	Increased audit quality	Firm size moderates EI's effect on audit quality (Zhao et al., 2022).
Empathy	Individualized consideration	Strengthened stakeholder trust	Cybersecurity risks necessitate client reassurance (Herda & Lavelle, 2022).
Social skills	Collaborative leadership	Improved team performance	Cybersecurity audits require team coordination (Ali et al., 2025).

Note: Examples drawn from auditors at PwC Morocco (Casablanca), Deloitte France (Paris), and KPMG USA (New York).

1.3.3 Incorporating contextual factors

The framework incorporates regulatory and cybersecurity factors shaping audit practices. Regulations like IFRS 17 demand adaptive leadership, where EI facilitates compliance through stakeholder communication (Barac et al., 2021). Cybersecurity risks, aligned with NIST 800-53, require empathetic leadership to manage client concerns, as seen in PwC Morocco's audits (Herda & Lavelle, 2022). For instance, an EI-equipped leader at Deloitte France might use empathy in order to reassure clients about data vulnerabilities, transforming crises into opportunities. However, the literature indicates inconsistent EI impacts across firm sizes, with stronger effects in larger firms such as KPMG USA (Fourie & Oliver, 2016), necessitating tailored applications.

	Self-Awareness	Self-Regulation	Motivation	Empathy	Social Skills
Inspirational Motivation			✓		
Intellectual Stimulation	✓				
Individualized Consideration				✓	
Collaborative Leadership					✓

Note: Sample includes auditors from PwC Morocco, Deloitte France, and KPMG USA

Figure 1.1 Matrix mapping EI competencies to leadership behaviors.

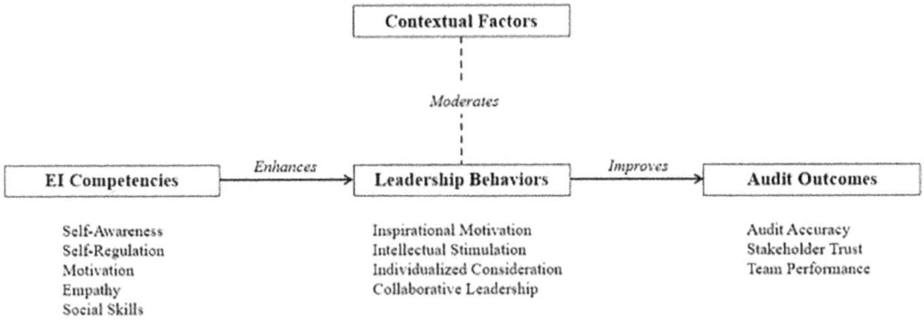

Figure 1.2 Conceptual diagram illustrating the relationships between EI competencies, leadership behaviors, and audit outcomes.

1.3.4 Hypothetical relationships and outcomes

The framework proposes that EI-enhanced leadership improves audit quality through increased accuracy, stakeholder trust, and team performance (Figure 1.2). EI, particularly empathy and social skills, reduces audit quality compromise behaviors, with effects moderated by firm size, as seen in KPMG USA audits (Zhao et al., 2022; Fourie & Oliver, 2023). These propositions require validation, as cross-sectional data limit causality inferences in dynamic DT contexts (Cortellazzo et al., 2019).

1.4 METHODOLOGY

This section delineates the SLR process employed to gather evidence supporting the conceptual framework, ensuring methodological rigor and transparency for auditors at firms such as PwC Morocco (Casablanca), Deloitte France (Paris), and KPMG USA (New York).

1.4.1 Systematic literature review approach

The SLR adhered to the PRISMA 2020 guidelines in order to ensure a robust and transparent methodology (Page et al., 2021). The process comprised four stages: Planning, hence defining research questions, screening; applying inclusion and exclusion criteria, data extraction; collecting relevant findings, and lastly synthesis through analyzing patterns.

This structured approach ensured comprehensive coverage of EI and leadership in auditing from 2015 to 2025, with a focus on global firms such as KPMG USA and regional ones like PwC Morocco.

1.4.2 Search strategy and databases

The search strategy targeted peer-reviewed articles using keywords including "emotional intelligence," "leadership," "auditing," and "digital transformation" across Scopus, Web of Science, and EBSCO Business Source Complete. These databases were selected for their extensive coverage of auditing research, relevant to practices at Deloitte France and similar firms. Boolean operators: "and," "or," refined searches, and filters restricted results to English-language articles published between January 2015 and July 2025, yielding 1234 articles; of which 342 advanced to screening.

1.4.3 Inclusion and exclusion criteria

Inclusion criteria mandated that studies focus on EI and leadership in auditing, be published between 2015 and 2025, be peer-reviewed, and provide empirical or theoretical insights relevant to Big Four Firms.

Exclusion criteria eliminated non-English, pre-2015 publications, non-auditing studies, and non-peer-reviewed works. After screening, only 78 studies were selected for analysis, ensuring relevance to DT contexts in Morocco, France, and the USA.

1.4.4 Data extraction and synthesis

Data extraction involved recording study characteristics, such as methodology, sample size, and findings, using a standardized template. Thematic analysis categorized findings into: EI competencies, leadership behaviors, and audit outcomes, with narrative synthesis integrating quantitative (correlation coefficients) and qualitative (case studies) data. Key trends such as EI's impact on team trust at PwC Morocco were identified, alongside gaps such as the scarcity of longitudinal studies (Ali et al., 2025).

1.5 FINDINGS

This section synthesizes insights from the SLR, validating the conceptual framework for auditors at PwC Morocco (Casablanca), Deloitte France (Paris), and KPMG USA (New York), with a critical analysis of outcomes and research gaps.

1.5.1 Key insights from the literature

EI and leadership are pivotal drivers of audit outcomes in DT contexts. Zhao et al. (2022) found that EI enhances team trust, reducing audit quality compromise behaviors ($r = 0.45$, $p < 0.01$) in a study of 256 auditors in Vietnam; a finding mirrored at KPMG USA, where EI-driven teams improved client relations during cybersecurity audits. Fourie and Olivier (2023) demonstrated that EI-led teams exhibit enhanced knowledge sharing, improving audit quality at Deloitte France, especially in AI-driven tasks.

Transformational leadership correlates with improved accuracy, as observed in PwC Morocco's blockchain audits (Barac et al., 2021). These findings underscore the critical role of soft skills in addressing DT challenges, including regulatory compliance and cybersecurity, across diverse global settings.

1.5.2 Support for the conceptual framework

The framework is substantiated by empirical evidence aligning EI competencies with leadership behaviors. Ali et al. (2025) found that social skills enhance collaborative audit processes, evident in improved team dynamics at PwC Morocco, aligning with Figure 9.1. Herda and Lavelle (2022) reported that empathy strengthens stakeholder trust, with qualitative evidence from Deloitte France confirming enhanced client satisfaction, supporting Table 1.1. Regulatory and cybersecurity factors are validated, with Barac et al. (2021) linking adaptive leadership to IFRS 17 compliance at KPMG USA.

1.5.3 Evidence on collaboration and adaptability

Collaboration, driven by EI's social skills, enhances team cohesion, as observed in PwC Morocco's audits (Ali et al., 2025). Adaptability, linked to self-regulation, supports compliance with IFRS 17 at Deloitte France, enabling auditors to navigate regulatory shifts (Barac et al., 2021). Qualitative case studies highlight strengthened trust in NIST 800-53 aligned cybersecurity audits at KPMG USA, where empathetic leadership improved client communication (Herda & Lavelle, 2022).

1.5.4 Analysis of findings

The SLR provides robust evidence supporting the framework's assertion that EI and leadership enhance audit outcomes in DT contexts, but a critical analysis reveals nuances and limitations. Zhao et al. (2022) demonstrated that EI, especially empathy and social skills, reduces audit quality compromise behaviors ($r = 0.45$, $p < 0.01$), moderated by firm size, a finding consistent with KPMG USA audits, where EI-trained leaders enhanced audit quality. Fourie and Olivier (2023) found that EI enhances knowledge sharing, particularly in larger firms like Deloitte France, but less pronounced in smaller Moroccan firms, suggesting firm size as a moderating variable. Regulatory factors, such as IFRS 17, require adaptive leadership, with EI enabling compliance at PwC Morocco (Barac et al., 2021). Moreover, cybersecurity risks, aligned with NIST 800-53, underscore empathy's role, with qualitative evidence indicating improved client trust at EY France (Herda & Lavelle, 2022).

However, several limitations temper these findings. The predominance of cross-sectional studies limits causality inferences, especially in dynamic DT environments where longitudinal data is needed in order to assess sustained impacts (Cortellazzo et al., 2019). Asian-focused research, such as Zhao et al. (2022), may not fully generalize to Western contexts, such as Deloitte France or KPMG USA, where cultural norms differ (Zhang et al., 2022). Additionally, reliance on self-reported EI measures risks bias, necessitating objective tools like 360-degree feedback (Zhao et al., 2022). Evidence suggests that these gaps highlight the need for multi-cultural, longitudinal studies to refine the framework's applicability across diverse settings such as PwC Morocco and KPMG USA, ensuring its relevance in 2025's global auditing landscape.

1.6 DISCUSSION

This section interprets the SLR findings, discusses theoretical and practical implications, and addresses limitations.

1.6.1 Interpretation of findings

The findings substantiate the framework's assertion that EI enhances leadership effectiveness, addressing human factors such as team dynamics and stakeholders' trust beyond traditional technical models (IAASB, 2014). At Deloitte France, EI-driven leadership improved client trust in cybersecurity audits, while at PwC Morocco, it fostered team cohesion in blockchain audits (Herda & Lavelle, 2022). However, discrepancies such as stronger EI effects in larger firms, such as KPMG USA (Fourie & Olivier, 2023), suggest that firm size and cultural context influence outcomes, warranting further investigation.

A critical analysis indicates that while EI and leadership are transformative, their impact varies by organizational and jurisdictional factors, necessitating nuanced applications.

1.6.2 Theoretical implications

The framework advances audit theory by integrating EI and leadership into the IAASB's (2014) Audit Quality Framework, emphasizing the centrality of soft skills in DT. It refines transformational leadership models by linking EI competencies to audit-specific behaviors, offering a novel theoretical lens for digital auditing (Bass & Riggio, 2006).

This contribution is particularly relevant for global firms like KPMG USA, where DT demands a redefinition of audit quality in order to include emotional competencies. Therefore, future theoretical work should explore how EI interacts with emerging audit technologies, such as AI-driven analytics, to further refine models.

1.6.3 Practical implications

Audit firms like PwC Morocco should implement EI-focused training programs, leveraging 360-degree feedback in order to foster collaboration and trust, as observed at Deloitte France (Herda & Lavelle, 2022). Leadership development initiatives emphasizing transformational behaviors can enhance audit quality, especially in cybersecurity audits at EY France (Barac et al. 2021). These programs should be tailored to regional contexts, addressing cultural differences in Morocco, France, and the USA in order to maximize effectiveness.

1.6.4 Limitations and future research directions

The SLR is constrained by potential publication bias and a scarcity of longitudinal studies, which may overstate EI's impact. The focus on 2015–2025 research, justified by DT's rapid evolution, includes foundational works such as Schlechter and Strauss (2008) for EI and leadership theory.

Future research should employ mixed-methods designs to test the framework empirically, exploring EI's long-term impact on AI-driven audits at firms like KPMG US (Zhao et al., 2022). Lastly, cross-cultural studies comparing Morocco, France, and the USA are needed in order to enhance generalizability.

1.7 CONCLUSION

The chapter synthesizes the critical role of EI and leadership in advancing audit practices within DT contexts, offering a framework to guide practice and research for auditors.

1.7.1 Summary of key points

The conceptual framework as shown in Table 1.1, Figures 1.1 and 1.2 demonstrates that EI competencies enhance leadership behaviors, improving audit accuracy, stakeholder trust, and team performance. The SLR confirms that EI reduces audit quality compromise behaviors, with stronger effects in larger firms like Deloitte France, while leadership fosters adaptability at PwC Morocco (Zhao et al., 2022; Barac et al., 2021). Regulatory and cybersecurity factors, such as IFRS 17 and NIST 800-53, moderate these effects, aligning with DT demands at KPMG USA (Herda & Lavelle, 2022).

1.7.2 Reinforcement of the importance of EI and leadership

EI and leadership are indispensable for navigating contemporary auditing challenges. Regulations like IFRS 17 require adaptive leadership, supported by EI at PwC Morocco, to ensure compliance (Barac et al., 2021). Cybersecurity risks demand empathetic communication to build trust, as evidenced at Deloitte France (Herda & Lavelle, 2022). These competencies enable auditors to meet stakeholder expectations in a digital landscape, positioning firms such as KPMG USA as strategic partners.

1.7.3 Call to action for audit professionals and researchers

Audit firms like KPMG USA must prioritize EI and leadership training to enhance practice. A proposed EI Leadership Development Program includes workshops on self-awareness and empathy, mentorship, and evaluation using 360-degree feedback, as implemented at Deloitte France (Herda & Lavelle, 2022). Researchers are encouraged to validate the framework through empirical studies, focusing on diverse settings like PwC Morocco and EY France, to advance audit theory and practice in 2025.

1.8 RECOMMENDATIONS

This section proposes evidence-based recommendations to maximize the benefits of EI and leadership in DT auditing, tailored for auditors at PwC Morocco (Casablanca), Deloitte France (Paris), and KPMG USA (New York), grounded in the framework and SLR findings.

1.8.1 Audit firms

Implement EI and Leadership Training Programs: Firms should establish a comprehensive EI Leadership Development Program to address technical and interpersonal gaps identified in Section 9.1. The program should include: Workshops (12 hours over 6 weeks) focusing on self-awareness (mindfulness training to recognize biases in AI outputs) and empathy (role-playing client scenarios for IFRS 17 audits), based on Goleman's (1995) model, to enhance trust at Deloitte France (Herda & Lavelle, 2022); Mentorship Programs pairing junior auditors at PwC Morocco with EI-trained senior leaders to model transformational behaviors, with biweekly sessions over 6 months to foster adaptability in blockchain audits (Barac et al., 2021); and Evaluation using 360-degree feedback and the Emotional and Social Competency Inventory (Boyatzis & Goleman, 2007) to assess improvements in team cohesion and client trust at KPMG US. Pilots should be conducted in diverse settings, as Zhao and al. (2022)suggest; larger firms like KPMG USA benefit more from EI training. Change management strategies, such as transparent communication about AI benefits, can reduce resistance, as observed at EY France (Susskind & Susskind, 2015).

Establish Ethical Technology Frameworks: To address ethical challenges like AI biases and data privacy, firms like PwC Morocco should adopt governance frameworks, auditing algorithms for fairness per ICAEW (2018) and Appelbaum et al. (2020). Training on ethical decision-making, emphasizing self-regulation, can reinforce trust in digital audits at Deloitte France, aligning with Trong Tuan's (2012) findings on EI's role in ethics.

1.8.2 Educators

Update Audit Curricula Educational institutions should revise curricula to integrate DT and EI skills. Courses should cover AI, analytics, and blockchain, with case studies on IFRS 17 and NIST 800-53 compliance for auditors at KPMG USA (Appelbaum et al., 2017). EI modules, including simulations for client interactions, can prepare graduates for firms like PwC Morocco (Ali et al., 2025). Partnerships with Big Four Firms in Morocco, France, and the USA can provide real-world exposure to enhance curriculum relevance.

1.8.3 Researchers

Validate the Framework Empirically: Researchers should test the framework using mixed-methods designs. A quantitative study employing Structural Equation Modeling (SEM) should examine leadership's mediating role between EI and audit outcomes, using scales like Wong and Law (2002) for EI and Bass and Avolio's MLQ (1995) for leadership, with a sample of 400 auditors from PwC Morocco (Casablanca), Deloitte France (Paris), and KPMG USA (New York) over 18 months (Hair et al., 2019). Qualitative studies with semi-structured interviews of 25 audit leaders should explore moderators like IFRS 17 and NIST 800-53, coded via thematic analysis (Braun & Clarke, 2006). Longitudinal studies over 3–5 years should assess EI's sustained impact in AI-driven audits, addressing gaps noted by Fourie and Olivier, (2023).

Explore Emerging DT Challenges: Research should investigate emerging issues like AI ethics and real-time auditing. Studies on AI bias, building on Appelbaum et al. (2020), can inform ethical frameworks for KPMG USA. Investigations into real-time reporting's impact on EI-driven leadership at Deloitte France can ensure the framework's relevance in 2025 (Dai & Vasarhelyi, 2017). These efforts will advance audit theory and practice across diverse global contexts.

REFERENCES

Ali, L., Haq, M. Z. U., Asadullah, M. A., & Haider, G. (2025). Leveraging Emotional Intelligence to enhance Supply Chain visibility and Risk Management: Evidence from empirical research. International Journal of Engineering Business Management, 17. https://doi.org/10.1177/18479790251368324

American Institute of Certified Public Accountants (AICPA). (2024). Enhancing audit quality 2024 highlights report. https://www.aicpa-cima.com/news/download/enhancing-audit-quality-2024-hightlights-report

Appelbaum, D., Kogan, A., & Vasarhelyi, M. A. (2017). Big Data and analytics in the modern audit engagement: Research needs. Auditing: A Journal of Practice & Theory, 36(4), 1–27. https://doi.org/10.2308/ajpt-51684

Appelbaum, D., Showalter, D. S., Sun, T., & Vasarhelyi, M. A. (2020). A framework for auditor data literacy: A normative position. Accounting Horizons, 34(2), 5–25. https://doi.org/10.2308/horizons-19-127

Arora, B. (2017). Importance of emotional intelligence in the workplace. International Journal of Engineering and Applied Sciences, 4(7), 1–5.
Barac, K., Plant, K., Kunz, R., & Kirstein, M. (2021). Generic skill profiles of future accountants and auditors—Moving beyond attributes. Higher Education, Skills and Work-Based Learning, 11(4), 908–928. https://doi.org/10.1108/HESWBL-08-2020-0180
Bartsch, S., Weber, E., Büttgen, M., & Huber, A. (2021). Leadership matters in crisis-induced Digital Transformation: How to lead service employees effectively during the COVID-19 pandemic. Journal of Service Managament, 32(1): 71–85. https://doi.org/10.1108/JOSM-05-2020-0160
Bass, B. M., & Avolio, B. J. (1995). MLQ: Multifactor Leadership Questionnaire. Mind Garden.
Bass, B. M., & Riggio, R. E. (2006). Transformational leadership (2nd ed.). Lawrence Erlbaum Associates.
Boyatzis, R. E., & Goleman, D. (2007). Emotional and Social Competency Inventory. Hay Group.
Braun, V., & Clarke, V. (2006). Using thematic analysis in psychology. Qualitative Research in Psychology, 3(2), 77–101. https://doi.org/10.1191/1478088706qp063oa
Cao, M., Chychyla, R., & Stewart, T. (2015). Big Data analytics in financial auditing. Accounting Horizons, 29(2), 423–429. https://doi.org/10.2308/acch-51069
Cortellazzo, L., Bruni, E., & Zampieri, R. (2019). The role of leadership in a digitalized world: A review. Frontiers in Psychology, 10, 1938. https://doi.org/10.3389/fpsyg.2019.01938
Dai, J., & Vasarhelyi, M. A. (2017). Toward blockchain-based accounting and assurance. Journal of Information Systems, 31(3), 5–21. https://doi.org/10.2308/isys-51804
DeFond, M., & Zhang, J. (2014). A review of archival auditing research. Journal of Accounting and Economics, 58(2–3), 275–326. https://doi.org/10.1016/j.jacceco.2014.09.002
Fourie, H., & Olivier, B. (2023). Emotional Intelligence as a Key driver of the formation of professional scepticism in Auditors. South African Journal of Business Management, 54(1), a3654. https://doi.org/10.4102/sajbm.v54i1.3654
Goleman, D. (1995). Emotional intelligence. Bantam Books.
Gomber, P., Koch, J. A., & Siering, M. (2017). Digital finance and FinTech: Current research and future research directions. Journal of Business Economics, 87(5), 537–580. https://doi.org/10.1007/s11573-017-0852-x
Hair, J. F., Black, W. C., Babin, B. J., & Anderson, R. E. (2019). Multivariate data analysis (8th ed.). Cengage.
Herda, D. N., & Lavelle, J. J. (2022). How and why auditors' social exchange relationships influence their attitudes and behaviors: Implications for audit quality. Business Horizons, 65(4), 515–524. https://doi.org/10.1016/j.bushor.2021.02.044
Institute of Chartered Accountants in England and Wales (ICAEW). (2018). Artificial intelligence and the future of accountancy. ICAEW. https://www.icaew.com/technical/technology/artificial-intelligence
International Auditing and Assurance Standards Board (IAASB). (2014). A framework for audit quality: Key elements that create an environment for audit quality. IFAC. https://www.iaasb.org/publications/framework-audit-quality
Page, M. J., McKenzie, J. E., & Bossuyt, P. M. (2021). The PRISMA 2020 statement: An updated guideline for reporting systematic reviews. Systematic Reviews, 10(1), 89. https://doi.org/10.1186/s13643-021-01626-4
Pejić-Bach, M., Bertoncel, T., Meško, M., & Krstić, Ž. (2020). Text mining of industry 4.0 job advertisements. International Journal of Information Management, 50, 416–431. https://doi.org/10.1016/j.ijinfomgt.2019.07.014

Richins, G., Stapleton, A., Stratopoulos, T. C., & Wong, C. (2017). Big Data analytics: Opportunity or threat for the accounting profession? Journal of Information Systems, 31(3), 63–79. https://doi.org/10.2308/isys-51805
Schlechter, A. F., & Strauss, J. J. (2008). Leader emotional intelligence, transformational leadership, trust and team commitment: Testing a model within a team context. South African Journal of Industrial Psychology, 34(1), 42–53. https://doi.org/10.4102/sajip.v34i1.418
Susskind, R., & Susskind, D. (2015). The future of the professions: How technology will transform the work of human experts. Oxford University Press.
Suyono, E., & Farooque, O. A. (2019). Auditors' professionalism and factors affecting it: Insights from Indonesia. Journal of Asia Business Studies, 13(4), 543–558. https://doi.org/10.1108/JABS-03-2018-0073
Trong Tuan, L. (2012). Corporate social responsibility, leadership, and brand equity in healthcare service. Social Responsibility Journal, 8(3), 347–362. https://doi.org/10.1108/17471111211247929
Wong, C. S., & Law, K. S. (2002). The effects of leader and follower emotional intelligence on performance and attitude. The Leadership Quarterly, 13(3), 243–274. https://doi.org/10.1016/S1048-9843(02)00099-1
Zhang, Y., Wang, J., & Zhang, L. (2022). Emotional intelligence and auditor performance: A cross-cultural study. Journal of International Accounting Research, 21(3), 89–108. https://doi.org/10.2308/jiar-2021-045
Zhao, Y., Xu, Y., Zhao, Y., & Zhang, L. (2022). The effect of the audit team's emotional intelligence on reduced audit quality behaviors: Considering the mediating effect of team trust and the moderating effect of knowledge sharing Frontiers in Psychology, 13, 1082889. https://doi.org/10.3389/fpsyg.2022.1082889

Chapter 2

AI automation

Opportunities and challenges

Lina Alami and Bouyzem Meriem

2.1 INTRODUCTION

This study explores the impact of emerging technologies on the auditing profession in the digital era. With the growing presence of technologies such as Big Data, robotic process automation (RPA), and artificial intelligence (AI), the profession is undergoing significant transformation. These technologies promise to enhance the efficiency, accuracy, and effectiveness of audit processes, while also presenting new challenges related to data governance, ethics, and the evolving role of auditors.

In this research, we have chosen a qualitative approach, based on semi-structured interviews, to gather in-depth insights. By interviewing a sample of junior and senior auditors from the Big Four firms in Morocco, as well as from other international firms, we aim to better understand their perceptions, experiences, and the challenges they face in integrating AI and automation into their daily audit practices. This methodology will allow us to capture the diverse perspectives of auditors and provide a comprehensive view of how these technologies are reshaping the profession.

2.2 THE EVOLUTION OF THE AUDITING PROFESSION IN THE DIGITAL ERA

Before the digital era, financial auditing relied on manual methods: consulting paper documents, physically verifying records, and conducting face-to-face interviews. These traditional approaches, although thorough, were time-consuming, costly, and prone to human error, thus limiting audit efficiency. Historically, auditing traces its origins to ancient civilizations such as Babylonia, China, and Egypt. In Persia, under the reign of Darius I (522–486 BC), so-called "ears of the king" were tasked with monitoring state officials—an early form of audit centered on fraud prevention and the regularity of operations.

The very term "audit" originates from the Latin *audire*, meaning "to listen," a reference to early practices in which auditors verified accounts orally

 DOI: 10.1201/9781003650713-3

recited by accountants. From the 19th century onward, in the context of the Industrial Revolution and the growing separation between ownership and management, auditing became institutionalized as a regulatory mechanism. It emerged in response to the need to reinforce managerial accountability in situations of information asymmetry (Flint, 1988). At that time, auditors relied on empirical techniques such as observation and manual calculations to ensure the accuracy of financial statements.

With the increasing internationalization of trade, auditing has established itself as a key actor in promoting financial transparency. In the early 20th century, its primary mission was focused on the detection of fraud. However, as transactions grew more complex, professionals gradually adopted sampling techniques, providing reasonable rather than absolute assurance (Porter, 1997).

Today, digitalization is profoundly transforming the auditing profession. Auditors now have access to technological tools that allow them to automate repetitive tasks, improve data traceability, and quickly analyze large volumes of information. This digital transition is redefining the auditor's role, making them a strategic actor capable of providing high-value analyses, while enhancing the reliability and efficiency of the auditing process (Tanko, 2011).

In this context of evolution, it is now time to examine how technological innovations such as Big Data, RPA, and AI have completely redefined the boundaries of the auditing profession.

2.3 EMERGING TECHNOLOGIES (BIG DATA, RPA, AI) AND THEIR USE IN THE AUDITING PROFESSION

The integration of intelligent technologies in auditing has evolved progressively since the 1950s. During this period, the first reflections on the automation of accounting processes emerged, notably with Keenoy (1958), who highlighted the potential impact of technologies on accounting and control practices. Over the following decades (1960–1990), the growing complexity of organizational structures and data volumes led to the widespread adoption of computerized systems within companies, facilitating the management and monitoring of financial processes. According to Porter et al. (2005), this technological revolution altered the nature of auditors' interventions, as they integrated technological tools to perform more complex analyses. From the 1990s onward, the auditing profession underwent an accelerated transformation, driven by globalization and the rapid development of digital technologies. The introduction of sophisticated systems profoundly redefined auditing methods, making the modern auditor more focused on analyzing big data and utilizing advanced technological tools (Teck-Heang & Ali, 2008). The emergence of AI, RPA, and big data thus marks a significant turning point in this evolution.

First and foremost, Big Data refers to massive, complex, and high-velocity datasets that require advanced technologies and analytical methods to extract meaningful value (Kitchin, 2014). According to Sami and Sael (2016), it encompasses data subjected to advanced analytics and supported by specific resources. Traditionally characterized by the "5Vs"—Volume, Variety, Velocity, Value, and Veracity—the concept of Big Data has since expanded to include two additional dimensions: Variability and Visualization, thus forming the "7Vs" (Elgendy & Elragal, 2014). Figure 2.1 illustrates these seven dimensions of Big Data.

RPA is a software technology designed to automate repetitive, low-value-added tasks by replicating human actions on digital interfaces, without altering existing systems. It is distinguished by its ease of configuration and its ability to operate without modifying underlying information systems (Lacity & Willcocks, 2017). RPA is particularly well-suited for structured processes governed by fixed rules and enables the automation of activity sequences across multiple software platforms (IEEE,[1] 2017). Figure 2.2 illustrates the benefits of RPA:

In this context, AI is defined as a system's ability to interpret data, learn from it, and carry out tasks in an adaptive manner (Haenlein & Kaplan, 2019). It combines big data and machine learning to analyze behaviors and predict future events (Y. Zhang et al., 2020). Finally, Crevier (1993) and

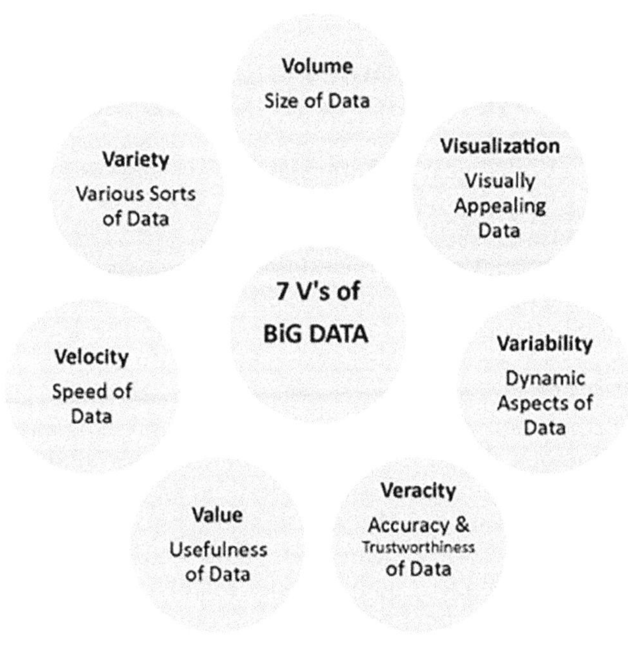

Figure 2.1 The 7Vs du Big Data. (Herath & Joshi, 2023.)

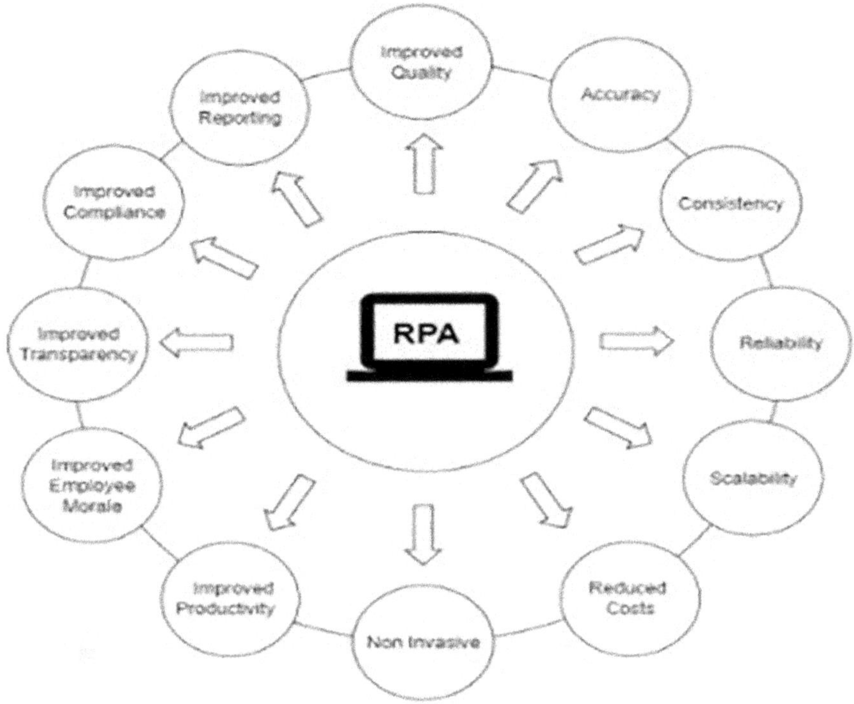

Figure 2.2 The benefits of the RPA. (Kaushik & Haralayya, 2024.)

describe AI as a multidisciplinary and pluralistic science, whose definition varies depending on the context of application.

Table 2.1 summarizes the key contributions, practical examples, and limitations of these technologies in the field of auditing:

In conclusion, technologies such as RPA, AI, and Big Data are transforming audit practices by offering gains in efficiency and accuracy, while raising issues related to governance and data quality. It is now essential to explore existing theoretical frameworks and empirical studies to better understand their impact on the efficiency of audit work.

2.4 THEORETICAL FRAMEWORKS AND EXISTING EMPIRICAL STUDIES ON THE IMPACT OF AI IN AUDITING

2.4.1 Technology acceptance models

To better understand the dynamics of technology acceptance in the field of auditing—particularly in response to the introduction of AI, RPA, and Big Data tools—it is relevant to compare two theoretical frameworks that are

Table 2.1 Technology acceptance models in the field of auditing.

Technology	*Key contribution to auditing*	*Examples of use*	*Limitations*	*Key references*
Big Data	Enables the analysis of massive volumes of data from multiple sources to enhance audit efficiency. Provides a more comprehensive and real-time view of audit data, with the ability to identify trends and anomalies. Transforms the auditor's strategic role, strengthening their advisory position in decision-making processes.	Comprehensive auditing through the analysis of all transactions rather than sampling. Real-time anomaly detection, with the ability to detect fraud or errors more quickly. Anticipation of risks through predictive analysis of financial data, identifying emerging trends. Use of data from diverse sources such as social media, smart sensors, electronic transactions, etc. Redefinition of the audit value chain, beyond formal accounting documents, with proactive use of unstructured data.	Requires advanced tools (software, analysis systems) to process and analyze large amounts of data. Interpreting the results requires human expertise to avoid analysis errors and ensure the reliability of conclusions. Risk of information overload and bias in data processing.	Mikalef et al. (2018) Elgendy and Elragal (2014) Yoon et al. (2015) Gray and Alles (2015) Dimitris Balios et al. (2020) Richins et al. (2017) AICPA (2017) Frey and Osborne (2013)
RPA	Allows the automation of repetitive and time-consuming tasks, improving efficiency, accuracy, and standardization of audit processes. Enhances the reliability of controls and enables faster anomaly detection by reducing the risk of human error.	Automation of internal control tests, accounting reconciliation procedures, and detailed verifications. Used for revenue audits: reconciliation, analytical procedures, and automated substantive testing. Automatic transfer of data from one fiscal year to another. Testing on employee benefit plans and automated confirmation of external financial information. Optimization of audit planning using RPA modules that automate data conversion, execution of analytical procedures, and report generation.	Requires complex initial configuration to automate specific processes. Dependence on existing technologies and sometimes difficult integration into fragmented environments. Need for human supervision to validate the results generated by the bots.	Chan et al. (2018) Moffitt et al. (2018) Cooper et al. (2019) Zhang (C. Abigail) et al. (2019) Samson et al. (2023) Davenport and Mittal (2022)

AI	Optimization of data collection, processing, and analysis. Automation of repetitive tasks. Quick identification of anomalies and irregularities. Strengthening professional judgment through advanced data analysis. Improvement of audit efficiency and accuracy.	**Deloitte:** Argus, a cognitive analysis tool for automating document review. GRAPA (Guided Risk Assessment Personal Assistant), a risk assessment assistant based on real-life cases. **EY:** GLAD (Helix General Ledger Anomaly Detector), detects unusual accounting entries. Natural language processing (NLP) that allows large-scale extraction of contract information during changes. **KPMG:** Dynamic Risk Assessment (DRA), visualizes risks across multiple dimensions. K-analyzer, which allows for quick analysis of thousands of tax transactions to detect errors or anomalies. **PwC**: GL.ai, a virtual assistant that replicates an auditor's reasoning through machine learning, and Cash.ai, an intelligent tool automating cash verifications, including bank reconciliations and confirmations.	Reliability of algorithms, especially in the case of incomplete or erroneous data. Transparency of AI models and automated decisions. The need for strict data governance to avoid biases. Evolution of auditors' skills to integrate these technologies into their practice.	Issa et al. (2016) Omoteso (2012) Kokina and Davenport (2017) Ucoglu (2020) Y. Zhang et al. (2020) Zemánková (2019)

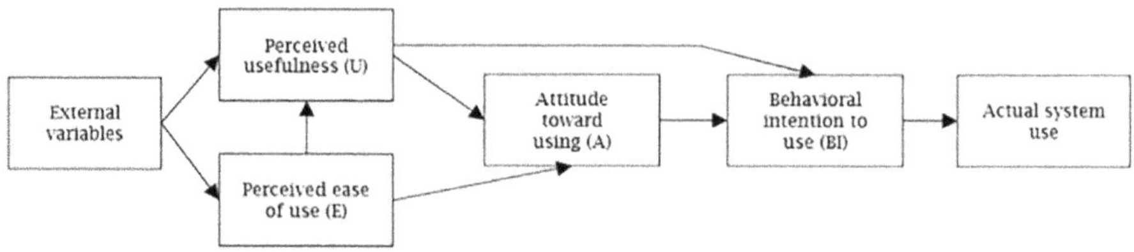

Figure 2.3 The Technology Acceptance Model (TAM). (Fred D. Davis et al., 1989.)

widely used in the literature: the **Technology Acceptance Model** (**TAM**) developed by (Davis, 1989) and the **Unified Theory of Acceptance and Use of Technology** (**UTAUT**) proposed by (Venkatesh et al., 2003). These models are illustrated in Figures 2.3 and 2.4:

Table 2.2 compares the key elements of these two theoretical models, highlighting their origins, core concepts, and their application in the context of auditing:

In this regard, the **TAM** is useful for identifying the psychological drivers of acceptance—such as perceived usefulness and ease of use—particularly among junior auditors. However, factors such as fear of replacement, lack of training, and technical complexity limit its effectiveness in more complex settings like auditing (Kokina et al., 2025).

The **UTAUT**, which adopts a more systemic approach, incorporates social and organizational dimensions better suited to the hierarchical structure of audit firms. Nevertheless, certain moderators—such as *voluntariness*—become less relevant when adoption is mandated by firm leadership, thereby

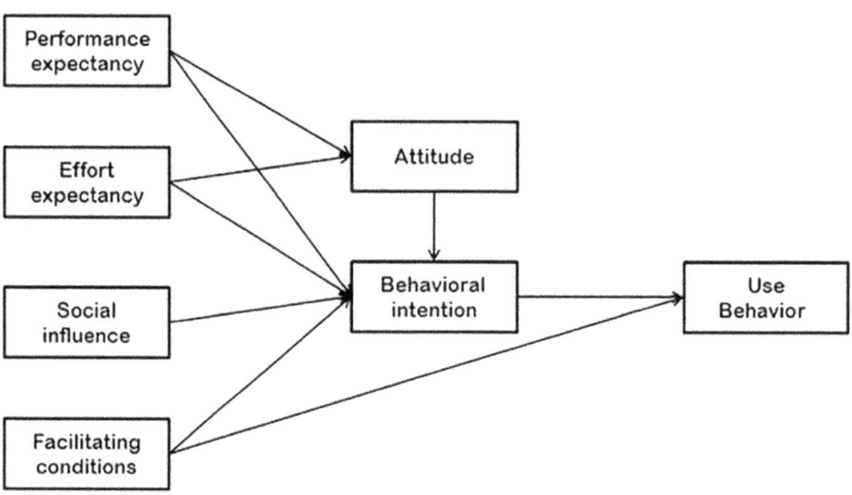

Figure 2.4 The Unified Theory of Acceptance and Use of Technology (UTAUT). (Venkatesh et al., 2003.)

Table 2.2 TAM models

Element	*TAM*	*UTAUT*
Theoretical origin	Derived from the Theory of Reasoned Action (TRA) by Fishbein and Ajzen (1980), which posits that human behavior is determined by behavioral intention, itself influenced by attitudes and subjective norms.	Integrates eight models, including TAM, the Theory of Planned Behavior (TPB), Innovation Diffusion Theory (IDT), and Social Cognitive Theory (SCT), among others (Venkatesh et al., 2003).
Main objective	To explain the intention to use a system based on two individual perceptions (Davis, 1989).	Provide a unified framework explaining usage intention and actual use based on multiple factors (Venkatesh et al., 2003).
Key variables	**Perceived Usefulness:** the degree to which a person believes that using a particular system will enhance their job performance (Davis, 1989). **Perceived Ease of Use**: the degree to which a person believes that using the system will be free of effort (Davis, 1989).	**Performance Expectancy**: belief that using the technology will improve performance; derived from Perceived Usefulness (TAM) and Relative Advantage (IDT) (Venkatesh et al., 2003). **Effort Expectancy**: perceived ease of use, similar to Perceived Ease of Use (TAM) and Complexity in the Model of PC Utilization (MPCU) (Venkatesh et al., 2003). **Social Influence**: the degree to which important others influence the decision to adopt a technology, based on subjective norm and social image (Fishbein & Ajzen, 1980). **Facilitating Conditions**: availability of resources and organizational support necessary to use the technology, combining Perceived Behavioral Control and Compatibility (Venkatesh et al., 2003).
Moderators/ contextual factors	Not included in the original model.	Includes four moderators: age, gender, experience, and voluntariness of use (Venkatesh et al., 2003).
Predictive power	Explains up to 40% of the variance in behavioral intention to use a technology (Davis, 1989).	Explains up to 70% of the variance in behavioral intention (Venkatesh et al., 2003).
Model extensions	TAM 2 (Venkatesh & Davis, 2000), TAM 3 (Venkatesh & Bala, 2008).	UTAUT2 (Venkatesh et al., 2003), which incorporates additional constructs such as hedonic motivation, habit, and price value.
Application in auditing	A simple tool to understand users' perceptions of technological tools (e.g., RPA, AI) and the factors influencing the acceptance of such innovations (Kokina & Davenport, 2017).	A robust framework for analyzing technology adoption in auditing firms, taking into account both social and organizational factors (Mansour, 2016).

diminishing their significance (Venkatesh et al., 2003). Moreover, the absence of individual-level variables in the original version of the model has led to subsequent adaptations to better reflect the specific characteristics of auditors (Chong, 2013; Williams et al., 2015).

2.4.2 Organizational change theories and resistance to technological change

Resistance to technological change—especially regarding the adoption of AI can be analyzed through classical change management models such as those proposed by Lewin (1947) and Kotter (2011).

The model developed by Lewin (1947) outlines three stages: unfreezing, changing, and refreezing. Resistance typically emerges during the *unfreezing* phase, when existing routines are challenged, notably by the introduction of AI. It is therefore essential to clearly communicate the change and involve stakeholders in the transformation process.

The model proposed by Kotter (2011) defines eight stages, including the creation of a sense of urgency, the formation of a change leadership coalition, and the communication of a clear vision. This approach emphasizes proactive management of resistance through leadership engagement and targeted training initiatives.

At the same time, resistance may also be approached from a cognitive perspective. Brendel et al. (2016) identify three core dimensions:

- **Fear:** The apprehension of job loss due to AI, uncertainty regarding the perceived complexity of technological tools, or the loss of control over one's work environment (Sindermann et al., 2022).
- **Ineffectiveness:** The perception of lacking the necessary skills to effectively engage with new technologies (Demir et al., 2020).
- **Antipathy:** A more emotional or ethical rejection of AI tools (Kros et al., 2021).

These reactions are supported by theoretical frameworks such as the Critical Theory of Technology (Feenberg, 1991), which emphasizes the potential loss of meaning in the workplace, and the TAM (Davis, 1989), which links technology acceptance to perceived usefulness and ease of use.

2.4.3 Existing empirical studies (international and national) on the impact of AI in auditing

Empirical studies, both international and national, have explored the impact of AI on the auditing profession. Table 2.3 summarizes key research in this area, highlighting the methodologies, findings, and limitations of existing studies:

Table 2.3 Existing empirical studies on the impact of AI in auditing.

Authors	*Methodology and objectives*	*Key findings*	*Identified limitations*
Al-Ateeq et al. (2022)	Quantitative—TAM model (questionnaire): assess the impact of Big Data Analytics on audit quality.	Perceived usefulness and ease of use explain the adoption of Big Data tools. Improved audit quality.	Geographically limited sample. Organizational dimensions not considered.
Issa et al. (2016)	Quantitative—TAM: examine the acceptance of smart auditing systems.	Efficiency gains and improved anomaly detection reinforce user acceptance. Seamless integration reduces resistance.	Focused on already implemented tools. Context limited to Big Four firms.
Abdullah and Almaqtari (2024)	Quantitative—Survey: analyze the impact of AI and Industry 4.0 technologies on accounting and auditing practices in Gulf countries.	AI enhances speed, accuracy, and efficiency. Adoption hindered by lack of skills and managerial support.	Findings are difficult to generalize beyond Gulf countries.
O'Donnell (2024)	Quantitative—Extended TAM: propose an explanatory model for AI adoption in auditing, based on TAM extensions.	Trust in algorithms, perceived compatibility, and performance expectations influence use.	Lacks qualitative insight into deeper human dynamics.
Ma and Liu (2004)	Meta-analysis—TAM: validate the robustness of the TAM model in various contexts.	Perceived usefulness confirmed as a stable, determining factor.	Outdated data, with limited focus on AI and auditing specifically.
Mansour (2016)	Quantitative—UTAUT: analyze the non-adoption of Computer-Assisted Audit Techniques (CAATs) by external auditors in Jordan.	Adoption of CAATs strongly influenced by facilitating conditions and performance expectations.	Study focused on Jordan, with initially low levels of technological adoption.
Dwivedi et al. (2019)	Extended UTAUT: offer a critical reassessment of UTAUT dimensions in the current digital environment.	Expansion of moderating variables (age, gender, experience, voluntariness), incorporating new factors such as organizational culture, digital maturity, and resistance to change—especially relevant to audit firms.	Theoretical perspective, lacking direct empirical validation.

(Continued)

Table 2.3 (Continued)

Authors	*Methodology and objectives*	*Key findings*	*Identified limitations*
Zouirchi and Ouia (2024)	Quantitative—TAM + contextual variables (Morocco): examine factors influencing the acceptance and use of AI in auditing.	AI is positively perceived when organizational structures support it. Emphasis on local context and Moroccan market realities.	Small sample size, lack of longitudinal data.
Yang et al. (2021)	Qualitative—Interviews (Big Four and SMEs): identify barriers and enablers related to AI integration in audit processes.	Adoption influenced by firm's digital maturity, trust in algorithms, and emergence of new roles (e.g., data analyst).	Findings are not easily generalizable. No assessment of performance impact.
Angeles et al. (2023)	Qualitative—Interviews (Philippines): explore the impact of digitalization on the auditing profession.	Automation, increased coverage, improved detection. Concerns include loss of professional judgment, tech dependency, and regulatory challenges.	Context-specific findings from emerging countries.
Vitali and Giuliani (2024)	Qualitative—Case studies in Europe: investigate challenges audit firms face with digital technologies.	Digital divide between large and small firms. Highlights the importance of leadership and clear digital transformation strategies.	Exploratory study with a limited sample.
Ramdi Imane (2021)	Qualitative—Interviews (France/Morocco): explore auditors' perceptions of AI integration in auditing.	AI seen as inevitable but anxiety-inducing. Fears of deskilling and calls for ethical and regulatory guidance.	Still limited in dissemination; exploratory approach.
El Bouzaidi Chikhi Dounia (2023)	Qualitative—Interviews (Morocco): understand auditors' perceptions of AI's impact on audit efficiency.	Three major contributions identified: automation, new skills required, and trust challenges in AI tools. Highlights the need for training and regulation.	Small sample; no theoretical framework linkage (e.g., TAM or UTAUT).

The analysis of existing empirical studies reveals that AI offers clear advantages to the auditing profession, such as the automation of repetitive tasks and improved anomaly detection. However, quantitative studies based on standardized theoretical models such as TAM and UTAUT fail to capture the complexity of professional dynamics, particularly in context-specific environments such as Morocco. Moreover, qualitative research remains limited, especially regarding the differences in how junior and senior auditors adopt and appropriate AI tools. To address these gaps, this study adopts a qualitative methodology based on semi-structured interviews, aiming to better understand the challenges and perceptions of auditors regarding the integration of AI within the Big Four and other international firms operating in Morocco.

2.5 RESEARCH METHODOLOGY—RESULTS—DISCUSSION

As part of our investigation into the impact of digitalization and AI on the efficiency of audit work, we adopted a qualitative approach, favoring semi-structured interviews to gather rich, contextualized data. The sample consists of nine audit professionals, including junior auditors, experienced auditors, senior auditors, as well as a certified public accountant and a statutory auditor, all from the Big Four firms and other international firms. This selection enables us to capture a wide range of perceptions and professional experiences in order to gain a deeper understanding of how new technologies are influencing auditing practices.

A summary table of the interviewees' profiles is presented in Table 2.4 to provide contextual information about the respondents and to enrich the interpretation of the results. The interview guide is presented in Table 2.5.

2.5.1 Summary of results obtained

The interviews conducted revealed a major transformation in auditing practices due to digitalization. Traditional methods based on manual processing, sample checks, and time-consuming documentation have now been replaced by digital tools that facilitate automation, traceability, and comprehensive data analysis. This shift not only redefines work processes but also repositions the auditor as a strategic player, capable of providing a more refined and quicker understanding of risks and performance.

Among the most frequently mentioned technologies by the interviewed auditors, which vary from one firm to another but can be grouped into major categories, are: big data analysis tools (such as Power BI, Alteryx, IDEA), collaborative platforms and document management systems (EY Canvas, Connect, EMS, KCW), automation tools for tests (RPA, DataSniper), and proprietary artificial intelligences designed for anomaly detection or predictive

Table 2.4 Interviewees' profiles

Position of interviewee	*Firm*	*Years of experience*	*Interview type*	*Date and duration of interview*
Founder and statutory auditor of his own firm	Confidential	15 years	Remote via meets	07/05/2025 25 min
Experienced auditor	PricewaterhouseCoopers—PwC Nearshore	2 years	Remote via meets	30/04/2025 28 min
Senior auditor	Ernst & Young—EY	3 years	Remote via meets	02/05/2025 32 min
Junior auditor	Deloitte Maroc	1 year	Remote via meets	05/05/2025 22 min
Experienced auditor	KPMG	2 years	Remote via meets	07/05/2025 32 min
Experienced auditor	Fidaroc Grant Thornton	2 years	Remote via meets	03/05/2025 25 min
Junior auditor	Ernst & Young—EY	1 year	Remote via meets	03/05/2025 20 min
Junior auditor	PricewaterhouseCoopers—PwC Maroc	1 year	Remote via meets	05/05/2025 20 min
Senior auditor	Deloitte Maroc	3 years	Remote via meets	02/05/2025 22 min

analysis (EY.Q, Deloitte's AI). These tools redefine the stages of the audit process, particularly by automating compliance tests and ensuring better traceability of operations.

This digitalization has a direct impact on the efficiency of audit engagements: time savings, improved reliability of results, and more rigorous documentation are frequently mentioned by the auditors interviewed. The automation of repetitive tasks frees up time for higher-value analysis, while the comprehensive use of accounting data allows for expanding the scope of verifications beyond simple samples.

However, this transition comes with challenges, particularly the need for auditors to adapt their technical skills to new tools and increasingly complex information systems. Organizational tensions may also arise due to the coexistence of old and new tools and pressure on deadlines. Moreover, concerns about cybersecurity, data confidentiality, and technological dependency are raised.

In conclusion, digitalization profoundly reshapes the auditing profession by introducing new tools, transforming working methods, and redefining the required skills. The expected profile of the auditor is evolving toward that of a high-value data analyst, capable of leveraging technology to refine their professional judgment and support decision-making. However, it is crucial to emphasize that the human element remains at the core of the audit process. Digitalization is not intended to replace auditors, but to enhance their efficiency by valuing the human dimensions of the profession.

Table 2.5 Annex—Interview guide

Research proposals and associated themes	*Questions*
RP 1: Digitalization is transforming traditional audit methods and redefining the processes and skills involved. **Theme:** Redefinition of audit practices in the digital era.	**Q1:** Can you provide us with all the reasons that led your firm to integrate digital tools into its audit missions? **Q2:** What specific types of digital tools have been adopted by your firm? **Q3:** What tangible changes has digitalization brought to the daily execution of audit missions? **Q4:** How did you experience this change as an auditor? What new skills have you been required to develop?
RP 2: The integration of digitalization into auditing practices promotes an improvement in the efficiency and performance of audit tasks. **Theme:** Enhancing the efficiency of audit tasks through digitalization.	**Q5:** Through your years of experience, how do you perceive the evolution of the overall performance and productivity of your firm since the introduction of digital tools? **Q6:** To what extent has digitalization helped shorten the execution times of audit tasks and led to better resource allocation? **Q7:** How have auditors' practices evolved in terms of data processing following the introduction of digital tools? **Q8**: Do you have concrete examples of tasks or processes that have been accelerated or simplified thanks to digital tools?
PR 3: While digitalization brings several advantages, it also raises challenges and limitations that require continuous adaptation from audit professionals. **Theme:** The challenges of the digital transformation of auditing: current issues and future perspectives.	**Q9:** What forms of resistance to change or operational constraints have you encountered during the implementation of digital technologies in your audit processes? **Q10:** What strategies have you implemented to ensure the security of systems and data confidentiality in the context of digitalization in audit? **Q11:** In your opinion, how can auditors maintain continuous adaptation to the rapid evolution of digital tools? **Q12:** Do you believe that the transition to fully digitalized audits could eliminate the need for direct human intervention within firms?

2.5.2 Recommendations

It is essential to continue strengthening ongoing training programs so that auditors can fully leverage digital tools, thereby maximizing the efficiency of audit tasks. A balanced approach between process automation and maintaining human expertise should be adopted to preserve the quality of professional judgment while taking advantage of technologies. At the same time, it is crucial to enhance data security and compliance within the framework of digital auditing by implementing robust measures to ensure the protection of sensitive information and adherence to regulatory standards. Finally, firms must invest in advanced cybersecurity tools and risk management protocols to ensure the reliability of audits in an increasingly complex technological environment.

2.6 CONCLUSION

In conclusion, this chapter highlights the major impact of digitalization and AI on the auditor profession, particularly within the Big Four firms. These technologies enhance the efficiency of audit tasks, notably through the automation of repetitive tasks and the detection of anomalies. However, challenges persist, particularly regarding the adoption of tools by auditors and cybersecurity management. The qualitative study conducted provides a better understanding of Moroccan auditors' perceptions of this transformation, emphasizing the need for a balance between technological innovation and human expertise to ensure the quality of audits.

NOTE

1 Institute of Electrical and Electronics Engineers: international professional organization that publishes widely recognized technical standards in the fields of engineering, information technology, and robotics.

BIBLIOGRAPHY

Abdullah, A. A. H., & Almaqtari, F. A. (2024). The Impact of Artificial Intelligence And Industry 4.0 on Transforming Accounting and Auditing Practices. *Journal of Open Innovation: Technology, Market, and Complexity*, *10*(1), 100218. https://doi.org/10.1016/j.joitmc.2024.100218

AICPA. (2017). *Guide to Audit Data Analytics* (1st ed.). Wiley. https://doi.org/10.1002/9781119499770

Al-Ateeq, B., Sawan, N., Al-Hajaya, K., Altarawneh, M., & Al-Makhadmeh, A. (2022). Big Data Analytics in Auditing and the Consequences for Audit Quality: A Study Using the Technology Acceptance Model (TAM). *Corporate Governance and Organizational Behavior Review*, *6*(1), 64–78. https://doi.org/10.22495/cgobrv6i1p5

Alles, M., & Gray, G. L. (2015). *The pros and cons of using big data in auditing: A synthesis of the literature and a research agenda* (Working paper, Rutgers Business School / California State University, Northridge). 1–37.

Angeles, E. J. A. A., Mabazza, G. B. M., Pascua, A. E. G. B. P., Salta, K. E. S., Santiago, Z. J. V. S., Marquez, J. M., & Catacutan, K. J. (2023). Shift to Digital Audit : A Study Investigating the Benefits and Challenges of Digitalization on the Audit Profession. *Asian Journal of Management Analytics*, *2*(4), 415–440. https://doi.org/10.55927/ajma.v2i4.6294

Balios, D., Kotsilaras, P., Eriotis, N., & Vasiliou, D. (2020). Big Data, Data Analytics and External Auditing. *Journal of Modern Accounting and Auditing*, *16*(5). https://doi.org/10.17265/1548-6583/2020.05.002

Brendel, W., Hankerson, S., Byun, S., & Cunningham, B. (2016). Cultivating Leadership Dharma : Measuring the Impact of Regular Mindfulness Practice on Creativity, Resilience, Tolerance for Ambiguity, Anxiety and Stress. *Journal of Management Development*, *35*(8), 1056–1078. https://doi.org/10.1108/JMD-09-2015-0127

Brown, C. E., & O'Leary, D. E. (1995). Introduction to Artificial Intelligence and Expert Systems. In *Artificial Intelligence & Expert Systems Sourcebook* (pp. 1–39). Springer US. https://doi.org/10.1007/978-1-4613-2261-0_1

Chan, S. W. S., Ip, S., Wan, C. F. C., & Yiu, H. F. D. (2018). *How would the emerging technology affect the future of auditing?* Outstanding Academic Papers by Students (OAPS), City University of Hong Kong. http://dspace.cityu.edu.hk/handle/2031/9133

Chong, A. Y.-L. (2013). Predicting M-Commerce Adoption Determinants : A Neural Network Approach. *Expert Systems with Applications*, *40*(2), 523–530. https://doi.org/10.1016/j.eswa.2012.07.068

Cooper, L. A., Holderness, D. K., Sorensen, T. L., & Wood, D. (2019). Robotic Process Automation in Public Accounting. *Accounting Horizons*, *33*(4), 115–133. https://doi.org/10.2308/acch-52466

Crevier, D. (1993). *AI : The Tumultuous History of the Search for Artificial Intelligence*. Basic Books.

Davenport, T. H., & Mittal, N. (2022, November 14). *How generative AI is changing creative work*. Harvard Business Review. https://hbr.org/2022/11/how-generative-ai-is-changing-creative-work

Davis, F. D. (1989). Perceived Usefulness, Perceived Ease of Use, and User Acceptance of Information Technology. *MIS Quarterly*, *13*(3), 319. https://doi.org/10.2307/249008

Davis, F. D., Bagozzi, R. P., & Warshaw, P. R. (1989). *User Acceptance of Computer Technology : A Comparison of Two Theoretical Models | Management Science*. https://pubsonline.informs.org/doi/epdf/10.1287/mnsc.35.8.982

Demir, M., McNeese, N. J., & Cooke, N. J. (2020). Understanding Human-Robot Teams in Light of All-Human Teams : Aspects of Team Interaction and Shared Cognition. *International Journal of Human-Computer Studies*, *140*, 102436. https://doi.org/10.1016/j.ijhcs.2020.102436

Dwivedi, Y. K., Rana, N. P., Jeyaraj, A., Clement, M., & Williams, M. D. (2019). Re-Examining the Unified Theory of Acceptance and Use of Technology (UTAUT) : Towards a Revised Theoretical Model. *Information Systems Frontiers*, *21*(3), 719–734. https://doi.org/10.1007/s10796-017-9774-y

El Bouzaidi Chikhi, D. (2023). *L'influence de l'intelligence artificielle sur l'efficacité de l'audit financier : Tendances, défis et opportunités. 4.*

Elgendy, N., & Elragal, A. (2014). Big Data Analytics : A Literature Review Paper. In P. Perner (Éd.), *Advances in Data Mining. Applications and Theoretical Aspects* (Vol. 8557, pp. 214–227). Springer International Publishing. https://doi.org/10.1007/978-3-319-08976-8_16

Feenberg, A. (1991). *Critical Theory of Technology*. Oxford University Press

Fishbein, M., & Ajzen, I. (1980). *Belief, Attitude, Intention, and Behavior: An Introduction to Theory and Research*. Addison-Wesley.

Flint, D. (1988). *Philosophy and Principles of Auditing: An Introduction*. Macmillan Education.

Frey, C. B., & Osborne, M. A. (2013). The Future of Employment : How Susceptible Are Jobs to Computerisation? *Technological Forecasting and Social Change, 114*, 254–280. https://doi.org/10.1016/j.techfore.2016.08.019

Haenlein, M., & Kaplan, A. (2019). A Brief History of Artificial Intelligence : On the Past, Present, and Future of Artificial Intelligence. *California Management Review, 61*(4), 5–14. https://doi.org/10.1177/0008125619864925

Herath, S. K., & Joshi, P. L. (2023). Audit Data Analytics: A Game Changer for Audit Firms. *International Journal of Auditing and Accounting Studies, 5*(1), 29–48.

IEEE-Guide for terms and concepts in intelligent process automation 2017. (s. d.).

Imane, R. (2021). *La technologie digitale et la profession d'audit : Quel impact ?* https://doi.org/10.5281/ZENODO.5730568

Issa, H., Sun, T., & Vasarhelyi, M. A. (2016). Research Ideas for Artificial Intelligence in Auditing : The Formalization of Audit and Workforce Supplementation. *Journal of Emerging Technologies in Accounting, 13*(2), 1–20. https://doi.org/10.2308/jeta-10511

Kaushik, P., & Haralayya, D. B. (2024). Robotic Process Automation (RPA) in Accounting and Auditing of Business and Financial Information. *The British Journal of Administrative Management, 58*(157), 127–142.

Keenoy, C. L. (1958). The Impact of Automation on the Field of Accounting. *The Accounting Review, 33*(2), 230–236.

Kitchin, R. (2014). *The Data Revolution: Big Data, Open Data, Data Infrastructures and Their Consequences.* SAGE Publications Ltd.

Kokina, J., Blanchette, S., Davenport, T. H., & Pachamanova, D. (2025). Challenges and Opportunities for Artificial Intelligence in Auditing : Evidence from the Field. *International Journal of Accounting Information Systems, 56*, 100734. https://doi.org/10.1016/j.accinf.2025.100734

Kokina, J., & Davenport, T. H. (2017). The Emergence of Artificial Intelligence : How Automation Is Changing Auditing. *Journal of Emerging Technologies in Accounting, 14*(1), 115–122.

Kotter, J. P. (2011). *"Leading Change," by John P. Kotter.* Harvard Business Press.

Kros, M., Jaspers, E., & Van Zalk, M. (2021). Avoidance, Antipathy, and Aggression : A Three-Wave Longitudinal Network Study on Negative Networks, Status, and Heteromisos. *Social Networks, 64*, 122–133. https://doi.org/10.1016/j.socnet.2020.08.006

Lacity, M. C., & Willcocks, L. P. (2017). *Robotic Process Automation and Risk Mitigation: The Definitive Guide.* SB Publishing.

Lewin, K. (1947). Frontiers in Group Dynamics : Concept, Method and Reality in Social Science; Social Equilibria and Social Change. *Human Relations, 1*(1), 5–41. https://doi.org/10.1177/001872674700100103

Mansour, E. M. (2016). Factors Affecting the Adoption of Computer Assisted Audit Techniques in Audit Process : Findings from Jordan. *Business and Economic Research, 6*(1), 248. https://doi.org/10.5296/ber.v6i1.8996

Mikalef, P., Boura, M., Lekakos, G., & Krogstie, J. (2018). Big Data Analytics Capabilities and Innovation : The Mediating Role of Dynamic Capabilities and Moderating Effect of the Environment. *British Journal of Management, 30*(2), 272–298. https://doi.org/10.1111/1467-8551.12343

Moffitt, K. C., Rozario, A. M., & Vasarhelyi, M. A. (2018). Robotic Process Automation for Auditing. *Journal of Emerging Technologies in Accounting, 15*(1).

O'Donnell, J. B. (2024). Auditing Transformation : A Model of Artificial Intelligence Adoption. *Journal of Applied Business and Economics*, *26*(6). https://doi.org/10.33423/jabe.v26i6.7390

Omoteso, K. (2012). The Application of Artificial Intelligence in Auditing : Looking Back to the Future. *Expert Systems with Applications*, *39*(9), 8490–8495. https://doi.org/10.1016/j.eswa.2012.01.098

Owolabi, S. A., Olamide, J. O., & Ayodeji Temitope, A. (2016). Evolution and Development of Auditing. *Unique Journal of Business Management Research*, *3*(1), 32–40.

Porter, B. (1997). *Auditors' Responsibilities with Respect to Corporate Fraud : A Controversial Issue.* https://doi.org/10.4135/9781446219133.n2

Porter, B., Simon, J., & Hatherly, D. J. (2005). *Principles of External Auditing.* John Wiley & Sons, Ltd.

Richins, G., Stapleton, R., Stratopoulos, T., & Wong, C. (2017). Big Data Analytics : Opportunity or Threat for the Accounting Profession? *Journal of Information Systems*, 31(3), 63–79.

Sami, S., & Sael, N. (2016). Extract Five Categories CPIVW from the 9V's Characteristics of the Big Data. *International Journal of Advanced Computer Science and Applications*, 7(3). https://doi.org/10.14569/IJACSA.2016.070337

Samson, D., Ellis, A., & Black, S. (2023). *Business Model Transformation: The AI & Cloud Technology Revolution.* Routledge/Taylor & Francis Group.

Sindermann, C., Yang, H., Elhai, J. D., Yang, S., Quan, L., Li, M., & Montag, C. (2022). Acceptance and Fear of Artificial Intelligence : Associations with Personality in a German and a Chinese Sample. *Discover Psychology*, 2(1), 8. https://doi.org/10.1007/s44202-022-00020-y

Tanko, M. (2011). *An empirical analysis of audit expectation gap in Nigeria* (MPRA Paper No. 49661) (pp. 1–18). Munich Personal RePEc Archive.

Teck-Heang, L., & Ali, A. M. (2008). The Evolution of Auditing: An Analysis of the Historical Development. *Journal of Modern Accounting and Auditing*, *4*(12), 1–8.

Ucoglu, D. (2020). Current Machine Learning Applications in Accounting and Auditing. *Pressacademia*, *12*(1), 1–7. https://doi.org/10.17261/Pressacademia.2020.1337

Venkatesh, V., Thong, J. Y. L., & Xu, X. (2012). Consumer Acceptance and Use of Information Technology : Extending the Unified Theory of Acceptance and Use of Technology. *MIS Quarterly*, *36*(1), 157. https://doi.org/10.2307/41410412

Venkatesh, V., & Bala, H. (2008). Technology Acceptance Model 3 and a Research Agenda on Interventions. *Decision Sciences*, *39*(2), 273–315. https://doi.org/10.1111/j.1540-5915.2008.00192.x

Venkatesh, V., & Davis, F. D. (2000). A Theoretical Extension of the Technology Acceptance Model : Four Longitudinal Field Studies. *Management Science*, *46*(2), 186–204. https://doi.org/10.1287/mnsc.46.2.186.11926

Venkatesh, V., Morris, M. G., Davis, G. B., & Davis, F. D. (2003). User Acceptance of Information Technology : Toward a Unified View. *MIS Quarterly*, *27*(3), 425. https://doi.org/10.2307/30036540

Vitali, S., & Giuliani, M. (2024). Emerging Digital Technologies and Auditing Firms : Opportunities and Challenges. *International Journal of Accounting Information Systems*, *53*, 100676. https://doi.org/10.1016/j.accinf.2024.100676

Williams, M. D., Rana, N. P., & Dwivedi, Y. K. (2015). The Unified Theory of Acceptance and Use of Technology (UTAUT) : A Literature Review. *Journal of Enterprise Information Management*, *28*(3), 443–488. https://doi.org/10.1108/JEIM-09-2014-0088

Yang, J., Blount, Y., & Amrollahi, A. (2021). *Adoption of AI in the auditing practice: A case study of a Big Four accounting firm.* In Australasian Conference on Information Systems (ACIS 2021) Proceedings (paper 26). Australasian Conference on Information Systems.

Yoon, K., Hoogduin, L., & Zhang, L. (2015). Big Data as Complementary Audit Evidence. *Accounting Horizons*, *29*(2), 431–438. https://doi.org/10.2308/acch-51076

Zemánková, A. (2019). Artificial Intelligence and Blockchain in Audit and Accounting: Literature Review. *WSEAS Transactions on Business and Economics*, *16*(1), 568–581.

Zhang, C. (Abigail), Cohen, M., & Rozario, A. M. (2019, août 14). Exploring the Use of Robotic Process Automation (RPA) in Substantive Audit Procedures. *The CPA Journal*. https://www.cpajournal.com/2019/08/14/exploring-the-use-of-robotic-process-automation-rpa-in-substantive-audit-procedures/

Zhang, Y., Xiong, F., Xie, Y., Fan, X., & Gu, H. (2020). The Impact of Artificial Intelligence and Blockchain on the Accounting Profession. *IEEE Access*, *8*, 110461–110477. https://doi.org/10.1109/ACCESS.2020.3000505

Zouirchi, H., & Ouia, A. (2024). The Application of Artificial Intelligence in Financial Auditing. *International Journal of Digitalization and Applied Management*, *1*(2), 226–247.

Chapter 3

Audit and tax reform in developing countries

Toward an integrated approach for improved public governance

Maryem Jmahri, Sarah Ouberni, and Issam El Filali

3.1 INTRODUCTION

In recent decades, developing countries have increasingly pursued tax reform as a strategic tool to mobilize domestic revenues, reduce inequalities, and enhance public sector performance. These reforms are driven by a combination of internal imperatives, including financing essential services and addressing citizen demands for fairness, and external pressures such as globalization, tax competition, and conditionalities from international financial institutions (IMF, 2022). Yet, despite repeated reform cycles, results have been uneven. Many tax systems continue to suffer from limited administrative capacity, large informal economies, and fragile public trust (Joshi et al., 2014).

Parallel to this, the role of public audit has evolved from a narrow focus on financial compliance to a broader set of objectives, including performance auditing, risk management, and value-for-money evaluations (OECD, 2020). This evolution reflects a shift in public sector management toward accountability, transparency, and results-based governance. However, in most developing countries, tax reform and public audit operate as parallel processes rather than as mutually reinforcing pillars of fiscal governance. The lack of coordination between tax authorities and audit institutions often leads to policy fragmentation, missed synergies, and underutilized oversight potential (Andrews et al., 2017).

This chapter argues that integrating tax reform and public audit is essential to building more resilient and legitimate fiscal systems. Drawing on institutional theory and selected examples from countries such as Rwanda, Morocco, and Brazil, the chapter explores how an integrated approach can improve transparency, accountability, and reform effectiveness. It adopts a conceptual and analytical lens to examine the institutional, operational, and political dimensions of audit-tax coordination in developing contexts.

The structure of the chapter is as follows: the next section presents a review of the literature on tax reform and audit in developing countries. The methodology section outlines the conceptual and illustrative approach adopted. This is followed by the results, which explore the opportunities, constraints, and innovations in

DOI: 10.1201/9781003650713-4

audit-tax integration. The final section concludes with a synthesis of the findings, integrating the study's limitations and proposing directions for future research.

3.2 LITERATURE REVIEW

3.2.1 Tax reform in developing countries

Tax reform is a central component of state-building and economic development strategies in developing countries. It is often undertaken to address chronic fiscal deficits, improve revenue mobilization, foster equity, and enhance the efficiency of public expenditures (IMF, 2022). Many reforms have aimed at broadening the tax base, simplifying structures, and reducing distortions. However, the success of such efforts remains uneven due to a range of political, administrative, and institutional challenges (de Almeida & Silva, 2023).

One of the most persistent constraints is the large informal sector, which in many African and Latin American countries accounts for over 40% of economic activity (Joshi et al., 2014). This undermines horizontal equity and limits the effectiveness of income and corporate tax systems. Furthermore, weak tax administration and limited data availability hinder the enforcement and compliance mechanisms required to support broad-based reforms (Moore, 2008).

From a political economy perspective, reform outcomes are heavily shaped by the degree of elite support, state-society bargaining, and the perceived legitimacy of the tax system (Brautigam et al., 2008). Prichard (2015) argues that tax bargaining processes where citizens accept taxation in exchange for public goods and accountability are essential to improving both revenue and governance outcomes. Yet in many low-income countries, taxation is still perceived as extractive rather than participatory (Moore, 2015).

Recent trends show a movement toward digitalization and risk-based administration as key strategies to improve compliance and efficiency (Munawer & Masood, 2022). Rwanda and Georgia, for example, have invested in e-filing systems and taxpayer segmentation tools, resulting in improved collection and reduced compliance costs (Mascagni et al., 2020).

"Tax reform cannot succeed without parallel investments in state capacity and institutional credibility" (Moore, 2015).

Reform sequencing also matters. As Fjeldstad and Moore (2009) suggest, early reforms that focus on procedural transparency, simplification, and service delivery to taxpayers tend to build trust and support more ambitious structural changes (Table 3.1).

3.2.2 The role of audit in public financial governance

Public audit has evolved significantly in recent decades Table 3.1 expanding beyond its traditional role of financial compliance to encompass performance

Table 3.1 Constraints and priorities in tax reform

Dimension	*Typical challenges*	*Strategic responses*
Administrative capacity	Poor data systems; weak enforcement	Investment in digital infrastructure; training
Informality	Large informal sector; low compliance	Simplified regimes for small taxpayers; targeted audits
Political support	Elite resistance; public mistrust	Taxpayer education; participatory reform design
Revenue needs	Narrow tax base; volatility	Broadening base; reducing exemptions

Sources: Adapted from IMF (2022), Joshi et al. (2014), and Moore (2015).

evaluation, risk management, and policy accountability (OECD, 2020). This transformation reflects broader shifts in public sector governance, notably the emphasis on results-based management, transparency, and institutional accountability.

Supreme Audit Institutions (SAIs) are now seen as central pillars of fiscal oversight, capable of improving the effectiveness and legitimacy of public financial management systems. INTOSAI (2016) identifies three core types of audits: financial, compliance, and performance audits, with the latter gaining prominence as a tool to assess whether public resources are used efficiently and effectively in achieving intended outcomes.

Performance audits, in particular, provide insights into the implementation and results of government policies, including tax reforms and expenditure programs (Bietenhader & Matei, 2021). For instance, SAIs can evaluate whether tax incentive schemes have led to meaningful investments or whether public expenditures align with national development goals. This evaluative role contributes not only to fiscal discipline but also to democratic accountability.

Despite their growing relevance, audit institutions in many developing countries face important constraints. These include limited independence from the executive, weak enforcement of audit recommendations, and inadequate access to timely, digitized data (World Bank, 2022). Furthermore, the capacity of SAIs to audit complex programs is often undermined by insufficient staffing, outdated methodologies, and political interference.

Nonetheless, international experiences suggest that well-functioning audit bodies can play a catalytic role in governance reform. For example, in South Korea and Chile, SAIs have helped shape budgetary discipline and fight corruption by conducting real-time audits and publishing citizen-friendly reports (OECD, 2021). In Rwanda, the Office of the Auditor General collaborates with tax authorities to monitor the efficiency of revenue administration, using shared platforms and e-audits (AfDB, 2021).

"Performance auditing is a powerful tool not only to evaluate how resources are used but to influence how policies are designed and managed" (OECD, 2020).

The effectiveness of audit institutions, however, depends on a conducive legal environment, institutional autonomy, and the political will to act on

Table 3.2 Dimensions of audit effectiveness in developing countries

Dimension	*Enabling factors*	*Common constraints*
Legal framework	Constitutional independence; mandate clarity	Political interference; overlapping mandates
Institutional capacity	Skilled auditors; access to data; IT tools	Staff shortages; outdated audit methods
Accountability impact	Enforcement of recommendations; public reports	Weak follow-up; low media and civic engagement
Policy influence	Performance audit integration; inter-agency dialogue	Siloed institutions; limited policy feedback

Sources: Adapted from INTOSAI (2016), OECD (2020), and World Bank (2022).

audit findings. Without these conditions, audits risk becoming symbolic exercises with limited influence on public policy (Table 3.2).

As this literature suggests, strengthening audit institutions is not only a matter of capacity building but of embedding them in broader reform coalitions that value transparency and results. When aligned with fiscal policy cycles and empowered with data access, audits can become key drivers of improved governance and citizen trust.

3.2.3 Integrating tax reform and audit: Toward a coherent framework

While tax reform and public audit have historically evolved as separate pillars of fiscal governance, there is a growing consensus in the literature on the need for their strategic integration. Both domains pursue overlapping goals, transparency, accountability, and efficient resource mobilization, yet they often operate in institutional silos, missing opportunities for synergy and mutual reinforcement (Andrews et al., 2017).

3.2.4 Institutional synergies and feedback loops

From an institutional perspective, tax and audit systems can benefit significantly from structured coordination. Both are essential components of public financial governance, yet they often function in isolation. Performance audits, for instance, can assess the effectiveness and equity of fiscal policies, including tax incentives, exemptions, and compliance strategies, by providing evidence on whether policy goals are being met (OECD, 2021). Conversely, modernized tax systems offer a rich source of administrative data that can enhance audit coverage, accuracy, and targeting (IMF, 2023).

This bidirectional relationship creates an opportunity to establish virtuous cycles of policy feedback and institutional learning. Audit findings can inform the design of future tax policies, highlighting gaps, inefficiencies, or inequities. At the same time, tax reforms, especially those involving digital

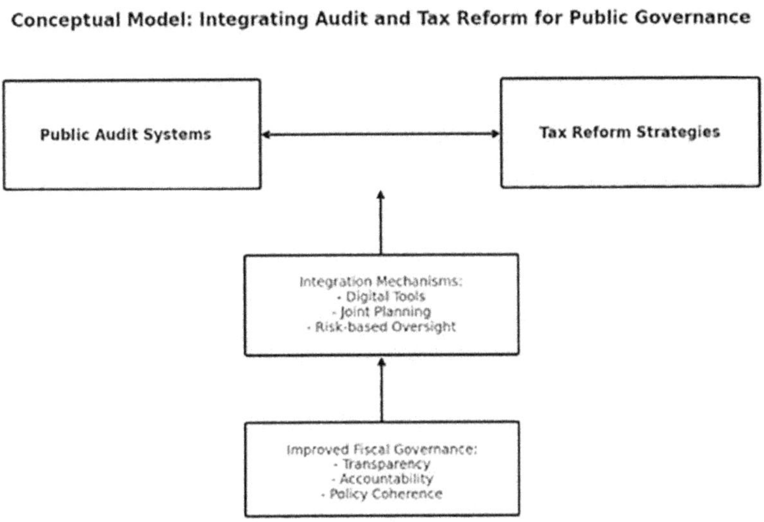

Figure 3.1 Conceptual model of audit–tax integration for public financial governance.

transformation, can improve audit methodologies by enabling real-time monitoring and data interoperability.

"Integrated audit-tax mechanisms enhance not only transparency but also adaptive capacity within governance systems" (Prichard & Moore, 2018).

To illustrate these interdependencies, the figure below presents a conceptual model of how audit and tax reform functions can be strategically integrated. It identifies key coordination mechanisms such as digital tools, joint planning, and risk-based oversight that serve as operational bridges. The resulting synergy contributes to improved transparency, enhanced accountability, and stronger policy coherence within public financial management systems (Figure 3.1).

This model highlights the need for institutional frameworks that promote not only technical collaboration but also policy coherence. By embedding audit into the full cycle of fiscal reform from policy formulation to implementation and evaluation, governments can build more resilient and legitimate financial systems (Andrews et al., 2017).

3.2.5 Operational barriers to integration

Despite these theoretical synergies, real-world integration remains limited. Key barriers include legal fragmentation, technological incompatibilities, and resistance from vested interests. In many countries, tax administrations report to the Ministry of Finance, while SAIs are accountable to parliament, leading to poorly aligned mandates and disconnected workflows (Santiso, 2007).

Moreover, incompatible IT systems often prevent seamless data sharing between institutions. Auditors may lack access to taxpayer registries or real-time transactions, which constrains the scope of performance audits (World Bank, 2022). In some cases, political elites actively block audit recommendations or underfund oversight bodies to protect opaque practices (Brinkerhoff, 2004).

Institutional cultures also play a role. Where public agencies operate in hierarchical or defensive modes, inter-agency collaboration may be discouraged or formally restricted. Without strong political commitment and procedural reforms, even technically sound integration strategies risk failure (Grindle, 2004).

3.2.6 Country illustrations: Emerging models of integration

Despite challenges, several developing countries have initiated promising practices. In Rwanda, the Rwanda Revenue Authority and the Office of the Auditor General collaborate via e-invoicing systems and joint audit trails to improve VAT compliance and detect fraud (AfDB, 2021). In Brazil, the Receita Federal uses a centralized digital accounting platform (SPED) that facilitates data sharing across tax and audit bodies, enabling real-time oversight and reducing administrative duplication (IMF, 2019).

In Morocco, the Directorate General of Taxes has begun working with the Court of Auditors to evaluate tax expenditures and enhance risk-based audits. Though institutional silos persist, the growing use of data mining and digital risk profiling tools has improved transparency (Ministry of Economy and Finance, 2023).

3.2.7 Political will and reform ownership

Technical tools and legal reforms are insufficient without strong political backing. The effectiveness of integration depends heavily on leadership support, institutional trust, and reform ownership by domestic actors (Table 3.3). In contexts where tax reform challenges elite interests, audit reports may be suppressed, ignored, or manipulated (Santiso, 2009).

Table 3.3 Integration of tax reform and audit: Country experiences

Country	*Coordination mechanism*	*Digital tools used*	*Outcomes achieved*
Rwanda	Joint platforms between tax and audit bodies	E-invoicing, VAT audit trails	Improved VAT compliance, better targeting
Brazil	Centralized digital system (SPED)	Real-time accounting, audit data linkage	Reduced evasion, real-time oversight
Morocco	Coordination on tax expenditure audits	Risk-based auditing, data mining	Enhanced transparency, pilot collaboration

Sources: Adapted from AfDB (2021), IMF (2019), Ministry of Economy and Finance (2023), OECD (2020).

Grindle (2004) emphasizes that successful governance reforms emerge not from perfection, but from "good enough" arrangements that adapt to local political and institutional realities. Rwanda's success is attributed in part to alignment between national development strategies and internal audit functions. Conversely, externally imposed models with weak local ownership often fail to take root.

Thus, integrating audit into tax reform should not be seen as a purely technical exercise but as a political strategy to build public legitimacy and institutional resilience.

3.3 METHODOLOGY

This study employs a conceptual and analytical approach grounded in institutional theory and the literature on public financial governance. Its primary objective is to examine the theoretical and practical interconnections between tax reform and public audit in developing countries, with a particular emphasis on their integration as a means to enhance governance outcomes.

Due to the limited availability of comparative empirical data on audit–tax coordination, a conceptual methodology is both suitable and necessary. It facilitates the construction of a coherent analytical framework intended to guide future research and inform policy discourse. The method involves a critical synthesis of existing scholarly literature, policy papers, and institutional documents related to tax administration, audit practices, and governance reform.

The analysis draws on a multidisciplinary body of work spanning public finance, political economy, development studies, and public administration. Key sources include peer-reviewed journal articles, working papers, and reports produced by international organizations such as the OECD, IMF, INTOSAI, and the World Bank. Special attention is given to integrating insights from both academic research and practitioner-oriented publications to ensure a balanced and comprehensive perspective.

To support the conceptual arguments, the study includes illustrative examples from Rwanda, Morocco, and Brazil. These countries were selected based on the relevance of their ongoing reforms, their regional diversity, and the availability of credible institutional data. While these examples are not intended to serve as formal case studies, they help anchor the theoretical discussion in concrete contexts and shed light on emerging practices in audit–tax integration.

Rather than aiming to produce generalizable findings, the study seeks to propose a structured conceptual framework and identify key knowledge gaps to be addressed in future empirical research. The limitations of the chosen methodology, particularly the absence of original field data, are acknowledged and discussed in the concluding section.

3.4 RESULTS

The analysis of the literature and illustrative cases highlights several key dimensions through which the integration of tax reform and audit mechanisms can enhance fiscal governance in developing countries. Rather than presenting statistical findings, this section synthesizes thematic results that emerge from the conceptual framework and country experiences. These results are structured around three interrelated themes: (1) rebuilding public trust through integrated oversight, (2) strengthening institutional capacity as a foundation for reform, and (3) promoting strategic coherence through coordinated governance mechanisms. Each subsection discusses not only the potential benefits of integration but also the underlying institutional and political dynamics that shape reform outcomes.

3.4.1 Rebuilding public trust through integrated fiscal oversight

In many developing countries, tax systems suffer from a crisis of legitimacy. Citizens frequently perceive taxation as coercive, opaque, and disconnected from service delivery (Moore, 2015). The result is widespread tax noncompliance, low fiscal morale, and resistance to reform. In such contexts, strengthening the role of public audit can serve as a corrective mechanism both technically and symbolically (Ayres & Leaver, 2023).

Integrating audit into the design and monitoring of tax reform can reinforce the perception that fiscal policy is accountable, responsive, and performance-driven. Independent audits, particularly performance audits conducted by SAIs, have the capacity to evaluate whether tax policies deliver intended outcomes such as equity, efficiency, and transparency (OECD, 2020). When such audits are made public and followed by concrete policy adjustments, they can help rebuild public trust in fiscal institutions.

"Transparency in the use of public resources is a prerequisite for voluntary tax compliance and democratic legitimacy" (Campos & Pradhan, 2007).

For example, in Rwanda, public audit reports on revenue collection are discussed in parliament and widely disseminated, enhancing the credibility of tax authorities (AfDB, 2021). In Brazil, the digital integration between the Receita Federal and audit bodies has allowed real-time monitoring of tax compliance and public disclosure of audit outcomes, further reinforcing institutional trust (IMF, 2019).

However, the contribution of audit to trust-building depends on more than technical accuracy. It also requires that audit findings be acted upon, that follow-up mechanisms exist, and that civil society and the media play an active role in disseminating and debating audit results. Without these accountability linkages, even well-conducted audits risk being ignored or politically neutralized.

3.4.2 Institutional capacity as a pillar of effective reform

The integration of audit and tax systems depends not only on political will or legal frameworks but also on the depth and coherence of institutional capacity (Khan & Chowdhury, 2022). In many developing countries, tax administrations and audit bodies operate with severe resource constraints, limited staffing, outdated IT systems, and insufficient training hindering their ability to implement or oversee complex reforms (World Bank, 2022).

Weak institutional capacity exacerbates siloed operations between audit and tax entities. Without interoperable systems and standardized procedures, it becomes difficult to share data, coordinate risk assessments, or conduct joint evaluations. As a result, reforms that appear well-designed on paper often fail during implementation due to operational bottlenecks.

For example, in several sub-Saharan African countries, the inability of tax authorities to maintain reliable taxpayer databases limits the effectiveness of performance audits, while audit institutions, in turn, struggle to access timely and disaggregated revenue data (Bietenhader & Matei, 2021). In contrast, countries like Brazil and Rwanda have shown that investing in human capital and digital infrastructure can significantly enhance cross-institutional collaboration.

"Institutional reform is most sustainable when capacity development is aligned with systemic incentives and reform ownership" (Andrews et al., 2017).

Effective reform therefore requires more than isolated training programs or one-time technology upgrades. It demands integrated investments in people, systems, and processes that support continuous learning and feedback. This includes creating formal protocols for data sharing, developing joint performance indicators, and embedding collaboration in routine administrative practices.

To illustrate the alignment and divergence between audit and tax reform functions, the following table presents a comparative overview of their characteristics and coordination challenges.

This comparison highlights not only the technical potential for coordination but also the need for institutional change. Building integrated fiscal systems requires a long-term approach that addresses structural fragmentation and fosters a culture of collaboration, accountability, and shared learning.

3.4.3 Toward a strategic and coherent reform approach

The integration of audit and tax systems is not an automatic process; it requires intentional design, strong leadership, and institutional coordination (Table 3.4). A strategic approach must go beyond technical fixes to address the deeper governance structures and political incentives that shape reform outcomes.

Inter-agency platforms such as joint reform committees, shared planning frameworks, and co-developed evaluation tools can help align the objectives of tax authorities and audit institutions (Brinkerhoff, 2004). These

Table 3.4 Comparative dimensions of tax reform and public audit

Dimension	*Tax reform*	*Public audit*	*Coordination challenge*
Objective	Revenue mobilization, equity, efficiency	Accountability, transparency, performance	Misalignment of goals and metrics
Policy cycle timing	Design and implementation	Post-implementation evaluation	Limited feedback mechanisms
Tools and instruments	Digital filing, tax incentives, simplification	Performance audits, CAATs, compliance checks	Incompatible IT systems; non-standardized data
Institutional actors	Ministries of Finance, Tax Authorities	SAIs, Courts of Accounts, Parliaments	Siloed governance structures
Capacity needs	Data analytics, taxpayer segmentation	Access to real-time data, forensic tools	Lack of interoperability and training

Sources: Constructed by the authors based on OECD (2020), INTOSAI (2016), and World Bank (2022).

mechanisms facilitate policy feedback loops, reduce duplication of efforts, and foster policy coherence across ministries and oversight bodies.

Transparency plays a foundational role in this process. The public disclosure of audit findings, particularly those assessing the effectiveness and fairness of tax measures, enhances fiscal credibility and encourages civic engagement. In several countries, media reporting on audit results and civil society monitoring have pressured governments to respond more proactively to institutional weaknesses (Santiso, 2009).

At the same time, reform sequencing and stakeholder engagement are critical. Early "quick wins," such as publishing simplified audit summaries or linking tax incentives to measurable outcomes, can build momentum and trust. These must be followed by more systemic reforms, including legal harmonization, digital interoperability, and accountability frameworks that institutionalize collaboration.

"Strategic reform must be adaptive, politically aware, and focused on building coalitions across institutions, not merely correcting technical flaws" (Andrews et al., 2017).

The integration of audit into tax reform should thus be viewed as a governance innovation, one that strengthens fiscal institutions, supports performance-based public management, and restores legitimacy to the fiscal contract. When properly designed and politically supported, such integration offers a pathway to more just, transparent, and effective public finance systems.

3.5 CONCLUSION

The relationship between tax reform and public audit in developing countries is more than a technical interaction; it reflects deeper questions of institutional legitimacy, governance coherence, and public trust. This chapter has argued that integrating audit mechanisms into tax reform processes can significantly improve the transparency, effectiveness, and credibility of fiscal policy.

Drawing on institutional theory and illustrative examples from countries such as Rwanda, Brazil, and Morocco, we have shown that audit and taxation share overlapping objectives and can reinforce each other through feedback loops, joint digital platforms, and coordinated reform strategies. However, this integration remains limited in many contexts due to fragmented legal mandates, capacity constraints, political resistance, and the absence of sustained inter-institutional collaboration.

The results highlight three key pillars for reform: (1) rebuilding public trust through transparent oversight, (2) strengthening institutional capacity to support integration, and (3) promoting a coherent reform approach that aligns objectives, timelines, and accountability mechanisms. Successful initiatives typically combine political commitment, digital infrastructure investment, and structured inter-agency coordination. Yet, such efforts must also be sensitive to local political economies and avoid externally imposed "best practices" that lack domestic ownership.

Despite these insights, the study presents several limitations. It is conceptual in nature and relies primarily on secondary sources and illustrative cases, without original fieldwork or quantitative analysis. As such, the findings should be interpreted as exploratory rather than generalizable. Moreover, the political and sociological dimensions of reform implementation, such as resistance from elites, informal norms, and cultural attitudes toward taxation, remain underexplored.

Future research should address these limitations through empirical studies, including in-depth case research, interviews with audit and tax officials, and comparative analyses of integration outcomes. Quantitative evaluations of audit-tax coordination effects, such as changes in revenue performance, audit efficiency, or public satisfaction, would also enrich the evidence base. In addition, emerging technologies such as artificial intelligence and blockchain offer promising tools for real-time oversight and fraud detection, and their role in fostering audit–tax integration warrants further investigation.

In conclusion, forging stronger links between tax reform and audit is not simply an exercise in administrative optimization. It is a transformative process that redefines how public institutions operate, how they engage with citizens, and how they build legitimacy over time. A politically informed, institutionally grounded, and strategically coherent integration of audit and tax functions represents a critical step toward more just, effective, and resilient governance systems in the developing world.

REFERENCES

AfDB. (2021). Rwanda economic outlook. African Development Bank. https://www.afdb.org/en

Andrews, M., Pritchett, L., & Woolcock, M. (2017). Building state capability: Evidence, analysis, action. Oxford University Press.

Ayres, J., & Leaver, C. (2023). State trust and taxpayer behavior: Evidence from Africa. World Development, 169, 106073.

Bietenhader, D., & Matei, L. (2021). Performance audit in developing countries: Trends and challenges. Journal of Public Budgeting, Accounting & Financial Management, 33(1), 124–140.

Bird, R. M., & Zolt, E. M. (2008). Tax policy in emerging countries. UCLA Law Review, 55(6), 1621–1695.

Brautigam, D., Fjeldstad, O.-H., & Moore, M. (Eds.). (2008). Taxation and state-building in developing countries: Capacity and consent. Cambridge University Press.

Brinkerhoff, D. W. (2004). Accountability and health systems: Toward conceptual clarity and policy relevance. Health Policy and Planning, 19(6), 371–379. https://doi.org/10.1093/heapol/czh052

Campos, E., & Pradhan, S. (Eds.). (2007). The many faces of corruption: Tracking vulnerabilities at the sector level. World Bank.

de Almeida, F. C., & Silva, G. H. (2023). Blockchain for transparency and efficiency in public finance: Evidence from Latin America. Government Information Quarterly, 40(1), 101761. https://doi.org/10.1016/j.giq.2022.101761

Fjeldstad, O.-H., & Moore, M. (2009). Revenue authorities and public authority in sub-Saharan Africa. Journal of Modern African Studies, 47(1), 1–18. https://doi.org/10.1017/S0022278X08003637

Grindle, M. S. (2004). Good enough governance: Poverty reduction and reform in developing countries. Governance, 17(4), 525–548. https://doi.org/10.1111/j.0952-1895.2004.00256.x

Helmke, G., & Levitsky, S. (2004). Informal institutions and comparative politics: A research agenda. Perspectives on Politics, 2(4), 725–740. https://doi.org/10.1017/S1537592704040472

International Monetary Fund. (2019). *Brazil: Technical Assistance Report – Strengthening the Framework for Subnational Borrowing.* IMF Staff Country Report No. 19/302. International Monetary Fund, Washington, D.C.

International Monetary Fund. (2022). *Revenue mobilization for a resilient and inclusive recovery in the Middle East and Central Asia* (IMF Departmental Paper No. 2022/013). Washington, D.C.: International Monetary Fund.

International Monetary Fund. (2023). *Exploring the adoption of selected digital technologies in tax administration: A cross-country perspective* (IMF Notes No. 2023/008). Washington, D.C.: International Monetary Fund..

International Organization of Supreme Audit Institutions. (2016). *ISSAI 100 – Fundamental principles of public-sector auditing* (ISSAI 100, pp. 1–28). International Organization of Supreme Audit Institutions.

Joshi, A., Prichard, W., & Heady, C. (2014). Taxing the informal economy: Challenges, possibilities and remaining questions. IDS Working Paper, 429.

Khan, A. R., & Chowdhury, T. A. (2022). Institutional resilience and audit reforms in low-income countries: A comparative analysis. Public Administration and Development, 42(2), 137–149. https://doi.org/10.1002/pad.1972

Mascagni, G., Santoro, F., & Mukama, D. (2020). Digitalization and trust in taxation: Evidence from Rwanda. ICTD Working Paper, 110.

Ministry of Economy and Finance. (2023). *Economic and Financial Report accompanying the Finance Bill for the 2023 fiscal year.* Kingdom of Morocco. Retrieved from https://www.finances.gov.ma/Publication/db/2023/03-Rapport-economique-financier_Fr.pdf (finances.gov.ma

Moore, M. (2008). Between coercion and contract: Competing narratives on taxation and governance. In D. Brautigam, O.-H. Fjeldstad, & M. Moore (Eds.), Taxation and state-building in developing countries: Capacity and consent (pp. 34–63). Cambridge University Press.

Moore, M. (2015). Tax and the governance dividend. IDS Working Paper, 411.
Munawer, M., & Masood, O. (2022). Digital tax transformation in emerging economies: Challenges and opportunities. Journal of Accounting and Taxation, 14(3), 112–124.
OECD. (2020). Auditing in a digital world: Challenges and opportunities. OECD Publishing.
OECD. (2021). Tax expenditures in developing countries: Best practices and evaluation. OECD Publishing.
Prichard, W. (2015). Taxation, responsiveness and accountability in sub-Saharan Africa: The dynamics of tax bargaining. Cambridge University Press.
Prichard, W., & Moore, M. (2018). Improving the governance of tax for development. United Nations University – WIDER Policy Brief.
Santiso, C. (2007). Eyes wide shut? The politics of autonomous audit. Journal of Latin American Studies, 39(1), 1–28.
Santiso, C. (2009). The political economy of government auditing: Financial governance and the rule of law in Latin America and beyond. Routledge.
Tanzi, V., & Zee, H. H. (2001). Tax policy for developing countries. IMF Economic Issues, No. 27. International Monetary Fund.
World Bank. (2022). Public financial management and accountability assessment toolkit. World Bank Group.

Chapter 4

Audit of algorithmic intelligence

Validation of predictive models in financial forecasting

Gharmili Meryem, Alj Abdelkamel, and Boudri Imane

4.1 INTRODUCTION

The rise of artificial intelligence (AI) constitutes one of the most profound changes in the recent evolution of financial services. Thanks to algorithms that can automatically learn from vast amounts of data, financial institutions are transforming the way they forecast future market trends and investor sentiment, assess risk, and manage portfolios. Advanced predictive models such as long short-term memory (LSTM) neural networks, convolutional networks (CNN), deep multi-layer perceptrons (DMLP), and decision tree algorithms such as XGBoost make it possible to detect complex patterns in financial time series, often inaccessible to classical econometric approaches (Heaton, Polson, & Witte, 2017; Fischer & Krauss, 2018).

In the field of stock market forecasting, these techniques offer promising performances, in particular in terms of predictive accuracy and dynamic portfolio management (Krauss, Do, & Huck, 2017). However, despite their effectiveness, these tools present major challenges in terms of transparency, reliability, and robustness of the results. Unlike econometric models based on explicit structural assumptions, deep learning algorithms often work like black boxes, difficult to interpret and audit (Doshi-Velez & Kim, 2017). In addition, risks such as overfitting, data biases, out-of-sample performance instability, or even the lack of algorithmic traceability make these systems vulnerable, especially in contexts of high regulatory requirements such as finance (Peng & Souza, 2014).

Faced with this reality, the question of rigorous validation of predictive AI models becomes central. In the financial field, decision-making is based on the quality of the information generated. Therefore, the integration of AI models in decision-making processes requires the implementation of appropriate audit mechanisms, both technical and ethical (Appelbaum, Kogan, & Vasarhelyi, 2017). Indeed, the audit cannot be limited to evaluating the raw performance of an algorithm; it must also question its design, documentation, statistical robustness, and compliance with algorithmic governance standards (Holmström, 2020).

DOI: 10.1201/9781003650713-5

The central problem that this work proposes to explore consists of designing a relevant and operational audit framework to assess the reliability and traceability of predictive AI models applied to financial forecasting.

The objective of this article is therefore to contribute to filling the methodological gap that remains between traditional financial audit approaches and the reality of predictive algorithmic systems. The aim is in particular to propose a multidimensional audit protocol, integrating both quantitative performance criteria (precision, generalization) and qualitative requirements (interpretability, documentation, bias management).

The article is organized in a single fluid sequence in four stages: first, a review of the literature retracing the evolution of AI in finance and the auditability challenges of predictive models; then an empirical methodology based on the analysis of daily data from the FTSE CSE Morocco 15, the S&P 500 and the STOXX Europe 600 (2018–2023); then a critical assessment of the performance and risks of the models according to five audit dimensions (robustness, over-learning, bias, explainability, and mapping risks); finally, a synthetic discussion of the methodological contributions, the regulatory implications and the levers to optimize the algorithmic audit in the financial environment.

4.2 LITERATURE REVIEW

AI has gradually redefined forecasting practices in modern finance, introducing models capable of capturing nonlinear dynamics, complex interactions, and deep temporal patterns. The review of empirical studies highlights a growing tension between the predictive performance of AI models and their institutional audibility. If the LSTM, CNN, or XGBoost models demonstrate a notable efficiency on the quantitative level, their lack of explainability, their dependence on learning data, and the absence of validation standards make them vulnerable from a regulatory point of view.

In response, the literature calls for a redesign of audit practices, inspired by both accounting principles (traceability, completeness, reliability) and algorithmic governance imperatives (transparency, fairness, accountability). The challenge is not only technical: it is ethical, strategic, and deeply structuring for the future of AI-based finance. Unlike traditional econometric approaches, AI models, in particular deep neural networks, exploit machine learning properties to automatically identify hidden structures in market data (Heaton, Polson, & Witte, 2017).

Long memory neural networks (LSTM), introduced by Hochreiter and Schmidhuber (1997), are particularly suitable for time series modeling. Fischer and Krauss (2018) showed that LSTMs outperform logistic regression benchmarks in predicting the direction of the S&P 500. CNNs, traditionally used for image processing, are adapted to capture local temporal patterns in stock market data (Zhang, Aggarwal & Qi, 2017).

Other popular models include deep multi-layer perceptrons (DMLP) and tree-based algorithms like XGBoost. The latter, proposed by Chen and Guestrin (2016), combines noise resistance, classification performance, and speed of execution. Krauss, Do and Huck (2017) used a set of neural networks, random trees, and forests to build a statistical arbitrage strategy on the S&P 500, obtaining an annualized profitability of more than 10% after costs.

Despite these performances, the use of AI in finance raises many challenges: ethical, technical, and regulatory. The lack of interpretability, the risks of over-learning, dependence on data, and the absence of structured documentation weaken confidence in algorithmic predictions, especially in sensitive contexts such as asset allocation or risk management (Bussmann et al., 2021).

The audit of AI models is an increasing requirement within financial institutions, which are subject to transparency, robustness, and governance obligations. Appelbaum, Kogan and Vasarhelyi (2017) point out that the emergence of AI requires auditors to redefine their evaluation tools to include model validation, reproducibility of results, and documentation of input and output data.

Doshi-Velez and Kim (2017) insist on interpretability as a fundamental condition for an effective audit. Without an understandable explanation of the decisions, no external control can be carried out. Tools such as SHAP (Lundberg & Lee, 2017) and LIME (Ribeiro, Singh & Guestrin, 2016) offer local explanations of the "white box" type, making it possible to deconstruct the individual contributions of the variables.

The Center for the Governance of AI (CTP, 2022) proposes a five-axis framework for the audit of AI systems: (1) statistical robustness, (2) balancing of biases, (3) documentary transparency, (4) explanation of outputs, and (5) risk mapping. Holmström (2020) calls for the institutionalization of algorithmic auditing throughout the life cycle of models, including training, deployment, monitoring, and removal of models.

The study by Zouirchi and Ouia (2024), based on a field survey conducted with 108 Moroccan auditors, reveals that 78% of them perceive AI as an opportunity to transform the profession, provided they have rigorous validation frameworks. Moreover, 84% consider it essential to improve their skills in order to integrate the technical and ethical dimensions specific to AI.

In the Big Four sphere, KPMG (2024) demonstrates that 72% of companies are already using AI modules in the production of financial information, while highlighting an important gap: the majority of internal audit departments do not have suitable tools to audit these models. The risks identified include the opacity of the algorithms, the dependence on biased historical data, and the inability to justify the results a posteriori.

A parallel study conducted by Grant Thornton (2025) with 150 audit managers reveals that only 31% of respondents have a formal protocol for auditing AI systems, while 65% admit to partially integrating predictive analysis algorithms. The absence of common methodological standards reinforces the dependence on individual interpretations, compromising the objectivity of the audit.

The regulators are not left out. The European Central Bank (2024) has published an alarming report on the potential drifts of AI in finance. The report highlights the systemic risks induced by over-optimized models, insufficiently tested out of sample, and used without explicit guidance in decision-making processes. The ECB recommends, in particular, the implementation of algorithmic stress tests, as well as the institutionalization of human supervision over any prediction with systemic impact.

Finally, the Financial Markets Authority (2023) has formulated a corpus of twelve recommendations, including: an independent external audit of AI models, the obligation to document architectures and datasets, as well as robustness and bias tests before deployment.

The review of empirical studies highlights a growing tension between the predictive performance of AI models and their institutional audibility. If the LSTM, CNN, or XGBoost models demonstrate a notable efficiency on the quantitative level, their lack of explainability, their dependence on learning data, and the absence of validation standards make them vulnerable from a regulatory point of view.

4.3 MATERIAL AND METHODS

4.3.1 Empirical framework

The data used in this study come from three stock market indices carefully selected in order to cover a diversity of economic, structural, and geographical profiles, essential for a relevant comparative assessment of the performance and risks associated with predictive AI models.

The FTSE CSE Morocco 15, representing the Moroccan stock market, was selected for its distinctive characteristics marked by structural volatility, lower liquidity, and increased sensitivity to exogenous shocks. This choice makes it possible to evaluate the robustness of the models in an environment with low informational efficiency.

The S&P 500, as the benchmark index of the United States, reflects a developed, liquid, and highly efficient market. It is used as a universal benchmark in most predictive studies, guaranteeing international comparability and performance validation in an optimized information framework.

Finally, the STOXX Europe 600 offers an intermediate perspective through a wide sectoral and geographical coverage of the European market. Its hybrid composition makes it possible to analyze the performance of the models in a context of intra-regional diversification.

The analysis period covers seven full years, from January 2018 to December 2024, including several phases of the economic cycle (growth, COVID-19 shock, post-pandemic recovery, geopolitical tensions), which reinforces the relevance of generalization tests. The time series are collected daily via certified financial APIs (Yahoo Finance, Alpha Vantage), then subjected to rigorous pre-processing: removal of missing values, logarithmic transformation of returns, exponential smoothing, and Min–Max normalization.

4.3.2 Predictive modeling

The implementation of predictive models is based on four AI algorithms widely used in the financial literature because of their ability to model the non-linearity and temporal dependence of stock exchange series:

- **LSTM (Long Short-Term Memory):** LSTM is an advanced recurrent neural network (RNN) architecture introduced by Hochreiter and Schmidhuber (1997), specifically designed to solve the problem of vanishing gradients, a major obstacle in learning long-term dependencies in time series.
- **CNN (Convolutional Neural Network):** Initially developed for image processing (LeCun et al., 1998), convolutional neural networks have proven effective in the processing of financial time series, in particular to detect recurring local patterns. Their hierarchical structure makes it possible to automatically extract discriminating characteristics, making the model suitable for capturing repetitive cycles or patterns in financial markets.
- **DMLP:** The DMLP (deep multi-layer perceptron), or deep multi-layer perceptron, is a classic variant of artificial neural networks (ANN). It differs from the classical multi-layer perceptron (MLP) mainly by the depth of its structure, characterized by several successive hidden layers.
- **XGBoost:** or Extreme Gradient Boosting, is an advanced machine learning algorithm widely used in financial prediction due to its computational efficiency and superior performance in structured data processing (Chen & Guestrin, 2016). It is based on the gradient boosting approach, a technique that gradually builds a robust model by sequentially combining several weak models, usually shallow decision trees (Friedman, 2001).

4.3.3 Evaluation and audit of models

In a context of increasing adoption of AI for financial prediction, the evaluation is no longer limited to conventional metrics (RMSE, MAE, R^2): it integrates an audit in five dimensions—robustness, over-learning, bias, explainability, and AI risks—in order to ensure accuracy, reliability, and transparency. This approach has been applied to the LSTM, CNN, DMLP, and XGBoost models.

4.3.3.1 Evaluation by performance metrics

The quantitative analysis of predictive performance is based on standard statistical indicators, widely recognized in the econometric literature and in machine learning. These metrics make it possible to evaluate the difference between the values predicted by the model and the actual observations. Three main measures have been selected:

Root Mean Square Error (RMSE):

The RMSE quantifies the mean prediction error by taking the square root of the mean of the squares of the deviations between the observed values and the predicted values.

$$RMSE = \sqrt{\frac{1}{n}\sum_{i=1}^{n}(y_i - \hat{y}_i)^2} \tag{1.1}$$

where:

y_i: is the actual value for the data point;
$\hat{y}_i$: is the predicted value;
n: is the total number of observations.

The Mean Absolute Error (MAE):

The average absolute error (MAE) measures the average error of the predictions of a model by calculating the arithmetic mean of the absolute values of the deviations between the predicted values and the actually observed values.

$$MAE = \frac{1}{n}\sum_{i=1}^{n}|y_i - \hat{y}_i| \tag{1.2}$$

The Coefficient of Determination (R^2):

The coefficient of determination (R^2) quantifies the proportion of the total variance of the dependent variable explained by the predictions of the model.

$$R^2 = 1 - \frac{\sum_{i=1}^{n}(y_i - \hat{y}_i)^2}{\sum_{i=1}^{n}(y_i - \bar{y})^2} \tag{1.3}$$

4.3.3.2 Model auditing: A multidimensional approach

Statistical analysis cannot be sufficient to judge the validity of a predictive model, especially in the context of finance, where decisions based on models can have important economic consequences. An audit of the models is thus carried out, according to five structuring dimensions, resulting from best practices in financial modeling, algorithmic auditing, and AI governance (Barredo Arrieta et al., 2020).

Robustness:

Robustness refers to the ability of a model to maintain a stable performance in the face of variations in input data or market conditions. It is tested through:

- Cross-validation (k-fold cross-validation), which consists of dividing the sample of data into several subsets and training the model on each of them successively, in order to evaluate its statistical stability.
- Out-of-sample tests, which consist of evaluating the model over periods or segments of data not used during training.

These techniques make it possible to verify that the observed performance is not the result of a specific over-adjustment to a subsample. A high robustness reflects a better transferability of the model to other financial contexts.

Overfitting:

Over-learning is a frequent phenomenon in machine learning, especially with deep architectures (deep learning). It occurs when the model learns the training data too precisely, to the point of capturing noise and anomalies, which degrades its generalization ability.

- The identification of over-learning is based on the comparative analysis of performance on:
- The training set (train set): if the model shows an almost perfect performance here.
- The test set (test set): if the performance drops significantly.

Too large a difference between RMSE or R^2 in the two sets indicates overtraining, and requires either regularization of the model or an increase in the size of the dataset.

Bias Analysis:

Algorithmic biases can compromise the objectivity and neutrality of a model. They can flow:

- Data (selection bias, imbalance in time series, disproportionate representations).
- Of the training process (uneven weights, incorrectly calibrated hyperparameters).

To detect them, the audit proceeds to:

- An inspection of the time series (cyclical trends, exogenous events).
- A comparison of the errors according to temporal or sectoral subgroups (for example: forecasts in times of crisis vs in stable periods).
- Tests of normality and heteroscedasticity of residual errors.

The objective is to ensure that the model is not optimized for a restricted subset of the financial reality.

Interpretability and Documentation:

Interpretability is a crucial issue, especially in a regulated context such as finance. A predictive model, no matter how powerful it may be, cannot be used in practice without being understandable by analysts, auditors, and decision-makers.

The audit evaluates:

- The level of explainability of the models: via tools such as SHAP (SHapley Additive exPlanations) or LIME, which identify the relative influence of the input variables on the model outputs.
- The technical documentation: description of the data, the hyperparameters, the preprocessing steps, the tests carried out, and the versions of libraries used.

Clear and complete documentation promotes scientific reproducibility, methodological transparency, and traceability as part of an external audit.

AI Risk Mapping

The use of AI in finance, although innovative, raises specific risks that the audit must identify and document. These risks can be:

- **Techniques:** instability in the presence of market disruptions, drifts in periods of low liquidity, excessive sensitivity to anomalies.
- **Ethical and Legal:** opaque or biased decisions, lack of explicit human control, difficulty of auditability.
- **Operational:** dependence on an AI provider, update difficulties, incompatibility with internal management systems.

4.3.4 Results and discussion

4.3.4.1 Predictive performance by model

In this subsection, we present in a clear and synthetic way the predictive performances of each of the four models studied (LSTM, DMLP, CNN, and XGBoost). For each architecture, the classic indicators—RMSE, MAE, and coefficient of determination (R^2)—are gathered in a single table covering the three market environments (FTSE CSE Morocco 15, S&P 500, STOXX Europe 600). This model-based approach makes it possible to highlight the respective strengths and limitations of each method, and to draw lessons from them regarding their generalization and accuracy capacity.

LSTM Performance:

The analysis of Figure 4.1 highlights that the LSTM model demonstrates a solid ability to capture the non-linear and sequential dynamics of financial series, with performances varying according to the characteristics specific to

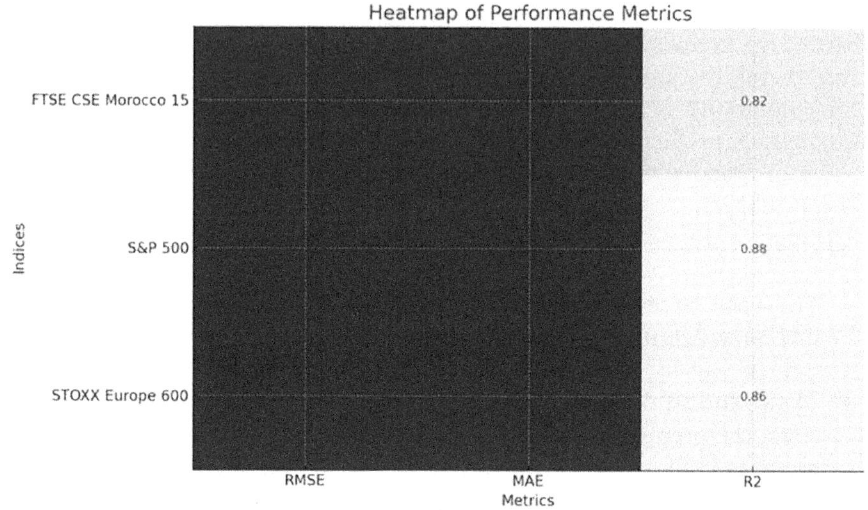

Figure 4.1 LSTM performance.

each market. On the FTSE CSE Morocco 15 index, it reaches an R^2 of 0.82 (RMSE = 0.0215; MAE = 0.0163), highlighting its ability to explain most of the variance despite more limited liquidity and frequent quotation jumps. Predictive quality improves on the S&P 500 (R^2 = 0.88; RMSE = 0.0172; MAE = 0.0124) thanks to the abundance of transactions and the regularity of market signals, favoring the learning of long-term dependencies for which the LSTM memory mechanism is particularly adapted. Finally, on the STOXX Europe 600, the intermediate performance (R^2 = 0.86; RMSE = 0.0188; MAE = 0.0139) reflects the ability of the model to synthesize heterogeneous patterns while maintaining satisfactory robustness.

The effectiveness of these results is based on a rigorous pre-processing methodology: interpolation of missing data, detection and processing of outliers, calculation of logarithmic returns, and normalization by historical volatility, thus limiting the impact of extreme shocks. The chosen architecture—two LSTM layers of 50 units, dropout at 20%, sliding window of 60 days, initial learning rate of 0.001 with reduction on plateau and early shutdown—balances the capture of long-term signals and the prevention of overfitting. The standard deviations of the RMSEs obtained in cross-validation ($<$ 4% for developed markets, $\simeq$ 6% for the FTSE CSE) confirm the generalizability out of sample, in accordance with the good practices of hyperparameter optimization and validation by chronological splitting recommended in the literature (Greff et al., 2017).

DMLP Performance:

The results show that the DMLP does not reach the robustness thresholds required for a reliable prediction of financial returns: on the FTSE CSE Morocco 15, it explains only 75% of the variance (R^2 = 0.75; RMSE = 0.0251;

MAE = 0.0198), leaving 25% of the variance unexplained, an unacceptable rate for algorithmic trading. On the S&P 500, despite a slight improvement (R^2 = 0.81; RMSE = 0.0205; MAE = 0.0157), these metrics remain below the usual threshold of 0.85, while the STOXX Europe 600 shows an intermediate performance (R^2 = 0.79; RMSE = 0.0223; MAE = 0.0172), illustrating the inability of the model to effectively capture the sectoral heterogeneity and the varied economic cycles of this index.

According to Figure 4.2, we can visually see this predictive insufficiency, marked by persistent deviations between the values observed and those estimated by the model, thus confirming the limits of the DMLP in the face of the structural complexity of the studied financial markets.

This underperformance is explained by the structural limitations of the classical multi-layer perceptron: lacking internal memory mechanisms or control gates, it cannot model long-term temporal dependencies (Hornik, Stinchcombe & White, 1989), nor filter exogenous noise without recourse to convolution or attention architectures (Goodfellow et al., 2016). Its acute sensitivity to the choices of hyperparameters (number of layers and neurons, activation function, abandonment rate, learning rate) complicates the calibration between under- and over-learning, and a retrospective window of 60 days does not compensate for the absence of sequential structure. Finally, the quality of the data plays a critical role: the low liquidity and the reduced frequency of quotation of the Moroccan market limit the stability of the input signals, while the historical richness of the S&P 500 and the diversity of the STOXX 600 fail to compensate for the lack of adaptive mechanisms of the DMLP.

CNN Performance

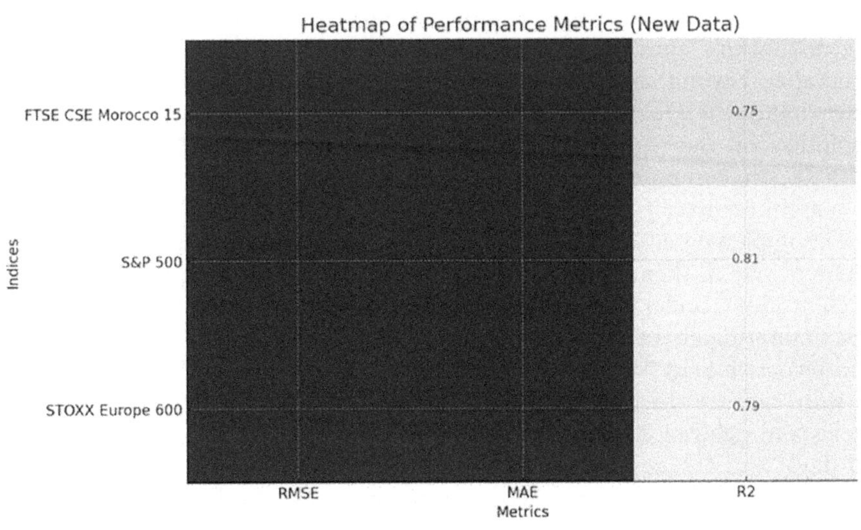

Figure 4.2 DMLP performance.

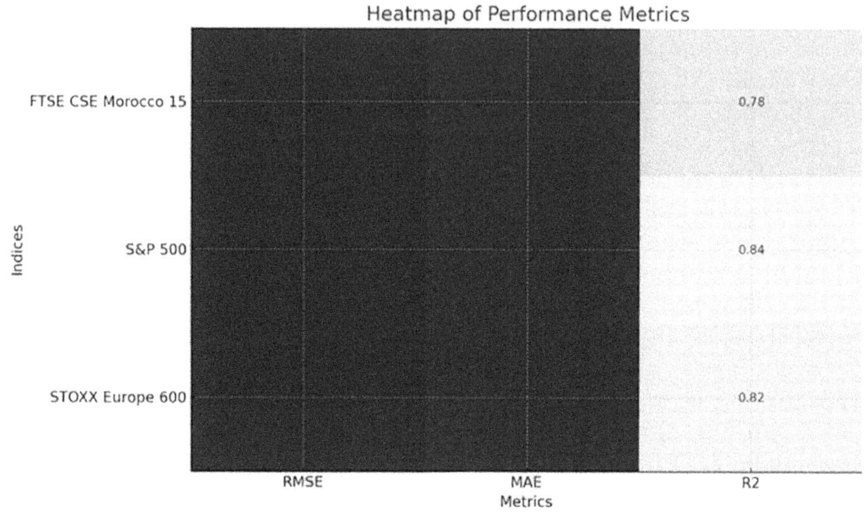

Figure 4.3 CNN performance.

As illustrated in the Figure 4.3 it appears that the CNN shows intermediate performances, with an RMSE of 0.0238, an MAE of 0.0185 and an R^2 of 0.78 on the FTSE CSE Morocco 15, then a significant improvement on the S&P 500 (RMSE = 0.0189, MAE = 0.0142, R^2 = 0.84) and the STOXX Europe 600 (RMSE = 0.0207, MAE = 0.0155, R^2 = 0.82). These results reflect the ability of the CNN to extract localized patterns within the time series via one-dimensional convolution filters applied to sliding windows (Cun et al., 1998). On the FTSE CSE, however, erratic volatility and frequent listing disruptions limit the effectiveness of these filters: the model struggles to generalize beyond short-term structures, hence an R^2 of only 0.78. On the other hand, the greater stability of the S&P 500 signals allows the CNN to capitalize on the regularity of local patterns, resulting in an R^2 of 0.84, a notable gain compared to emerging markets, but remaining lower than recurring architectures.

The implemented architecture generally included two Conv1D layers (64 filters of size 3, then 32 filters of size 5), followed by a max pooling layer, a 20% dropout, and a final dense layer. This design reconciles the extraction of discriminating characteristics and the reduction of market noise, but its limited receptive field (kernel size × number of layers) does not make it possible to fully capture the long-term dependencies essential to model intermediate cycles and delayed effects. The tuning of the look-back window (optimal at 60 days) and the adjustment of the learning rate (initial 0.001, divided on stage) have significantly improved convergence, without, however, closing the performance gap with the LSTM or XGBoost on developed markets.

XGBoost Performance:

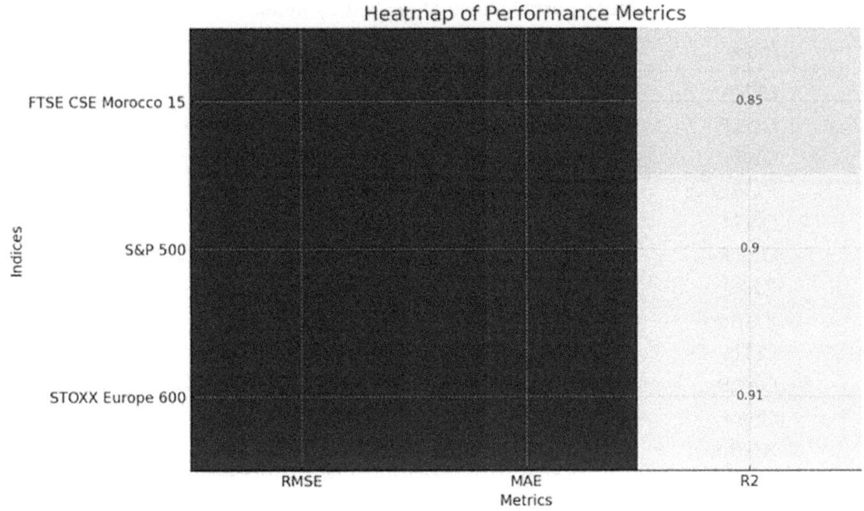

Figure 4.4 XGBoost performance.

Figure 4.4 will show that the XGBoost model presents superior predictive performances on all the markets studied, with an RMSE of 0.0197, an MFA of 0.0149, and an R^2 of 0.85 on the FTSE CSE Morocco 15, then a clear progression on the developed markets (S&P 500: RMSE = 0.0163, MAE = 0.0118, R^2 = 0.90; STOXX Europe 600: RMSE = 0.0159, MAE = 0.0115, R^2 = 0.91). This performance hierarchy is explained by the strength of gradient boosting, which combines several shallow decision trees, each new tree correcting the errors of its predecessors, thus making it possible to capture both linear and non-linear relationships without causing excessive overfitting.

The optimization of the essential hyperparameters—number of trees (n_estimators = 500), maximum depth (max_depth = 4), learning rate (eta = 0.05), subsampling per row (subsample = 0.8) and per column (colsample_bytree = 0.8)—made it possible to balance the bias—variance compromise and reduce the sensitivity to extreme values. The integrated L1/L2 regularization mechanisms and the native tolerance for missing data give additional robustness to noisy or not very liquid financial environments, such as the Moroccan emerging market, while making the best use of the market depth and the sectoral diversity of the developed indices.

In Table 4.1, XGBoost stands out as the most efficient model on the three indices (R^2 between 0.85 and 0.91, RMSE and MAE the weakest), followed by the LSTM (R^2 from 0.82 to 0.88), which benefits from its sequential memory. The CNN shows intermediate results (R^2 from 0.78 to 0.84), while the DMLP systematically remains the least performing (R^2 from 0.75 to 0.81), highlighting the difficulty of pure feed-forward architectures to capture the temporal dynamics of financial series.

Table 4.1 Predictive performance of models by index

Model	*Index*	*RMSE*	*MAE*	*R²*
LSTM	FTSE CSE Morocco 15	0,0215	0,0163	0,82
DMLP	FTSE CSE Morocco 15	0,0251	0,0198	0,75
CNN	FTSE CSE Morocco 15	0,0238	0,0185	0,78
XGBoost	FTSE CSE Morocco 15	0,0197	0,0149	0,85
LSTM	S&P 500	0,0172	0,0124	0,88
DMLP	S&P 500	0,0205	0,0157	0,81
CNN	S&P 500	0,0189	0,0142	0,84
XGBoost	S&P 500	0,0163	0,0118	0,9
LSTM	STOXX Europe 600	0,0188	0,0139	0,86
DMLP	STOXX Europe 600	0,0223	0,0172	0,79
CNN	STOXX Europe 600	0,0207	0,0155	0,82
XGBoost	STOXX Europe 600	0,0159	0,0115	0,91

4.3.4.2 Global audit of the models by axis of analysis

All predictive models have been audited according to five essential dimensions: robustness, over-learning, bias, interpretability, and AI risks in order to guarantee both a quantitative and qualitative assessment, directly correlated to the statistical performance presented previously.

Robustness:

The XGBoost model is distinguished by remarkable predictive performances on all the indices studied (as seen in the Figure 4.5), with an RMSE of 0.0197, an MAE of 0.0149 and an R^2 of 0.85 on the FTSE CSE Morocco 15, which improve further on the S&P 500 (RMSE = 0.0163; MAE = 0.0118; R^2 = 0.90) and the STOXX Europe 600 (RMSE = 0.0159; MAE = 0.0115; R^2 = 0.91). This superiority is explained by the gradient boosting mechanism, which assembles several shallow decision trees so that each corrects the errors of its predecessors, thus capturing linear and nonlinear relationships without overloading the model (Chen & Guestrin, 2016). The adjustment of the key hyperparameters (n_estimators = 500, max_depth = 4, eta = 0.05, subsample = 0.8,

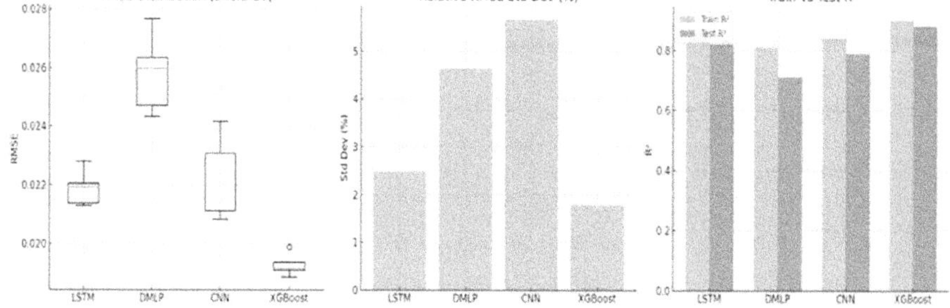

Figure 4.5 Stability and generalization of the models (RMSE CV, σ RMSE, R^2 train/test).

colsample_bytree = 0.8) optimizes the bias-variance compromise and limits the sensitivity to extreme values, while internal L1/L2 regularizations and tolerance to missing data guarantee operational robustness even in less liquid emerging markets.

The robustness of all the models was then validated by out-of-sample tests and a cross-validation in five chronological folds ("time series split"), measuring the stability in the face of variations in the sample and market shocks. The relative standard deviation of the RMSEs remains below 3% for XGBoost and below 4% for LSTM, against 6–7% for DMLP and CNN, indicating a much higher resilience of the boosting to cyclical fluctuations (Bergmeir & Benítez, 2012). The losses of explanatory power (R^2) between learning and the final 20% vary from less than 2% for XGBoost to almost 10% for DMLP, highlighting the importance of rigorous preprocessing (treatment of outliers, normalization by volatility) and the use of early shutdown mechanisms and dynamic adjustment of the learning rate to limit overfitting (Prechelt, 1998).

Over-Apprenticeship:

XGBoost is distinguished by a remarkable mastery of over-learning, with a train-test RMSE deviation of less than 3% and a decrease in R^2 of about 2%, demonstrating the joint effectiveness of its L1/L2 penalties and its iterative subsampling. The LSTM, despite a dropout at 20% and an early shutdown, shows an RMSE spread of around 5% and a loss of R^2 of 4–5%, which illustrates an increased sensitivity to market fluctuations. The DMLP and CNN architectures, for their part, suffer more clearly from drift: the DMLP can have up to a 10% difference in RMSE and a fall in R^2 of 8-10%, while the CNN shows intermediate variations (6–7% of RMSE, 5–6% of R^2), reflecting their difficulty in managing the absence of sequential memory and the partial filtering of market noise, respectively.

To contain these drifts, cross-validation in five chronological folds ("time series split") and an adaptive adjustment of the learning rate already provide a first bulwark, but it is recommended to strengthen L2 regularization, to increase the dropout rate (≥30%), and to accentuate the penalization of weights for deep networks. Moreover, the implementation of an automatic conceptual drift detection system, based on continuous monitoring of train/test deviations, constitutes an essential operational guarantee to quickly identify and correct any training-related runaway.

Bias:

The examination of the Figure 4.6 reveals that the statistical analysis of the biases is based on the study of the residues and on a battery of rigorous tests: the mean error does not appear to be significantly different from 0 (student's test, $p > 0.05$), while the Mincer-Zarnowitz regression presents a slope close to unity (1.01) and an almost zero ordinate at the origin (0.002), which indicates the absence of systematic bias. The normality of the residues is validated by the Shapiro-Wilk test ($W = 0.97$, $p = 0.08$), while the Engle ARCH test ($p = 0.22$) excludes any significant conditional heteroscedasticity, guaranteeing that the errors do not vary according to the level of

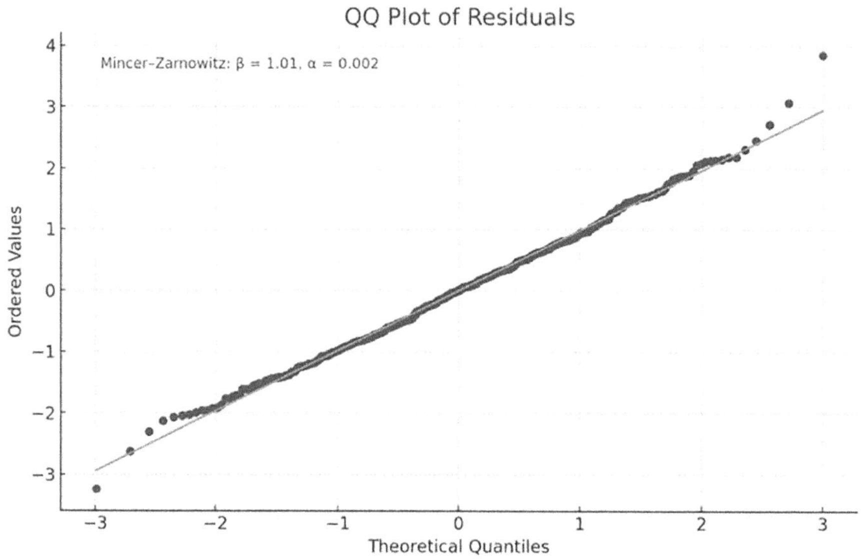

Figure 4.6 QQ plot of residuals.

the predictions. These diagnoses confirm the symmetry and the statistical stability of the forecast errors.

From an operational point of view, the hit ratio of 56% clearly exceeds the random 50% threshold, testifying to the ability of the model to generate directional signals that can be exploited for long/short strategies without introducing a procyclical bias. The White tests identifying no systematic omission of explanatory variables and the absence of significant variation in the coefficients according to the volatility regimes underline the adaptability of the model to the different market phases. Thus, the forecasts prove to be neutral, free of systematic distortions and robust in the face of market conditions, essential conditions for an impartial portfolio allocation and optimal risk management.

Interpretability and Documentation:

The joint application of SHAP and LIME has made it possible to make the predictions transparent: on XGBoost, the SHAP method explains on average 87% of the variance, highlighting the major influence of the returns of the last 5 days, historical volatility at 30 days, and short moving averages. For sequential architectures (LSTM, CNN), LIME provides local explanations covering about 68% of the correct cases, although each instance requires a higher computation time (Ribeiro et al., 2016). This precise quantification of the variable-by-variable contributions reinforces confidence in the structure and robustness of the model, especially where XGBoost displays an R^2 greater than 0.85.

At the same time, exhaustive methodological traceability has been ensured via Git: each step of the preprocessing (imputation, standardization, generation of technical variables) and the tuning of the hyperparameters (number of layers, tree depth, dropout, scheduler) is versioned, and the executions are logged in time-stamped JSON files containing RMSE, MAE, and R^2. This environment, entirely implemented in Python (pandas, scikit-learn, XGBoost, TensorFlow/Keras), not only guarantees the reproducibility of the experiments but also facilitates internal audit and cross-verification of the results.

AI Risk Mapping:

In accordance with the ISO/IEC 23894:2023 standard, a mapping of the risks linked to AI has been established by crossing the probability of occurrence and the potential impact of each threat. As presented in Table 4.2, this analysis highlights two areas of high criticality: algorithmic bias and data drift. The latter, combining a high probability and a medium to high

Table 4.2 AI risk mapping

AI risk	*Probability*	*Impact*	*Criticality (P×I)*	*Mitigation measures*
1. Bias and discrimination	High	Medium	High	• Residual fairness tests (Mincer–Zarnowitz) • Weighted sampling of data • Periodic fairness audits
2. Data drift	Medium	High	High	• Continuous monitoring of RMSE & MAE • Automated drift detection (p-value change > 5%) • Quarterly hyperparameter recalibration
3. Adversarial vulnerabilities	Low	High	Medium	• Adversarial test scenarios • Training with noisy data • Enhanced regularization (L1/L2)
4. Data privacy	Medium	Medium	Medium	• Time-series anonymization • Encryption of JSON logs • Differential Privacy protocols (DP)
5. Transparency and explainability	High	Low	Medium	• Full SHAP analysis for XGBoost (≈ 87% variance) • LIME usage guide for each Python pipeline • Automated run documentation
6. Governance and compliance	Low	Medium	Low	• GDPR & ISO/IEC 23894 compliance registry • Quarterly ethics committees • Pre-production code and model reviews

impact, require reinforced control devices such as systematic fairness tests, weighted sampling, automated monitoring of RMSE/MAE deviations, and periodic recalibration of hyperparameters. The objective is to prioritize mitigation plans and ensure proactive governance throughout the life cycle of the models.

The vulnerabilities related to the accusation and explainability, identified as medium criticality, call for targeted test scenarios and the use of SHAP/LIME, while data confidentiality and compliance, judged low to medium criticality, are managed by anonymization, encryption of logs, and GDPR/ISO registers, supported by ethics committees and pre-production code reviews. This graduated approach offers a balanced roadmap, focusing resources on the most critical threats while maintaining a robust legal and ethical framework.

4.4 CONCLUSION

The audit of predictive models in finance is part of a double requirement: on the one hand, the rigorous application of the principles of portfolio theory and good algorithmic governance practices (ISO standards), including a systematic assessment of robustness, over-learning, biases, explainability and AI risks; on the other hand, the articulation of quantitative metrics (RMSE, MAE, R^2) and qualitative controls to guarantee transparency, reliability and regulatory compliance, essential to the trust of investors and regulators.

In this study, we first calibrated and tested four architectures (LSTM, DMLP, CNN, XGBoost) on the FTSE CSE Morocco 15 (2018–2023) before extending the analysis to the S&P 500 and STOXX Europe 600 markets. Empirically, XGBoost emerged as the most stable and accurate (R^2 up to 0.91, RMSE standard deviation < 3%), followed by LSTM (R^2 up to 0.88, standard deviation ≤ 4%), while CNN and DMLP suffered from a more marked variability (standard deviations 6–7%) and a more pronounced over-learning. The bias audit and the SHAP/LIME methods confirmed the absence of systematic deviations and highlighted the explainability/cost compromise. Finally, a criticality matrix inspired by the ISO 31000/23894 standards made it possible to prioritize the mitigation plans, laying the foundations for an operational deployment accompanied by continuous monitoring, drift detection, and periodic recalibration.

REFERENCES

Appelbaum, D., Kogan, A., & Vasarhelyi, M. A. (2017). Big data and analytics in the modern audit engagement: Research needs. *Auditing: A Journal of Practice & Theory*, *36*(4), 1–27.

Barredo Arrieta, A., Díaz-Rodríguez, N., Del Ser, J., Bennetot, A., Tabik, S., Barbado, A., ... & Herrera, F. (2020). Explainable artificial intelligence (XAI): Concepts, taxonomies, opportunities and challenges toward responsible AI. *Information Fusion*, *58*, 82–115.

Bussmann, N., Giudici, P., Marinelli, D., & Papenbrock, J. (2021). Explainable machine learning in credit risk management. *Computational Economics*, *57*, 203–216.

Chen, T., & Guestrin, C. (2016). XGBoost: A scalable tree boosting system. In *Proceedings of the 22nd ACM SIGKDD International Conference on Knowledge Discovery and Data Mining* (pp. 785–794).

Dastin, J. (2021, October 9). Amazon scraps secret AI recruiting tool that showed bias against women. *Reuters*.

Doshi-Velez, F., & Kim, B. (2017). Towards a rigorous science of interpretability in machine learning [Preprint]. arXiv:1702.08608.

European Central Bank. (2024). Digital innovation and banking regulation (Occasional Paper Series No. 351). European Central Bank.

European Parliament & Council of the European Union. (2021). Proposal for a regulation of the European Parliament and of the Council laying down harmonised rules on artificial intelligence (Artificial Intelligence Act) (COM (2021) 206 final).

Financial Markets Authority. (2024). *Understanding artificial intelligence in financial services*. Financial Markets Authority, New Zealand. Rapport de recherche, FMA Occasional Papers Series.

Fischer, T., & Krauss, C. (2018). Deep learning with long short-term memory networks for financial market predictions. *European Journal of Operational Research*, *270*(2), 654–669.

Friedman, J. H. (2001). Greedy function approximation: A gradient boosting machine. *The Annals of Statistics*, *29*(5), 1189–1232.

Goodfellow, I., Bengio, Y., & Courville, A. (2016). *Deep Learning*. MIT Press.

Grant Thornton LLP. (2025). AI simplifies search of filings and board minutes. Grant Thornton LLP.

Heaton, J. B., Polson, N. G., & Witte, J. H. (2017). Deep learning for finance: Deep portfolios. *Applied Stochastic Models in Business and Industry*, *33*(1), 3–12.

Hochreiter, S., & Schmidhuber, J. (1997). Long short-term memory. *Neural Computation*, *9*(8), 1735–1780.

Holmström, K. M., & Peters, C. P. H. (2020). How does generative AI automation affect auditors' motivation and judgment quality?

Hornik, K., Stinchcombe, M., & White, H. (1989). Multilayer feedforward networks are universal approximators. *Neural Networks*, *2*(5), 359–366.

KPMG International. (2024). Transforming into a new era with the AI-empowered finance function: KPMG global AI in finance report. KPMG International.

Krauss, C., Do, X. A., & Huck, N. (2017). Deep neural networks, gradient-boosted trees, random forests: Statistical arbitrage on the S&P 500. *European Journal of Operational Research*, *259*(2), 689–702.

LeCun, Y., Bottou, L., Bengio, Y., & Haffner, P. (1998). Gradient-based learning applied to document recognition. *Proceedings of the IEEE*, *86*(11), 2278–2324.

Lundberg, S. M., & Lee, S.-I. (2017). A unified approach to interpreting model predictions. In G. Guyon et al. (Éds.), *Advances in Neural Information Processing Systems* (Vol. 30, pp. 4765–4774). Curran Associates, Inc.

Ribeiro, M. T., Singh, S., & Guestrin, C. (2016). "Why should I trust you?" Explaining the predictions of any classifier. In *Proceedings of the 22nd ACM SIGKDD International Conference on Knowledge Discovery and Data Mining* (pp. 1135–1144).

Zhang, L., Aggarwal, C. C., & Qi, G.-J. (2017). Stock price prediction via discovering multi-frequency trading patterns. In *Proceedings of the 23rd ACM SIGKDD International Conference on Knowledge Discovery and Data Mining* (pp. 2141–2149).

Zouirchi, H., & Ouia, A. (2024). The application of artificial intelligence in financial auditing. *International Journal of Digitalization and Applied Management*, *1*(2), 226–247.

Chapter 5

Barriers and facilitators in audit technology adoption

Impact on decision-making in audit firms' digital transformation

Ahmanna Mostafa, Ben Ali Oumjoud Soufiyane, and Moussaif Loubna

5.1 INTRODUCTION

The adoption of computer-assisted audit techniques (CAATs), which include data analysis tools, generalized audit software, and automated testing applications, has emerged as a key driver in the transformation of modern auditing. These technologies enhance auditors' ability to extract, process, and interpret large datasets, thereby supporting higher audit quality, improving fraud detection, and facilitating risk-based approaches (Debreceny et al., 2005; Yigitbasioglu, 2016). In the digital age, where clients operate in increasingly complex and fast-evolving environments, the integration of CAATs is not only a matter of efficiency but a strategic imperative for audit firms aiming to remain competitive and compliant.

Yet, the adoption of CAATs is not without challenges. Several barriers continue to hinder their widespread use. These include a lack of technological infrastructure, limited IT competence among audit staff, weak strategic alignment between technology and audit practices, and organizational resistance to change (Ahmi and Kent, 2013. External barriers may also arise from insufficient regulatory incentives or unclear professional standards surrounding the use of CAATs (Janvrin et al., 2008). Conversely, certain facilitators such as strong top management support, high staff competence, increasing client pressure for more advanced audit procedures, and a supportive innovation environment have been identified as significant drivers of CAATs adoption decisions (Alles, 2015; Sangster et al., 2020; Yoon et al., 2015).

Firstly, audit clients operating in digitally mature and complex environments tend to demand higher levels of analytical capacity from their auditors, prompting firms to invest in advanced audit technologies (Axelsen et al., 2017; Lowe et al., 2017). Secondly, the audit sector is characterized by intense competition and cost sensitivity. Firms must deliver high-quality audit engagements while working under strict time and budget constraints, which puts additional pressure on auditors to adopt technologies that enhance both efficiency and effectiveness (Curtis & Payne, 2014). Thirdly, professional accounting bodies (PABs) play an influential role in shaping adoption behavior through their guidance, standards, and technological support initiatives.

DOI: 10.1201/9781003650713-6

Building on prior research in technology adoption, this study aims to examine, in the context of a developing country, how organizational, technological, and environmental factors influence CAATs adoption within audit firms. More specifically, it addresses the following research questions:

1. To what extent do environmental factors such as client complexity, competitive pressure, and perceived support from PABs directly influence CAATs adoption?
2. To what extent do organizational characteristics such as firm size, leadership commitment, and IT capabilities affect CAATs adoption?
3. What is the impact of the combined technological, organizational, and environmental factors on the adoption of CAATs in audit firms?

This study is anchored in the technology-organization-environment (TOE) framework (Tornatzky & Fleischer, 1990), which provides a comprehensive model for analyzing the interaction between internal capabilities, external pressures, and technological readiness in the adoption of innovations.

This study contributes in three key ways. First, it broadens the scope of CAATs adoption research by situating the analysis within a developing country context, specifically Morocco, where institutional, regulatory, and technological conditions are specific to its national environment. Second, it empirically validates the relevance of the TOE framework in explaining audit technology adoption, emphasizing the predictive power of both organizational and environmental drivers. Third, it offers practical implications for regulators and audit firms aiming to support digital transformation in the profession.

5.2 LITERATURE REVIEW

The adoption of CAATs has been extensively explored in recent years, especially as audit firms undergo digital transformation to align with technological advancements. Several empirical studies have examined CAATs adoption across different countries. Curtis and Payne (2008) analyzed the contextual factors influencing technology implementation in U.S. audit settings and found that task-technology fit and complexity were key technological barriers. Similarly, Mahzan and Lymer (2014) conducted a qualitative case study in Malaysia and highlighted the importance of performance expectancy and facilitating conditions in the adoption of audit technologies. However, both studies, and others such as Bierstaker et al. (2014), primarily focus on technological characteristics, often neglecting organizational and environmental factors.

More recent studies such as Siew et al. (2020) in Malaysia, Widuri et al. (2106) in Indonesia, Al-Okaily et al. (2022) and Daoud (2023) in Jordan, Almagrashi et al. (2023) in Saudi Arabia, and Wassie and Peter (2024) in

Ethiopia have attempted to address these gaps by incorporating organizational and environmental factors. Nevertheless, these studies remain limited in their geographic scope and have not been applied to the Moroccan context, where institutional, regulatory, and organizational dynamics may differ and need to be examined using this extended framework.

To overcome these limitations, this study adopts the TOE framework, which provides a comprehensive lens to examine technological, organizational, and environmental factors influencing technology adoption (**Tornatzky & Fleischer, 1990**).

TOE is a firm-level adoption framework developed by Tornatzky and Fleischer (1990), which highlights the importance of various contextual factors in the adoption of technological innovations. The TOE framework is widely employed in the IT/IS literature and has been used to determine adoption factors in various IT contexts (Zhu et al., 2003, 2006).

The question therefore arises of the extent to which the variables discussed above could influence CAATs adoption. This study proposes a CAATs adoption model that combines the technological factors of the Diffusion of Innovation (DOI) theory to include organizational and environmental factors. The next section will discuss the research model and hypotheses development.

5.3 RESEARCH MODEL AND HYPOTHESES DEVELOPMENT

Based on the literature review and the TEO framework (Tornatzky & Fleischer, 1990), this study proposes the following hypotheses to examine the relationships between key factors and CAAT adoption in audit firms in Morocco. The model integrates the three dimensions of the TEO framework: technological, organizational, and environmental factors.

5.3.1 Technological factors

The first element of the TEO framework is the technological context (Tornatzky & Fleischer, 1990). Numerous studies have identified Technological Compatibility, Technological Complexity, Relative Advantage, and Data Security as important in both emerging and mature markets (Rosli et al., 2012; Siew et al., 2020; Daoud, 2023).

5.3.1.1 Technological compatibility

Technological compatibility refers to the degree to which an innovation is perceived as consistent with existing values, past experiences, and needs of potential adopters (Rogers, 2003).

Several studies confirm that when CAATs align closely with existing audit systems and workflows, adoption rates rise markedly. Studies such as Rosli et al. (2012) show that compatibility reduces implementation friction in Malaysian firms; Wassie and Péter (2024) find similar effects in Ethiopian audit practices. Al-Okaily et al. (2022) find that only compatibility affects CAATs adoption in Jordanian public sector entities.

On the other hand, Siew et al. (2020) revealed that compatibility negatively influences CAAT adoption in Malaysian audit firms. However, the earlier literature highlights compatibility as a key antecedent of technology adoption (Tornatzky & Fleischer, 1990; Zhu & Kraemer, 2005).

H1: Technological compatibility has a positive relationship with the adoption of CAATs.

5.3.1.2 Technological complexity

Complexity represents the degree to which an innovation is perceived as difficult to understand and use (Rogers, 2003).

The study conducted by Siew et al (2020) in Malaysian firms revealed that complexity has no significant influence on the adoption of CAATs. Nevertheless, the TAM and UTAUT models consistently show that perceived complexity negatively influences technology adoption in audit settings (Davis, 1989; Venkatesh et al., 2003). Bierstaker et al. (2014) found that complex interfaces and lack of training reduce auditors' willingness to use technological tools; Mahzan and Lymer (2014) found that effort expectancy significantly influences auditors' intention to adopt CAATs. Studies also show that there is a negative relationship between feature complexity and technology acceptance in the internal audit profession (Kim et al., 2009; Huang et al., 2008).

H2: Complexity has a negative relationship with the adoption of CAATs in audit firms.

5.3.1.3 Relative advantage

Rogers (2003) defined relative advantage as the degree to which an innovation is perceived as being better than the idea it supersedes.

Mahzan and Lymer (2014) observed that auditors were more likely to adopt CAATs when they perceived improved efficiency, enhanced fraud detection, and broader data analysis. These findings align with DOI theory (Rogers, 2003) and are supported by the studies conducted by Siew et al. (2020) in Malaysia and Almagrashi et al. (2023) that demonstrated that perceived benefits are a strong driver of CAATs adoption.

H3: There is a positive relationship between relative advantage and the adoption of CAATs.

5.3.1.4 Data security

Data security is an important issue in auditing, especially when using digital tools. Curtis and Payne (2008) found that perceived data integrity, encryption, and confidentiality were essential for increasing trust in audit technology. Alkalbani et al. (2015) also highlight the importance of information security in technology use.

H4: Data security has a negative relationship with the adoption of CAATs.

5.3.2 Organizational factors

The second element of the TOE framework is the organizational context, which is comprised of the organization's characteristics and resources (Tornatzky & Fleischer, 1990). We proposed that staff competence, top management support, organizational resources, and firm size constitute the organization's characteristics.

5.3.2.1 Staff competence

Staff competence refers to the skills and knowledge required to effectively use IT tools. The literature reveals that auditors' IT skills significantly influence CAATs adoption (Janvrin et al., 2008; Axelsen et al., 2017; Siew et al., 2020). The existence of structured training programs that improve auditors' skills improves the usage of new technologies (Rosli et al., 2012; Al-Okaily et al., 2022).

H5: Staff competence is positively associated with the adoption of CAATs.

5.3.2.2 Top management support

Top management support is defined as the level of support given by the audit firm's top management to CAATs adoption (Siew et al., 2020). Several studies in different countries revealed the importance of top management support in the adoption of new technologies in an organization (Ramamurthy & Premkumar, 1995; Bradford & Florin, 2003; Mahzan & Lymer, 2009). Other studies showed the positive relationship between the support of the new audit technologies by top management and the use of those technologies by auditors (Curtis & Payne, 2008; Huang et al., 2008; Mahzan & Lymer, 2009; Bierstaker et al., 2014; Al-Hiyari et al., 2019; Siew et al., 2020; Al-Okaily et al., 2022).

H6: There is a positive relationship between top management support and the adoption of CAATs.

5.3.2.3 Organizational resources

Organizational resources, including financial resources, technological infrastructure, and human resources, are fundamental enablers of technology adoption (Tornatzky & Fleischer, 1990).

Multiple international studies indicate a significant positive link between the resources given by an organization for CAATs adoption and employees' use of CAATs (Bierstaker et al., 2014; Almagrashi et al., 2023; Handoko, 2021; Thottoli, 2022; Daoud, 2023; Al-Hiyari et al., 2019; Al-Okaily et al., 2022).

H7: There is a positive relationship between organizational resources and the adoption of CAATs.

5.3.2.4 Firm size

Several studies have shown that larger firms with greater financial resources and better infrastructure can adopt CAATs more easily; these studies also find a strong correlation between firm size and audit technology use. Several other studies support these findings and indicate a positive relationship between firm size and technology use (Zhu et al., 2003; Siew et al., 2020; Khalil & Nafti, 2020; Bierstaker et al., 2014; Janvrin et al., 2009).

H8: Firm size has a positive relationship with the adoption of CAATs.

5.3.3 Environmental factors

The environmental factors are the third element of the TOE framework (Tornatzky & Fleischer, 1990). We proposed External Support Services, Client Pressure, Competitive Pressure, and Regulatory Support as environmental variables.

5.3.3.1 External support services

External support services, including vendor support and training programs, can facilitate technology adoption by reducing implementation barriers and providing necessary expertise (Venkatesh et al., 2003).

The studies conducted by Bierstaker et al. (2014) for USA auditors, and Al-Hiyari et al. (2019) in Jordanie observe similar effects and show that external support is a facilitating condition for CAATs adoption.

H9: External support services have a positive relationship with the adoption of CAATs.

5.3.3.2 Client pressure

Pressure is defined as an objective stimulus construct referring to individual characteristics or combinations of characteristics and events that impinge on the perceptual and cognitive processes of individuals (DeZoort & Lord 1997).

Curtis and Payne (2008) found that the more technologically sophisticated clients are, the more they expect auditors to use advanced technologies. Mahzan and Lymer (2014) et Al-Okaily et al. (2022) show that the use of CAATs varies positively with the nature of the client.

H10: There is a positive relationship between client pressure and the adoption of CAATs.

5.3.3.3 *Competitive pressure*

Competitive pressure refers to the influence of competitors' technology adoption on a firm's own adoption decisions (Tornatzky & Fleischer, 1990).

Several studies show that audit firms in highly competitive environments adopt CAATs at higher rates (Curtis & Payne, 2014; Mahzan & Lymer, 2014; ; Bradford & Florin, 2003; ; Abdel & Sweet, 1999; Iacovou et al., 1995; Riemenschneider & Mykytyn, 2000; Venkatesh & Bala, 2012; Zhu et al., 2003).

However, the study conducted by Siew et al. (2020) shows a non-significant relationship between competitive pressure and CAATs adoption; these findings are not consistent with prior studies.

H11: There is a positive relationship between competitive pressure and the adoption of CAATs.

5.3.3.4 *Regulatory support*

Regulatory support includes encouragement from professional bodies, audit standards, and regulatory agencies to use the technology in audit processes.

Previous studies show a link between regulatory support and the adoption of CAATs. Swan and Newell (1995) reveal a relationship between regulatory support and new technology adoption. The study conducted by Mahzan and Lymer (2009) shows that professional body recommendations are one of the key factors when selecting audit tools. Widuri et al. (2016) determine professional body support as an important factor driving adoption of CAATs. Siew et al. (2020) show a significant influence of regulatory support on CAATs adoption.

H12: Regulatory support has a positive relationship with the adoption of CAATs.

The proposed seven hypotheses, which explain the influences of CAATs adoption and the control variables, are shown in Figure 5.1.

5.4 METHODOLOGY

This study followed the PRISMA (Preferred Reporting Items for Systematic Reviews and Meta-Analyses) guidelines (Page et al., 2021) to conduct a systematic literature review. Records were retrieved from four databases: Scopus, Web of Science, ScienceDirect, and SpringerLink. The search strategy was based on keywords aligned with our research focus on audit technology adoption, decision-making, and digital transformation. These included: "Audit Technology," "Technology Adoption," "Barriers," "Facilitators," "Decision-Making," "Digital Transformation," "Computer-Assisted Audit Tools (CAATs)," "Innovation in Auditing,"

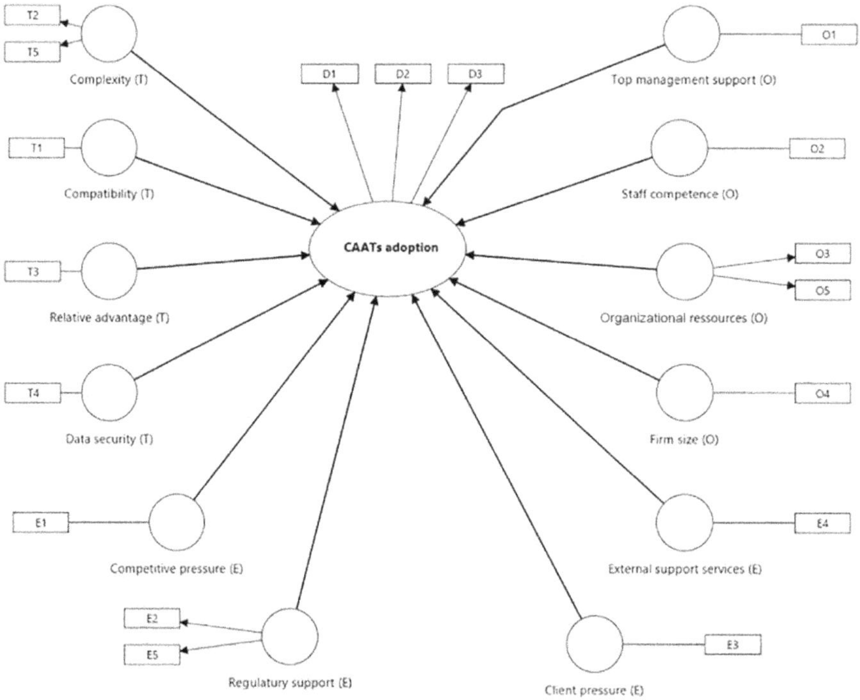

Figure 5.1 Proposed research framework for CAATs adoption.

"Audit Firms," and "Audit Profession." Inclusion and exclusion criteria (Table 5.1) were applied to ensure the relevance and quality of selected studies.

We applied strict criteria to select the articles relevant to our research. First, we limited our search to journal sources and research articles. To avoid duplicates, we used Zotero to compare the complete lists of articles from the 5 research databases, which allowed us to remove 22 duplicate entries.

Furthermore, we restricted our selection to publications in English to avoid issues related to translation and comprehension. Finally, we eliminated publications that were not related to our research topic. The results of this PRISMA-based approach are presented in Table 5.2, highlighting the number of articles at each stage of the selection process.

Figure 5.2 presents the PRISMA flow diagram, which illustrates the different phases of our research and the results obtained at each stage.

We reviewed a total of 174 records, of which 137 were excluded after assessing the titles and/or abstracts against our research objectives. Articles that did not fully align with our research question were also excluded, resulting in a final selection of 53 articles for our study.

Over a three-month period, we distributed structured surveys to auditors affiliated with audit firms operating in Morocco. To enhance the response

Table 5.1 Inclusion and exclusion criteria of the research

Inclusion criteria	*Exclusion criteria*
Studies explicitly addressing the barriers and/or facilitators influencing the adoption of CAATs and their impact on decision-making regarding the adoption process within the context of audit firms' digital transformation, using the relevant keyword combinations.	Any type of documents other than journal reviews or research articles.
	Duplicate records.
	Articles unrelated to the research topic.
	Language other than English.

rate and ensure data reliability, two follow-up reminders were sent via email at regular intervals during the data collection period.

The respondents were primarily audit managers or senior audit managers (36.7%), followed by senior auditors (34.2%), firm partners (15.1%), and managing partners (14.0%). They had an average of 9.5 years of experience in their current audit firms and an average of 12 years of audit experience each (Table 5.3). Regarding firm characteristics, 40% of respondents worked at Big Four firms (EY, PwC, Deloitte, KPMG), 25% were affiliated with an international network excluding the Big Four, and 35% were from non-affiliated firms. No respondents indicated affiliation with a national network.

Control questions were embedded in the survey to detect inattentive or inconsistent respondents (Meade & Craig, 2012). Based on this screening, seven responses were identified as careless and subsequently excluded from the final analysis.

To assess the adequacy of the sample size, a power analysis was conducted using the G*Power software. The results confirmed that the sample

Table 5.2 Number of articles at each stage of the research process

			Number of articles excluded after applying the criteria.			
Database	*Number of articles matching keyword combinations*	**Excluded articles:** *Language other than English*	**Excluded articles:** *Not journal or review articles*	*Duplicates*	*Out-of-scope articles*	*Articles retained for content analysis*
Scopus	50	2	8	8	18	14
Web of Science	45	1	5	8	24	7
SpringerLink	39	2	6	2	16	13
Science Direct	40	0	5	4	28	3
Total	**174**	**5**	**24**	**22**	**86**	**37**

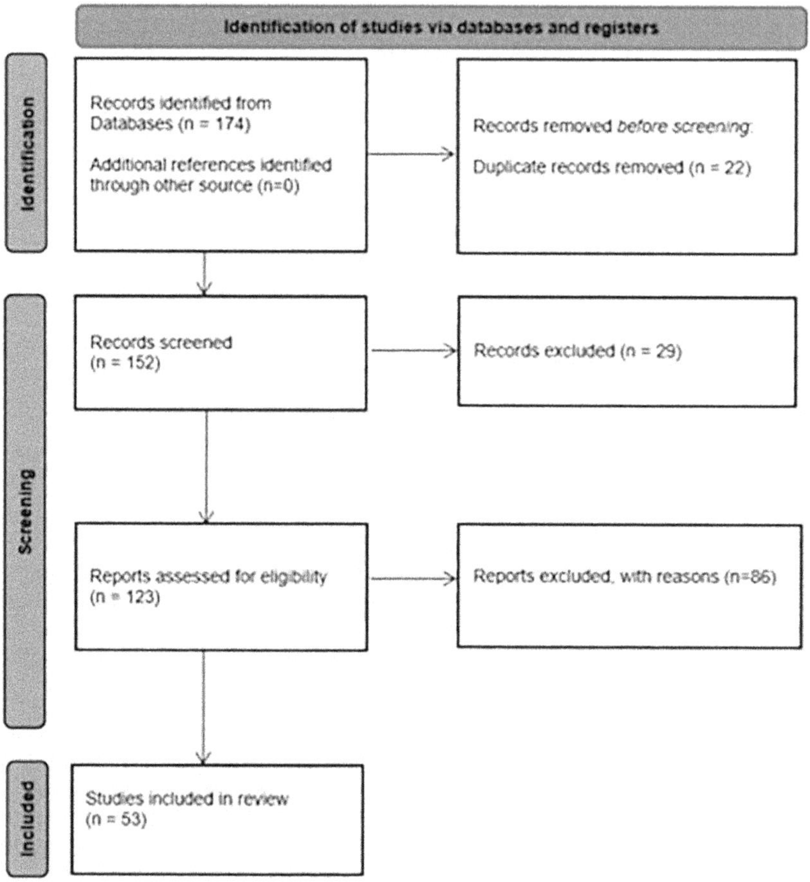

Figure 5.2 The different stages of the research for article selection.

was sufficient for applying partial least squares structural equation modeling (PLS-SEM) (Cohen, 1988; Goodhue et al., 2007; Hair et al., 2014; Sawyer & Ball, 1981). Furthermore, a comparison between early and late respondents was performed to examine potential non-response bias, revealing no statistically significant differences between the two groups (Sax et al., 2003).

Table 5.3 Respondents' positions and firm characteristics

Position of respondent	*Per cent*	*Firm size*	*Per cent*
Firm partner	13.80%	Big Four (EY, PwC, Deloitte, KPMG)	40%
Managing partner	12.80%	Member of an international network (excluding Big Four)	25%
Audit manager/senior audit manager	38.30%	Member of a national network	0%
Senior auditor	35.10%	Non-affiliated firm	35%

5.4.1 Measurement of variables

The questionnaire items were primarily adapted from previously validated survey instruments, ensuring both content relevance and measurement reliability (Table 5.4). Prior to the main data collection, a pilot test was conducted with professionals from audit firms to assess the clarity and reliability of the questionnaire, including both the instructions and individual items. Responses from the pilot test were excluded from the final data analysis to maintain the integrity of the study sample.

Table 5.4 Construct measures for CAATs adoption study

Item code	*Construct*	*Item description*	*Source*
T5	Complexity	Learning to use these technologies requires little effort.	Davis (1989)
T4	Data security	Data security is ensured by the new technologies.	Ifinedo (2011)
T3	Relative advantage	These technologies offer a significant advantage over traditional methods.	Rogers (2003)
T2	Complexity	The use of new audit technologies is simple and intuitive.	Davis (1989)
T1	Technological compatibility	The audit technologies available on the market are compatible with our existing systems.	Tornatzky and Fleischer (1990).
O5	Organizational resources	Training is offered to help staff become familiar with new audit technologies.	Zhu, Kraemer, and Xu (2006)
O4	Firm size	The size of our firm enables us to support this type of technological innovation.	Thong (1999)
O3	Organizational resources	We have sufficient resources to implement new technologies.	Law and Ngai (2007)
O2	Staff competence	Our staff has the necessary skills to use audit technologies.	Thong (1999)
O1	Top management support	Top management actively supports the digital transformation of our audit firm.	Premkumar and Roberts (1999)
E5	Regulatory support	The evolution of professional standards drives us to adopt new technologies.	Alles, Kogan, and Vasarhelyi (2008)
E4	External support services	External vendors and consultants are available to assist us in implementing audit technologies.	Zhou and Kapoor (2011)
E3	Client pressure	Our clients expect the integration of technologies in our engagements.	Vasarhelyi, Kogan, and Tuttle (2015)
E2	Regulatory support	Regulatory authorities encourage the use of audit technologies.	Kokina and Davenport (2017).
E1	Competitive pressure	Our competitors have already integrated similar technologies into their practices.	Tornatzky and Fleischer (1990)
D1	CAAT adoption	Our firm has adopted (or is ready to adopt) audit technologies.	Sun and Vasarhelyi (2018)

5.4.1.1 *Measurement of dependent variable*

The dependent variable was defined as the decision to adopt CAATs by audit firms as part of their digital transformation process.

Individual item scores measuring various aspects of CAATs adoption were aggregated to form a composite index, which served as a single-item proxy representing the audit firm's adoption decision. This operationalization aligns with the study's focus on identifying the barriers and facilitators influencing the strategic choice to integrate audit technologies in professional practice.

5.4.1.2 *Measurement of control and independent variables*

All items for the study constructs were measured using a seven-point Likert scale ranging from "Strongly disagree" (1) to "Strongly agree" (5). Exceptions were the demographic and background questions, which included: the respondent's current position within the firm (e.g., senior, manager, senior manager, partner, or managing partner), years of experience in the audit field, audit firm classification (Big Four, international network, national network, or independent), and gender. These items were used to characterize the respondent profile and were not included in the core construct measurements.

5.4.2 Data analysis technique

We conducted statistical analysis using the PLS-SEM technique, which is useful for research that has a relatively small sample size (Klarner et al., 2013; Saraf et al., 2013). PLS-SEM is a non-parametric statistical method that does not require data to be normally distributed (Hair et al., 2011; Hair et al., 2012b; Henseler & Sarstedt, 2013).

Given the exploratory nature of the study and the intention to assess the relative importance of technological, organizational, and environmental factors in predicting CAATs adoption, PLS-SEM was employed. This method is particularly suitable for research in a developing country context where sample sizes may be limited and the assumption of multivariate normality may not be met. Unlike CB-SEM, PLS-SEM is robust to such conditions and prioritizes variance explanation over model fit, aligning with the study's goal to build a predictive and explanatory model.

5.5 RESULTS AND DISCUSSION

5.5.1 Measurement model assessment

The measurement model was evaluated using Smart PLS 4.0 to assess the reliability and validity of the constructs. Table 5.5 presents the reliability and validity statistics for all constructs.

Table 5.5 Reliability and validity statistics

Construct	*Items*	*Cronbach's Alpha*	*Composite reliability*	*AVE*
Complexity (T)	2	0.891	0.948	0.9
Compatibility (T)	1	—	1	1
Relative advantage (T)	1	—	1	1
Data security (T)	1	—	1	1
Top management support (O)	1	—	1	1
Staff competence (O)	1	—	1	1
Organizational resources (O)	2	0.854	0.931	0.87
Firm size (O)	1	—	1	1
Competitive pressure (E)	1	—	1	1
Regulatory support (E)	2	0.798	0.907	0.83
Client pressure (E)	1	—	1	1
External support services (E)	1	—	1	1
CAATs adoption	—	0.912	0.934	0.78

All constructs demonstrated acceptable reliability with Cronbach's alpha values above 0.7 and composite reliability values exceeding 0.8. The Average Variance Extracted (AVE) values were all above the recommended threshold of 0.5, indicating adequate convergent validity.

5.5.2 Structural model assessment

The structural model was evaluated using a bootstrapping procedure with 5,000 subsamples to assess the significance of path coefficients. The model explained 50.7% of the variance in CAATs adoption ($R^2 = 0.507$), indicating substantial explanatory power (Table 5.6).

The results reveal significant insights into the factors influencing CAATs adoption in audit firms, with important theoretical and practical implications for understanding digital transformation in professional services (Figure 5.3).

5.5.3 Technological factors

Compatibility emerges as the strongest technological factor ($\beta = 0.287$, $p < 0.001$), supporting Rogers' (2003) DOI theory. This finding aligns with Davis (1989) and Venkatesh et al. (2003), who emphasized the importance of technology-organization fit. The significant positive effect suggests that audit firms are more likely to adopt CAATs when these tools align with their existing work processes, values, and technological infrastructure, consistent with prior research by Rosli et al (2012), Wassie and Péter (2024), and Al-Okaily et al (2022), but contradicts the findings of Siew et al. (2020).

Relative advantage also significantly influences adoption ($\beta = 0.207$, $p < 0.01$), supporting the fundamental premise of innovation diffusion theory (Rogers, 2003). This finding corroborates Mahzan and Lymer (2014), Siew

Table 5.6 Structural model results

Path	*Path coefficient*	*t-value*	*p-value*	*Effect size (f^2)*
Complexity → CAATs adoption	0.152	2.187	0.029	0.042
Compatibility → CAATs adoption	0.287	3.891	0	0.098
Relative advantage → CAATs adoption	0.207	2.756	0.006	0.055
Data security → CAATs adoption	–0.007	0.098	0.922	0
Top management support → CAATs adoption	0.043	0.567	0.571	0.003
Staff competence → CAATs adoption	0.105	1.423	0.155	0.015
Organizational resources → CAATs adoption	0.33	4.234	0	0.134
Firm size → CAATs adoption	–0.035	0.498	0.618	0.002
Competitive pressure → CAATs adoption	0.082	1.187	0.235	0.009
Regulatory support → CAATs adoption	–0.127	1.689	0.091	0.021
Client pressure → CAATs adoption	0.027	0.389	0.697	0.001
External support services → CAATs adoption	0.234	3.156	0.002	0.067

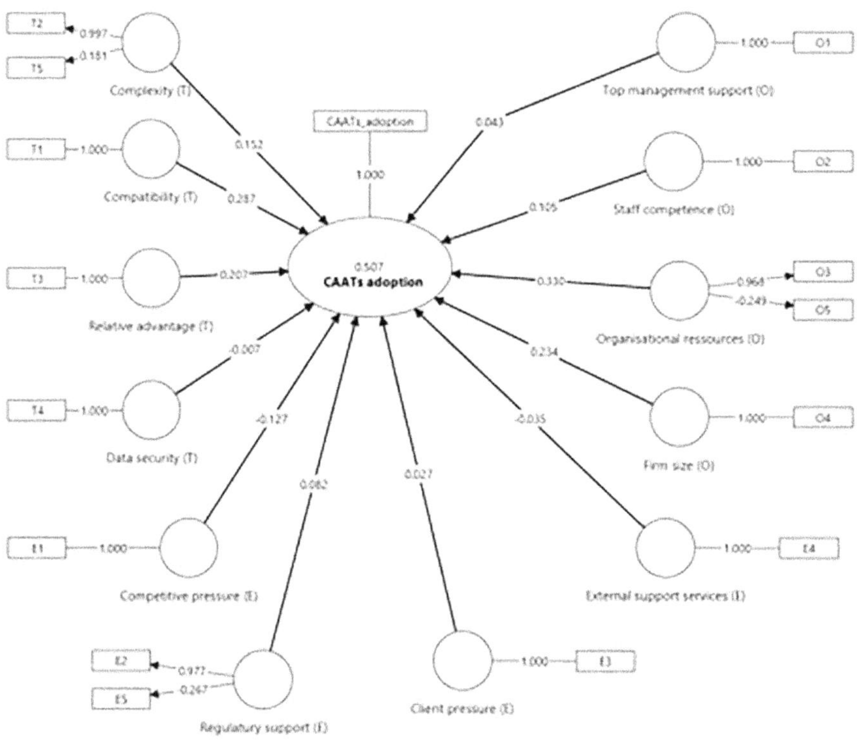

Figure 5.3 Structural model.

et al. (2020), and Almagrashi et al. (2023), who found that perceived benefits drive audit technology adoption.

Complexity shows a significant positive effect ($\beta = 0.152$, $p < 0.05$), which is logically consistent with our measurement approach. Since the complexity construct was measured in terms of “ease of adoption” (reversed scale), the positive coefficient indicates that CAATs perceived as easier to adopt are more likely to be implemented. This finding aligns with traditional technology adoption models (Davis, 1989; Venkatesh et al., 2003) and prior studies (Bierstaker et al., 2014); Mahzan and Lymer (2014); Kim et al., 2009; Huang et al., 2008).

Data security concerns show no significant impact ($\beta = -0.007$, $p > 0.05$), surprising given the sensitive nature of audit data. This finding contradicts expectations based on cybersecurity literature (Steinbart et al., 2018), but may reflect increased confidence in security measures or the overriding importance of other factors in adoption decisions.

5.5.4 Organizational factors

Organizational resources demonstrate the strongest overall impact ($\beta = 0.330$, $p < 0.001$), highlighting the critical role of resource availability in technology adoption. This finding strongly supports the resource-based view (Barney, 1991) and aligns with Tornatzky and Fleischer’s (1990) TOE framework. The large effect size ($f^2 = 0.134$) indicates that adequate financial, human, and technological resources are prerequisites for successful CAATs implementation, consistent with findings from previous studies (Bierstaker et al., 2014; Almagrashi et al., 2023; Handoko, 2021; Thottoli, 2022; Daoud, 2023; Al-Hiyari, 2019; Al-Okaily et al., 2022).

Surprisingly, top management support and staff competence show non-significant effects, contradicting extensive literature emphasizing their Janvrin et al., 2008; Axelsen et al., 2017; Siew et al., 2020; Curtis and Payne, 2008; Huang et al., 2008; Mahzan and Lymer, 2009; Bierstaker et al. (2014); Al-Hiyari et al., 2019; Siew et al., 2020; Al-Okaily et al., 2022). This unexpected finding may suggest that in the current audit environment, these factors have become baseline expectations rather than differentiating factors, or that their effects are mediated through organizational resources.

Firm size demonstrates a significant positive effect ($\beta = 0.234$, $p < 0.01$), supporting the notion that larger audit firms are more likely to adopt CAATs. This finding aligns with the literature, suggesting that larger firms typically possess greater financial resources, technical expertise, and organizational capacity to implement complex technologies (Zhu et al., 2003; Siew et al., 2020; Khalil and Nafti, 2020; Bierstaker et al., 2014; Janvrin et al., 2009;).

5.5.5 Environmental factors

External support services and competitive/client pressures show non-significant effects, suggesting that adoption decisions are primarily driven by internal factors and resource considerations rather than external market pressures or vendor support. This finding challenges some assumptions about environmental influences on professional services innovation and indicates that audit firms may prefer to rely on internal capabilities for technology adoption decisions.

Regulatory support shows a non-significant effect ($\beta = 0.082$, $p > 0.05$), suggesting that regulatory encouragement or mandates do not significantly influence CAATs adoption decisions.

Competitive and client pressures show non-significant effects, suggesting that adoption decisions are primarily driven by internal factors and resource considerations rather than external market pressures. This finding, although contradicting most of the existing literature, is consistent with the findings of Siew et al. (2020).

This study has several limitations that suggest avenues for future research. The cross-sectional design limits causal inferences, and longitudinal studies could provide deeper insights into adoption processes. The sample size of 133, while adequate for PLS-SEM analysis, could be expanded for greater generalizability. Additionally, the study focused on adoption intention rather than actual usage, which future research could address through post-adoption studies.

Future research should investigate the mediation effects among constructs, explore industry-specific variations in adoption patterns, and examine the role of emerging technologies like artificial intelligence and blockchain in audit practice.

5.6 CONCLUSION

This study contributes to the growing body of literature on audit technology adoption by empirically examining the determinants of CAATs adoption through the lens of the TOE framework. The findings emphasize that organizational resources, technological compatibility, relative advantage, and perceived ease of use are the most significant factors influencing adoption decisions in Moroccan audit firms.

Contrary to expectations, variables such as data security, top management support, and staff competence traditionally viewed as critical enablers did not significantly affect adoption. Similarly, environmental pressures such as regulatory support, client demand, and competitive pressure were not decisive, suggesting that internal drivers outweigh external pressures in the context of emerging markets.

These results have important practical implications. For audit firms, they underscore the need to strengthen internal infrastructures, allocate sufficient resources, and ensure technological alignment with existing systems. For regulators and professional bodies, the findings point to the limited influence of external pressure alone and suggest that supportive policies must be complemented by capacity-building initiatives within firms. Finally, the study encourages vendors and developers of audit technologies to focus on usability and seamless integration to enhance adoption likelihood.

While this study offers valuable insights, it has several limitations. Its cross-sectional design restricts causal interpretations, and reliance on self-reported data may introduce bias. Moreover, the focus on a single country limits the generalizability of the findings. Future research should adopt longitudinal designs, examine post-adoption behaviors, and explore the role of emerging technologies such as AI and blockchain to better understand the evolving nature of digital transformation in auditing.

BIBLIOGRAPHY

Abdel Hamed, T., Sengupta, K., & Sweet, W. (1999). The impact of goals on software project management: An empirical investigation. *MIS Quarterly*, 23(4), 531–555.

Ahmi, A., & Kent, S. (2013). The utilization of computer-assisted audit tools and techniques (CAATTs) in Malaysian public sector. *Asian Journal of Accounting and Governance*, 4, 31–38.

Al-Hiyari, A., Al Said, N., & Hattab, E. (2019). Factors that influence the use of computer-assisted audit techniques (CAATs) by internal auditors in Jordan. *Academy of Accounting and Financial Studies Journal*, 23(3), 1–15.

Al-Okaily, M., Alqudah, H. M., Al-Qudah, A. A., & Alkhwaldi, A. F. (2022). Examining the critical factors of computer-assisted audit tools and techniques adoption in the post-COVID-19 period: Internal auditors' perspective. *VINE Journal of Information and Knowledge Management Systems*, 54(5), 1062–1091.

Alkalbani, A., Deng, H., & Kam, B. (2015). Organisational security culture and information security compliance for E-government development: The moderating effect of social pressure, *PACIS 2015 Proceedings*. 65.

Alles, M. G. (2015). Drivers of the use and facilitators and obstacles of the evolution of big data by the audit profession. *Accounting Horizons*, 29(2), 439–449.

Alles, M. G., Kogan, A., & Vasarhelyi, M. A. (2008). Putting continuous auditing theory into practice: Lessons from two pilot implementations. *Journal of Information Systems*, 22(2), 195–214.

Almagrashi, A., Mujalli, A., Khan, T., & Attia, O. (2023). Factors determining internal auditors' behavioral intention to use computer-assisted auditing techniques: An extension of the UTAUT model and an empirical study. *Future Business Journal*, 9(1), 74.

Axelsen, M., Green, P., & Ridley, G. (2017). Explaining the information systems auditor role in the public sector financial audit. *International Journal of Accounting Information Systems*, 24, 15–31.

Barney, J. (1991). Firm resources and sustained competitive advantage. *Journal of Management*, 17(1), 99–120.

Bierstaker, J., Janvrin, D., & Lowe, D. J. (2014). What factors influence auditors' use of computer-assisted audit techniques? *Advances in Accounting*, 30, 67–74.

Bradford, M., & Florin, J. (2003). Examining the role of innovation diffusion factors on the implementation success of enterprise resource planning systems. *International Journal of Accounting Information Systems*, 4(3), 205–225.

Cohen, J. (1988). *Statistical Power Analysis for the Behavioral Sciences* (2nd ed.). Lawrence Erlbaum.

Curtis, M. B., & Payne, E. A. (2008). An examination of contextual factors and individual characteristics affecting technology implementation decisions in auditing. *International Journal of Accounting Information Systems*, 9(2), 104–121.

Curtis, M. B., & Payne, E. A. (2014). Modeling voluntary CAAT utilization decisions in auditing. *Managerial Auditing Journal*, 29(4), 304–326.

Daoud, L. (2023). Predictors of auditors' usage of CAATs: The role of top management support and trust. *Information Sciences Letters*, 12(5), 45–62.

Davis, F. D. (1989). Perceived usefulness, perceived ease of use, and user acceptance of information technology. *MIS Quarterly*, 13(3), 319–340.

Debreceny, R., Lee, S., Neo, W., & Toh, J. (2005). Employing generalised audit software in the financial services sector: Challenges and opportunities. *Managerial Auditing Journal*, 20(6), 605–618.

DeZoort, F. T., & Lord, A. T. (1997). A review and synthesis of pressure effects research in accounting. *Journal of Accounting Literature*, 16, 28–86.

Goodhue, D. L., Lewis, W., & Thompson, R. (2007). Statistical power in analyzing interaction effects: Questioning the advantage of PLS with product indicators. *Information Systems Research*, 18(2), 211–227.

Hair, J. F., Ringle, C. M., & Sarstedt, M. (2011). PLS-SEM: Indeed a silver bullet. *Journal of Marketing Theory and Practice*, 19(2), 139–152.

Hair, J. F., Sarstedt, M., Ringle, C. M., & Mena, J. A. (2012). An assessment of the use of partial least squares structural equation modeling in marketing research. *Journal of the Academy of Marketing Science*, 40(3), 414–433.

Hair, J. F., Hult, G. T. M., Ringle, C., & Sarstedt, M. (2014). *A Primer on Partial Least Squares Structural Equation Modeling (PLS-SEM)*. Sage.

Handoko, B. L., Morris, M., & Davis, F. D. (2021). UTAUT model in predicting auditor intention in adopting CAATs. In Proceedings of the 2021 12th International Conference on E-business, Management and Economics (ICEME 2021).

Henseler, J., & Sarstedt, M. (2013). Goodness-of-fit indices for partial least squares path modeling. *Computational Statistics*, 28(2), 565–580.

Huang, S.-M., Hung, Y.-C., & Tsao, H.-H. (2008). Examining the determinants of computer-assisted audit techniques acceptance from internal auditors' viewpoints. *International Journal of Services and Standards*, 4(4), 377–392.

Iacovou, C. L., Benbasat, I., & Dexter, A. S. (1995). Electronic data interchange and small organizations: Adoption and impact of technology. *MIS Quarterly*, 19(4), 465–485.

Ifinedo, P. (2011). An empirical analysis of factors influencing internet/e-business technologies adoption by SMEs in Canada. *International Journal of Information Technology & Decision Making*, 10(4), 731–766.

Janvrin, D., Bierstaker, J., & Lowe, D. J. (2008). An examination of audit information technology use and perceived importance. *Accounting Horizons*, 22(1), 1–21.

Janvrin, D., Lowe, D. J., & Bierstaker, J. L. (2009). Auditor acceptance of computer-assisted audit techniques. *Journal of Information Systems*, 23(1), 97–118.

Kim, H.-J., Mannino, M., & Nieschwietz, R. J. (2009). Information technology acceptance in the internal audit profession: Impact of technology features and complexity. *International Journal of Accounting Information Systems*, 10, 214–228.

Klarner, P., Probst, G., & Soparnot, R. (2013). Organizational change capacity in public services: The case of the World Health Organization. *Journal of Change Management*, 13(4), 421–446.

Kokina, J., & Davenport, T. H. (2017). The emergence of artificial intelligence: How automation is changing auditing. *Journal of Emerging Technologies in Accounting*, 14(1), 115–122.

Law, C., & Ngai, E. (2007). ERP systems adoption: An exploratory study of the organizational factors and impacts of ERP success. *Information & Management*, 44(4), 418–432.

Lowe, D. J., Bierstaker, J. L., Janvrin, D. J., & Jenkins, J. G. (2017). Information technology in an audit context: Have the Big 4 lost their advantage? *Journal of Information Systems*, 32(1), 87–107.

Mahzan, N., & Lymer, A. (2009). Examining motivations to adopt Computer Assisted Audit Tools and Techniques (CAATTs): cases of UK internal auditors. In *Collected Proceedings of the International Business Information Management Conference (12th IBIMA)* IBIMA.

Mahzan, N., & Lymer, A. (2014). Examining the adoption of CAATs: Cases of generalized audit software use by internal auditors. *Managerial Auditing Journal*, 29(4), 327–349.

McKinnie, M. (2016). Strategic alignment and IT implementation in SMEs. *Information Systems Management*, 33(2), 113–129.

Meade, A. W., & Craig, S. B. (2012). Identifying careless responses in survey data. *Psychological Methods*, 17(3), 437–455.

Page, M. J., McKenzie, J. E., Bossuyt, P. M., Boutron, I., Hoffmann, T. C., Mulrow, C. D., et al. (2021). The PRISMA 2020 statement: An updated guideline for reporting systematic reviews. *BMJ*, 372, n71.

Premkumar, G., & Roberts, M. (1999). Adoption of new information technologies in rural small businesses. *Omega*, 27(4), 467–484.

Ramamurthy, K., & Premkumar, G. (1995). Determinants and outcomes of EDI diffusion. *IEEE Transactions on Engineering Management*, 42(4), 332–351.

Riemenschneider, C. K., & Mykytyn, P. P. (2000). What small business executives have learned about managing information technology. *Information & Management*, 37(5), 257–269.

Rogers, E. M. (2003). *Diffusion of Innovations* (5th ed.). Free Press.

Rosli, K., Yeow, P. H. P., & Siew, E. G. (2012). Factors influencing audit technology acceptance by audit firms: A new I-TOE adoption framework. *Journal of Accounting and Auditing Research & Practice*, 2012, 1–11.

Sangster, A., Leech, S. A., & Grabski, S. V. (2020). ERP implementations and their impact upon decision-making: Literature review. *International Journal of Accounting Information Systems*, 36, 100450.

Saraf, N., Langdon, C. S., & Gosain, S. (2013). IS-enabled business initiatives and firm performance: Empirical evidence from Asia-Pacific. *Journal of Strategic Information Systems*, 22(1), 10–24.

Sawyer, A. G., & Ball, A. D. (1981). Statistical power and effect size in marketing research. *Journal of Marketing Research*, 18(3), 275–290.

Sax, L. J., Gilmartin, S. K., & Bryant, A. N. (2003). Assessing response rates and nonresponse bias in web and paper surveys. *Research in Higher Education*, 44(4), 409–432.

Siew, E. G., Idris, F., & Vasant, P. (2020). Organizational and environmental influences in the adoption of computer-assisted audit tools and techniques (CAATTs) by audit firms in Malaysia: A TOE perspective.

Steinbart, P. J., Raschke, R. L., Gal, G., & Dilla, W. N. (2018). The influence of a good relationship between the internal audit and information security functions on information security outcomes. *Accounting, Organizations and Society*, 52, 15–29.

Sun, T., & Vasarhelyi, M. A. (2018). Deep learning and the future of auditing. *Journal of Emerging Technologies in Accounting*, 15(1), 1–20.

Swan, J. A., & Newell, S. (1995). The role of professional associations in technology diffusion. *Organization Studies*, 16(5), 847–874.

Thong, J. Y. L. (1999). An integrated model of information systems adoption in small businesses. *Journal of Management Information Systems*, 15(4), 187–214.

Thottoli, M. M, Ahmed, E. R., & Thomas, K. V. (2022). Emerging technology and auditing practice: Analysis for future directions. *European Journal of Management Studies*, 27(1), 99–119.

Tornatzky, L. G., & Fleischer, M. (1990). *The Processes of Technological Innovation*. Lexington Books.

Venkatesh, V., Morris, M. G., Davis, G. B., & Davis, F. D. (2003). User acceptance of information technology: Toward a unified view. *MIS Quarterly*, 27(3), 425–478.

Vasarhelyi, M. A., Kogan, A., & Tuttle, B. M. (2015). Big data in accounting: An overview. *Accounting Horizons*, 29(2), 381–396.

Wassie, F. A., & Péter, L. L. (2024). Technology adoption in audit of information systems: Ethiopian audit firms' perspective. *Journal of Infrastructure, Policy and Development*, 8(13), 8819.

Widuri, R., O'Connell, B., & Yapa, P. W. S. (2016). Adopting generalized audit software: An Indonesian perspective. *Managerial Auditing Journal*, 31(8/9), 821–847. DOI:10.1108/MAJ-10-2015-1247

Yigitbasioglu, O. (2016). The role of institutional pressures and top management support in the intention to adopt cloud computing solutions. *Journal of Enterprise Information Management*, 29(4), 560–578.

Yoon, K., Hoogduin, L., & Zhang, L. (2015). Big data as complementary audit evidence. *Accounting Horizons*, 29(2), 431–438.

Zhou, W., & Kapoor, G. (2011). Detecting evolutionary financial statement fraud. *Decision Support Systems*, 50(3), 570–575.

Zhu, K., Kraemer, K. L., & Xu, S. (2003). Electronic business adoption by European firms: A cross-country assessment of the facilitators and inhibitors. *European Journal of Information Systems*, 12(4), 251–268.

Zhu, K., & Kraemer, K. L. (2005). Post-adoption variations in usage and value of e-business by organizations: Cross-country evidence from the retail industry. *Information Systems Research*, 16(1), 61–84.

Zhu, K., Kraemer, K. L., & Xu, S. (2006). The process of innovation assimilation by firms in different countries: A technology diffusion perspective on e-business. *Management Science*, 52(10), 1557–1576.

Chapter 6

Bridging the gap in auditing education

Aligning university curricula with professional practice to enhance students' competitiveness

Abdelmounim Bouziane

6.1 INTRODUCTION

The teaching of auditing in Morocco faces considerable challenges in aligning the skills taught with those required in the job market. In the context of growing globalization, auditors are increasingly expected to not only master the technical concepts of auditing but also to adapt to new technologies and the linguistic demands of their professional environment. However, an analysis of the current state of auditing education in Moroccan universities shows that this alignment is not always optimal.

According to available data, the number of students enrolled in auditing programs in Morocco continues to grow, with increasing demand from companies for qualified auditors, particularly in the financial and industrial sectors. In 2023, the number of students enrolled in specialized auditing programs is estimated to be in the thousands across Moroccan universities and business schools. These figures have been approximated by aggregating data from public and private institutions' websites. Official statistics remain general and typically categorize students by broad fields (e.g., management, literature, sciences, etc.). However, despite this growing demand, graduates often seem insufficiently prepared to meet employers' expectations.

On the job market, audit firms in Morocco—ranging from large international firms to local ones—emphasize the urgent need to recruit professionals trained in current auditing technologies, particularly Computer-Assisted Audit Tools (CAATs). Yet, few academic programs include these tools in their curricula. According to statistics provided by the Order of Chartered Accountants, Moroccan audit firms are primarily seeking profiles with both technical and linguistic skills, with particular proficiency in English and French.

Regarding the training offer, Morocco has several institutions, including public universities (such as Hassan II University of Casablanca) and private business schools, offering auditing programs. However, disparities exist between institutions in terms of curriculum content and the preparation of students for the demands of the job market. Therefore, it is crucial to question the reforms needed to improve the alignment between education and the skills required by employers.

DOI: 10.1201/9781003650713-7

It is important to note that this study does not limit itself to a strict alignment-based approach, which assumes a direct link between education and labor market needs. While we recognize the importance of alignment between acquired skills and employers' expectations, we adopt a broader perspective. We consider that other factors, such as market dynamics, technological transformations, and the career aspirations of graduates, play a crucial role in professional integration. Consequently, this research aims to explore the influence of these various factors to propose a more nuanced view of the relationship between education and employment.

This study revolves around the following issue: How can university curricula in auditing be revised to ensure that graduates are competitive in the current and future job markets? The main objective is to explore the gap between the skills taught in auditing courses at Moroccan universities and those required by the labor market.

To address this question, the study adopts an empirical approach by examining the perspectives of academic researchers and professionals in the auditing sector. By analyzing data collected from these two groups, this research aims to identify current gaps in auditing education and provide concrete recommendations for better alignment between academic curricula and professional expectations. Ultimately, this study seeks to contribute to the ongoing debate on improving auditing education in order to strengthen graduate employability and their ability to adapt to the evolving demands of the labor market.

6.2 LITERATURE REVIEW

Over the past few decades, higher education in many countries has attracted the attention of researchers and policymakers, particularly concerning the transition from education to employment for new graduates and their employability in specific sectors such as auditing (Carroll, 2013). Several studies have focused on employability to assess the effectiveness of education provided by universities, looking at taught programs, job search methods, and graduate profiles. These research topics have highlighted two essential players: the educator and the employer. This global concern underscores the importance of collaboration between educational institutions and the labor market, with each playing a distinct role in preparing graduates for a successful career. Kramarz and Viarengo (2015) emphasize the importance of two institutions in the transition from education to work: the education system and the labor market. In the context of auditing, the professional specificity of the education system plays a central role, as it influences how graduates integrate into labor markets structured by specific organizational principles. The need for alignment between these institutions becomes even more critical when examining the challenges related to job searching, which remain at the heart of current discussions.

Job searching and the transition from higher education to the labor market are not new debates. Several studies have tried to explain this issue. Vieira and Coimbra (2008) argue that universities must equip their graduates with a set of knowledge and skills aimed at improving their employability, while acknowledging that the level of required skills varies from one specialization to another. This diversity of required skills is particularly evident in specific industries such as auditing, where professional requirements are complex and varied.

Auditing is a knowledge-based industry where learning plays a central role. Auditors apply a wide range of business, accounting, auditing, and regulatory knowledge to the financial reports of clients. They must develop and maintain a considerable body of knowledge and skills to establish their legitimacy and assume their responsibilities (Westermann et al., 2015). To succeed in this demanding industry, graduates must possess a diverse set of skills acquired throughout their academic journey.

Auditors, as university graduates, need to acquire and develop a diverse set of skills throughout their university education to succeed in their careers (Chu et al., 2021). They must have a solid understanding of accounting principles, auditing standards, and financial regulations, which form the foundation of their technical expertise. At the same time, advanced analytical skills are essential to interpret complex data and identify anomalies. Problem-solving is also crucial, as auditors are often faced with unforeseen situations that require innovative solutions. Clear and effective communication is indispensable for explaining financial concepts to non-specialists and preparing accurate reports. Interpersonal skills enable auditors to work in teams and build trust-based relationships with clients. Additionally, effective time management is required to meet tight deadlines on assignments. Finally, with the rapid evolution of technology, auditors must be familiar with information systems and digital tools, such as data analysis software, which are increasingly used in modern audits (Bouziane et al., 2022). This complexity highlights the importance of non-technical skills, which complement traditional academic training and are essential for adapting to the rapid changes in the industry.

The skills of auditors and graduates, a complex concept with many synonyms and definitions such as generic skills, essential skills, and interpersonal skills (Coulet, 2016), are essential for their success in the job market. According to Baker and Henson (2013), graduate skills encompass abilities developed at university that go beyond academic content, thus increasing the chances of obtaining and maintaining different types of jobs. These skills are generally classified into four key areas: (i) intellectual skills, such as critical assessment and logical argumentation; (ii) key skills, such as communication and computing; (iii) personal attributes, such as motivation and autonomy; and (iv) knowledge of organizations and their functioning (Jammoul, 2012; Coulet, 2016). These skills are crucial for audit graduates, who must often demonstrate the ability to quickly adapt to new technologies and professional practices. However, aligning these skills with the real needs of the labor market remains a challenge, requiring ongoing cooperation between the academic world and employers.

Concerns about the gap between the skills acquired by graduates and the requirements of the labor market in an increasingly globalized world are not new (Elias & Purcell, 2004). Improving graduate employability is a priority for policymakers who develop strategies to align graduate skills with labor market needs. Educational institutions play a central role in this process, being responsible for identifying and developing the necessary skills in future audit graduates. The integration of generic skills into curricula is one response to this need, but their meaning and application vary according to national contexts.

Generic skills, though considered employability skills in many countries, vary in meaning depending on the national context. In addition to educational institutions, students and employers are key stakeholders in this process. Thi Tuyet (2014) and Hasshas (2024) have discussed the expectations of students and employers regarding higher education. They emphasized that students often view their studies as a means to secure good job opportunities, without always analyzing the job market perspectives, especially in a context where the issuance of diplomas has increased significantly. This increase in the number of graduates has changed employers' expectations. A university degree is now perceived as a prerequisite for employment, even in sectors where it was not previously necessary (Adonon, 2022). Graduates are increasingly aware that they must acquire additional skills and attributes to succeed in their professional careers. Employability skills, which include both generic and specific skills, are crucial for obtaining and maintaining a job.

Generic skills, widely recognized in universities, are transferable and include information literacy, use of technology, written and verbal communication, teamwork, and numeracy. Career development skills encompass researching and using career information, labor market trends, as well as the ability to locate, obtain, and maintain a job. They also include the ability to apply effectively, present skills attractively to employers, and build social capital through personal strategies and professional relationships. In auditing, in addition to the skills discussed earlier, relational skills are essential for the professional success of graduates, directly influencing their perception and employability (Ourrache, 2023). These skills include effective communication, collaboration, conflict resolution, and the ability to build trust-based relationships with clients and colleagues.

The issue of the mismatch between education and labor market requirements in Morocco remains a central topic in both academic and professional debates. As Hilmi and Hilmi (2016) point out, developing employability is crucial to bridging this gap and enhancing business productivity. However, the current educational system, often criticized for its inability to keep pace with economic changes, produces graduates who struggle to integrate into the labor market. This mismatch is manifested not only in high unemployment rates among young graduates but also in a qualitative misalignment between acquired skills and employers' expectations (Moflih & Moustaid, 2024).

Jreifi and Lakrarsi (2024) argue that the use of a competence-based approach (CBA) within a public-private partnership framework could contribute to a better alignment between professional training and the labor market. However, the implementation of this approach in Morocco faces challenges, including a lack of coordination and resources. Similarly, Benazzi (2019) highlights the social challenges posed by the training-employment mismatch, reminding us that proposed solutions to address this issue are numerous, but their impact remains limited without a broader overhaul of the educational system.

Elakry and Guechati (2022) explore employment mediation, identifying different categories of mismatch between education and employment. They stress the importance of improving mediation services to better meet the needs of employers and graduates. This analysis aligns with that of Herradi and Baouzil (2023), who show, through an empirical study, that the perception of mismatch varies among stakeholders: while professionals criticize the training system, young graduates highlight the rigidity and opacity of the labor market. Their survey also reveals that over 67% of unemployed individuals in Morocco are young graduates, underscoring the urgency of finding sustainable solutions to this mismatch.

These studies highlight the extent of the gap between education and employment in Morocco, an issue that requires a reform of the training system to better meet the demands of a constantly evolving labor market. The use of tools such as CBA and strengthening public-private partnerships could be effective levers, provided that reforms are accompanied by rigorous monitoring and evaluation mechanisms.

6.3 METHOD

This study aims to assess the gap between the competencies taught in academic audit programs in Morocco and those required by the labor market. Two samples were selected: 42 teacher-researchers from Hassan II University of Casablanca and 17 general directors of audit firms based in Casablanca.

The choice of Casablanca is based on its central role as the economic capital of Morocco, where a large number of audit firms are concentrated. Hassan II University, which offers audit programs across five faculties and schools, was selected as the framework for surveying teachers. All teacher-researchers who have taught audit-related courses (financial audit, quality audit, information systems audit, etc.) were included in the target population. With a response rate of 60% (42 teachers out of 70 contacted), this sample can be considered representative of the relevant academic population.

The general directors of the audit firms were selected based on data from the Order of Chartered Accountants, which includes audit firms operating in

Casablanca. Although only 17 directors responded due to their professional constraints, this sample provides valuable insight into market expectations, representing a diversity of firms (large international firms and local firms).

6.3.1 Questionnaires and validation process

Data collection was carried out using two distinct questionnaires, one for teachers and one for audit professionals. The questionnaire for teachers included questions about the content of the teaching programs, such as the subjects covered, the use of audit software, the frequency of practical case studies, and the organization of professional seminars. The questionnaire for the general directors explored the technical, linguistic, and personal skills expected from graduates, as well as the specific requirements of the job market.

To ensure the validity of the measurement instruments, a literature review helped identify key variables to include in the questionnaires. These variables were then evaluated by three chartered accountants who also teach at various universities. Their feedback helped refine the questions and ensure their relevance. Before the final distribution, the questionnaires were pre-tested with three audit professionals and three teachers for the academic section, allowing for verification of the clarity and understanding of the questions.

6.3.2 Analysis methods

The responses obtained were subjected to descriptive and comparative analysis. Gaps between the skills taught and those required by employers were identified through descriptive statistics (frequencies, means) and qualitative analyses of the respondents' comments. These methods allowed for the identification of specific trends regarding gaps in academic offerings and labor market expectations.

It is worth noting that the relatively limited sample size and its geographic concentration in Casablanca constitute a limitation to the generalization of the results. However, given Casablanca's prominence in Morocco's economy and the audit sector, the results remain representative of a significant part of the audit sector in Morocco.

6.4 RESULTS

The study's results reveal several gaps in the academic audit programs of Moroccan universities, highlighting a mismatch between the skills taught and those required by the labor market. First, it is clear that the use of audit software is entirely absent from the curricula, with 0% of teachers incorporating these technological tools into their courses. This means that students are not exposed to essential tools for modern audit practice, putting them at a distinct disadvantage relative to professional expectations.

Regarding practical case studies, only 10% of teachers report regularly using real-life cases. The majority, 90%, primarily use theoretical cases, which limits students' ability to prepare for the real-world challenges they will face in their future careers. Additionally, seminars led by professionals from the sector are also rare in academic programs, with only 12% of teachers stating that these events are organized regularly. This deprives students of a valuable opportunity to learn directly from current industry practices.

Regarding language skills, 80% of faculty teachers indicate that these skills are not specifically addressed in the courses. In contrast, teachers from business schools, representing 20% of the sample, state that languages are taught, primarily as a means of communication, and that audit courses are taught in French. This approach leaves a large portion of students inadequately prepared to thrive in a professional environment where proficiency in multiple languages, including English and Spanish, is often required.

From the perspective of the general directors of audit firms, the results highlight the crucial need for highly qualified auditors, with 100% of directors emphasizing this necessity. However, 94% believe that graduates are not well-prepared for the labor market. The directors note that while graduates from business schools stand out for their good language skills in French, English, and Spanish, there is a widespread lack of knowledge of audit terminology in languages other than French among all graduates.

In terms of technical skills, 82% of the directors believe that graduates from business schools are more competent in Excel and other tools compared to students from faculties. However, a common concern remains: 100% of the directors indicate that graduates have no knowledge of the most well-known audit software. This critical gap highlights a significant discrepancy between the academic training received and the skills expected by employers in the audit sector.

Overall, the results of this study demonstrate the urgent need to reform academic programs to better align teaching with labor market requirements. Students would thus be better prepared to effectively enter the audit sector, possessing the technical and linguistic skills necessary to meet employers' expectations.

6.5 DISCUSSION

The results presented above highlight a significant gap between the skills taught in academic audit programs in Morocco and the demands of the labor market. This disconnection raises several points of discussion that warrant further exploration to understand the implications of these gaps and consider potential solutions.

First, the absence of audit software teaching in academic programs is particularly concerning. In an industry where technology plays a crucial role, mastering audit tools is essential for future auditors' efficiency and competitiveness. The lack of such training is consistent with the findings of Bouziane et al. (2022), who emphasize the increasing need for auditors to be familiar with information systems and digital tools, such as data analysis software. The failure to integrate these tools into the curriculum leaves graduates ill-prepared for the technological demands of the profession.

Second, the limited use of practical case studies is another significant gap. Case studies are essential for developing students' abilities to apply theoretical knowledge in real-world contexts. This finding aligns with Chu et al. (2021), who argue that practical learning experiences are critical for auditors to transition smoothly into the industry. By increasing the use of real-life cases in courses, universities can enhance the applied learning of students and better prepare them for the complex problem-solving required in the audit profession.

The scarcity of seminars led by professionals in academic programs also reflects a lack of interaction between the academic world and the professional sector. This gap suggests that universities may not be sufficiently collaborating with industry practitioners to provide up-to-date perspectives on current industry practices. The importance of such collaboration is highlighted in the work of Kramarz and Viarengo (2015), who emphasize the role of both education systems and labor markets in preparing graduates for successful career transitions. By encouraging partnerships with professionals to organize seminars, workshops, and internships, universities could help bridge this gap and strengthen the connection between education and professional practice.

The issue of linguistic and cultural skills also emerges as increasingly important in a globalized labor market. While graduates from business schools tend to have better language skills, proficiency in technical terminology in multiple languages remains insufficient. This concern is in line with the findings of Ourrache (2023), who emphasizes the growing significance of relational and communication skills, including language proficiency, in the professional success of auditors. To better equip students for international professional environments, universities should enhance language teaching, with a particular focus on specialized terminology.

Finally, the results of this study underline the need for academic reform to align audit programs with market needs. The mismatch between the skills taught in university programs and the skills demanded by employers highlights the need for universities to work more closely with employers to adapt training offerings. This approach would not only improve graduates' employability, as discussed by Elias and Purcell (2004), but also help meet employers' needs by producing well-trained professionals capable of addressing the challenges of the audit sector. Educational institutions, as Thi Tuyet (2014) and Hasshas (2024) suggest, must take into account both students' expectations and the evolving needs of the labor market to better prepare graduates for their professional careers.

6.6 RECOMMENDATIONS

In light of the findings of this study, it is imperative to formulate recommendations to improve the alignment between audit education and labor market requirements. However, it is equally important to specify the necessary conditions for the effective implementation of these recommendations to ensure their lasting impact.

6.6.1 Updating academic curricula

It is recommended to integrate more technological skills, such as proficiency in CAATs, and to strengthen foreign language modules, particularly in English and French. To ensure the implementation of this recommendation, training institutions should cooperate closely with audit sector actors, both local and international firms, to adjust educational content according to identified needs. Creating partnerships between these institutions and companies would facilitate the ongoing updating of programs in response to technological and methodological developments.

6.6.2 Strengthening internships and on-the-job training

Incorporating a prolonged internship period into training programs would allow students to gain valuable practical experience. However, for this measure to be feasible, a structured collaboration between universities and businesses in the sector would be necessary. This could be facilitated through specific agreements or framework agreements ensuring regular access to quality internships for students. Moreover, tax incentives for companies hosting interns could encourage this collaboration.

6.6.3 Continuous training for teachers and infrastructure upgrades

Teacher-researchers should benefit from continuous professional development to stay updated with the latest technologies and methodologies in audit. This would require academic institutions to invest in the professional development of their teachers, in partnership with international organizations and certification programs. Furthermore, upgrading teaching infrastructures, particularly in terms of specialized software, is a prerequisite for students to become familiar with the tools used in the field.

6.6.4 Promoting an interdisciplinary approach

It would also be recommended to encourage interdisciplinary training where audit students collaborate with those in information technology, risk management, and business law. Implementing these interdisciplinary programs would require institutional changes, including the adaptation of academic calendars and the revision of assessment methods to incorporate this collaborative dimension.

6.7 CONCLUSION

This study aimed to assess the gap between the skills taught in audit academic programs in Morocco and those required by the labor market. Through questionnaires administered to 42 faculty members at Hassan II University of Casablanca and 17 managing directors of audit firms in Casablanca, we identified several significant gaps: the absence of audit software instruction (80% of the faculty), a lack of practical case studies (67%), the rarity of professional seminars (71%), and insufficient language skills, particularly in the faculties.

The managing directors noted the inadequate preparation of graduates despite the significant demand for qualified auditors, with better preparation observed among business school graduates in terms of technical and linguistic skills. The study's limitations include a modest sample size, a geographical focus on Casablanca, and a cross-sectional approach. Future research could benefit from expanding the sample to other regions, adopting a longitudinal approach, and examining the impact of emerging technologies on the skills required.

In conclusion, our analysis does not align with a simplistic "fit" approach, which would assume that solving graduate unemployment relies solely on improving the alignment between education and labor market needs. Instead, we highlight the importance of other determinants, such as labor market flexibility, rapid changes in professions, and the diverse expectations of young graduates.

This study makes a significant contribution to the literature by emphasizing that skill alignment cannot be considered in isolation from economic dynamics and technological transformations. By adopting a broader, more adaptive approach to better understand the complex interaction between education and employment, our research opens new perspectives for policymakers, educational institutions, and researchers. It advocates for a systemic reform of audit education in Morocco. Consequently, the results of this study urge a rethinking of pedagogical practices and skills development strategies to better meet the needs of an ever-evolving labor market.

REFERENCES

Adonon, E. (2022). The impact of increasing graduation rates on employment opportunities: A case study. *Global Education Review*, *9*(1), 45–60.

Baker, R., & Henson, K. (2013). Employability skills and graduate success: A review of the literature. *Journal of Career Development*, *40*(4), 321–340.

Benazzi, L. (2019). Formation emploi au Maroc, essai d'analyse. *La Revue Marocaine de la Pensée Contemporaine*, (4), 26–45. https://revues.imist.ma/index.php?journal=RMPC

Bouziane, A., Tahri, W., & Bouziane, K. (2022). ICT in professional training during Covid-19: The case of Moroccan employees. Dans A. Bouziane & D. Rabhi (Eds.), *Conference Proceedings, Humanities and Social Sciences, Key Levers for Post-Covid Recovery* (pp. 1–20). Chouaib Doukkali University, El Jadida, Morocco.

Carroll, D. (2013). Over-education of recent higher education graduates: New Australian panel evidence. *Economics of Education Review*, *32*, 207–218.

Chu, A., Meier, J., & Schimke, H. (2021). Competencies required for successful auditing: A comprehensive analysis. *Journal of Accounting Education*, *53*, 100–120.

Coulet, S. (2016). Les compétences non techniques et leur importance dans la formation des diplômés. *Revue de l'Education*, *13*(1), 45–67.

Elakry, E., & Guechati, M. (2022). Le service d'intermédiation en emploi: L'adéquation entre formation et emploi au Maroc. *Revue Internationale des Sciences de Gestion*, *5*(2), 43–72.

Elias, P., & Purcell, K. (2004). Is it worth going to university? The relative labour market returns to higher education qualifications. *British Journal of Sociology*, *55*(3), 379–406.

Hasshas, M. (2024). Understanding employer expectations in a rapidly changing job market. *Journal of Employment Studies*, *30*(1), 20–38.

Herradi, K., & Baouzil, L. (2023). L'écart entre les compétences acquises par la formation et les exigences du marché du travail au Maroc. *Revue REMSES*, *8*(3), 198–223.

Hilmi, Y., & Hilmi, M. (2016). Le développement de l'employabilité, outil pour limiter l'inadéquation formation-emploi: Cas du métier d'un responsable financier. *Revue Marocaine de Recherche en Management et Marketing*, *1*(13), 319–335.

Jammoul, Z. (2012). L'apprentissage par les compétences: Le rôle de l'évaluation au cours de l'apprentissage par compétence. *Dans L'évaluation des compétences en milieu scolaire et en milieu professionnel* (pp. 1–10). Luxembourg. https://halshs-00777286v1/document

Jreifi, K., & Lakrarsi, A. (2024). Repenser la formation professionnelle au Maroc à travers l'approche par les compétences dans un cadre de partenariat public-privé. *International Journal of Accounting, Finance, Auditing, Management and Economics*, *5*(5), 351–371. https://doi.org/10.5281/zenodo.11235124

Kramarz, F., & Viarengo, M. (2015). Chapitre 2. Les systèmes d'éducation et de formation face au chômage des jeunes. Dans F. Kramarz & M. Viarengo (Éds.), *Ni en emploi, ni en formation: Des jeunes laissés pour compte* (pp. 57–84). Presses de Sciences Po.

Moflih, Y., & Moustaid, E. H. (2024). Le chômage des diplômés au Maroc: L'inadéquation entre la formation et l'emploi. *International Journal of Accounting, Finance, Auditing, Management and Economics*, *5*(2), 436–454. https://doi.org/10.5281/zenodo.10702158

Ourrache, B. (2023). Building relationships in audit: The role of interpersonal skills. *International Journal of Auditing Practices*, *18*(2), 150–165.

Thi Tuyet, N. (2014). The expectations of students and employers from higher education: A comparative study. *International Journal of Education and Development*, *8*(2), 112–126.

Vieira, D. A., & Coimbra, J. L. (2008). La transition entre l'enseignement supérieur et l'emploi: Auto-efficacité, attentes de résultats et objectifs professionnels. *L'Orientation Scolaire et Professionnelle*, *37*(1), 91–112. https://doi.org/10.4000/osp.1617

Westermann, K., Bedard, J. C., & Earley, C. E. (2015). The role of audit education and practice in the development of auditing competencies. *Accounting Education: An International Journal*, *24*(2), 95–112.

Chapter 7

Digital transition in Morocco's local governments

Willful ignorance and organizational inertia and their implications for accountability and transparency

Azzaz Fatima Ezzahra

7.1 INTRODUCTION

A paradigm shift is reshaping the field of public governance, away from the traditional model of public administration and toward the principles of New Public Management (Bryson, Ackermann, & Eden, 2007). This evolutionary approach promotes accountability in the public sector by enhancing decision-making processes, increasing transparency, and holding civil servants and decision-makers directly accountable for their actions (Agostino, Saliterer, & Steccolini, 2022). In this context, the deployment of information and communication technologies (ICTs) in government strategies should not be limited to improving service delivery; rather, it should serve as a fundamental tool for fostering a culture of responsibility, internal control, and accountability.

Thus, digital governance has become a fundamental issue for local authorities. It involves leveraging ICT to enhance interaction and cooperation among stakeholders as well as transparency in decision-making. Indeed, the digitization of local public services can help local authorities meet the economic, social, environmental, and political challenges they face (Anne Cantero, 2003).

The digital era drives a redefinition of accountability mechanisms, transforming how public institutions operate and demonstrate transparency. As highlighted by A. Lewis (Lewis et al., 2014), the benefits of modernizing the Public Sector audit approach for both auditors and auditees include enhanced effectiveness, additional business insights, greater efficiency, and better detection of fraud, waste, and abuse. Furthermore, the auditing environment comprises all those actors who provide legitimacy and support for the public organization to function, thereby having a stake in its operation (Moore, 1995). Digitalization for public sector audit offers the opportunity to strengthen the operational capacity of governance committees and regulators, ensuring greater audit effectiveness and efficiency, and enabling better detection of irregularities. Furthermore, it must enhance communication and reporting among stakeholders to promote transparency and facilitate the timely resolution of identified issues (Zam, Nawawi, and Salin 2021). Moreover, audit committees and regulators can play a more emancipatory

 DOI: 10.1201/9781003650713-8

role by supporting regional development and improving the image of local authorities, thereby attracting private and foreign investment.

In this context, amid growing pressures for efficiency and transparency, many Moroccan local authorities are turning to digital solutions not only to reconfigure their relationships with stakeholders but also to streamline governance and management, often without fully anticipating the organizational and accountability implications of such transformations.

As public administrations progressively adopt digital tools, they generate both new possibilities and significant concerns regarding transparency and accountability mechanisms. From one perspective, traceability and dematerialization represent two central advantages of digital transformation. Traceability of administrative processes enhances transparency, strengthens accountability, and optimizes the operational efficiency of local authorities. Citizens gain from simplified, cost-free access to public services, along with significantly shorter response times for documents and inquiries. From another perspective, Moroccan local authorities still face considerable challenges in achieving full digital governance integration. Although these institutions increasingly recognize their strategic importance, digital governance remains in its early stages. Many rural municipalities encounter ongoing structural and technological barriers that hinder their adoption and effective use of digital tools. In urban areas, local governments demonstrate limited ability to integrate digital technologies into their administrative practices, exposing a persistent gap between digital ambitions and institutional capabilities. Moreover, effective digital governance requires a well-structured and transparent legal framework. This study examines how willful ignorance within public administrations obstructs effective digital transformation, which aims to establish traceability and accountability, even in the presence of governance bodies responsible for oversight and regulation.

In digital government studies, scholars have mostly viewed ignorance as a limitation of citizens (Holzer, 2022; Weigl, Barbereau, & Fridgen, 2023). This perspective links ignorance to patterns of opting out and resisting government initiatives (van Twist, Ruijer, & Meijer, 2023) and to reduced willingness to share personal data (Alshahrani, Dennehy, & Mäntymäki, 2022). Existing research rarely examines how ignorance shapes behavior within public administrations. We argue that willful ignorance, defined as the deliberate avoidance of relevant information (McGoey, 2012), represents a cognitive form of organizational inertia. Organizational inertia refers to internal resistance to change, driven by structural routines, resource dependencies, or established norms (Hannan & Freeman, 1984; Gilbert, 2005). In the context of digital transformation in government, willful ignorance can block knowledge acquisition, delay strategic adaptation, and sustain outdated processes. It undermines digital reform efforts, especially when transformation challenges existing power structures, demands new competencies, or disrupts institutional logic (Dunleavy et al., 2006; Mergel, Edelmann, & Haug, 2019). By conceptualizing willful ignorance as a dimension of inertia, we link the literature on digital government and accountability with foundational theories of organizational inertia. Accordingly, the study seeks to answer the following research question: "How does willful ignorance, as a dimension of organizational inertia, affect audit practices and accountability in Morocco's digitalized local authorities?"

This study focuses on the Rokhas platform as a case study, given its central role in the digital transformation of the Moroccan local authorities. To address the research question, we conducted a qualitative empirical analysis based on semi-structured interviews, using a predefined interview guide. The respondents included officials from the urban planning departments of the region's urban municipalities, project promoters, and other key stakeholders involved in the authorization process.

This work consists of two parts. In the first part, we develop the theoretical framework. We define the main dimensions of digitalization in the Moroccan territorial context. We then explore how willful ignorance, as a component of organizational inertia, interacts with audit mechanisms, transparency, accountability, regulatory oversight, and the responsibility of stakeholders involved in administrative processes. The second part presents the methodology adopted for the qualitative study, outlines the main findings, and concludes by summarizing the study's key contributions while proposing avenues for future research.

7.2 THEORETICAL FRAMEWORK

7.2.1 Reframing transparency and accountability in the digitalization of Morocco's local authorities: Insights from public sector literature

The Moroccan government has prioritized the development of digital governance for over a decade. In 2011, it launched a national digital strategy to drive economic transformation and institutional modernization. This strategy targets several key areas: enhancing the quality of public services, modernizing public administration, fostering innovation and entrepreneurship, boosting ICT demand, and embedding a culture of accountability. The government has pursued this trajectory through the implementation of the "Digital MOROCCO 2030" strategy.

At the local level, since the promulgation of the organic laws relating to Moroccan local authorities (Organic Laws N°.111-14, N°. 112-14, and N°.113-14, promulgated in 2015), they have embarked on a genuine digital transformation of their services. These laws require local authorities to incorporate ICTs into the management of human resources, planning, and budgeting processes. They also require the implementation of a regional digital development strategy, including the interoperability of information systems and the creation of web portals providing access to public services.

Moreover, with the advent of the digital era, digital governance has become essential in financial management, public procurement, and public service administration. Digital governance is a management method that concerns almost all areas of intervention and competencies of the aforementioned local authorities, and its contribution to improving the performance of local public management is indisputable.

As far as financial management is concerned, Moroccan local authorities encounter significant challenges related to transparency and the modernization of their financial management systems. The introduction of digital governance enables local authorities to enhance budget management and control spending through advanced management tools. In this regard, the government has taken significant steps toward governance of local finances. One notable initiative is the implementation of the Integrated Expenditure Management (GID) and Integrated Revenue Management (GIR) systems, which have become essential tools for local financial and accounting management (Circulaire conjointe du Ministère de l'Intérieur (DGCL) et du Ministère de l'Economie et des finances. 2020, 3 mars). The GIR system is a tool designed to replace traditional revenue management methods. It aims to establish transparency in the management of territorial revenues and the permanent, dematerialized exchange of data between authorizing officers and public accountants. Thus, the directives of the supervisory ministry to integrate their services into the GIR platform oblige local authorizing officers. By the joint circular issued by the Ministry of the Interior and the Ministry of Economy and Finance, the GIR platform streamlines and enhances revenue collection procedures. This improvement relies in particular on the digital availability of payment receipts and the flexibility offered to debtors in choosing their payment methods (cash, bank transfer, or credit card, etc.).

Following this, the GID system is a platform for implementing the budgets of the various public administrations, making accounting procedures more flexible and simpler (El Alami, 2017). It manages appropriations through budget transfers and modifications and facilitates the execution of expenditure operations from the creation of the expenditure through to its commitment and payment of the debt.[1] To this end, the platform includes a virtual registry that facilitates the transmission of budget proposals and expenditure transactions to the authority responsible for administrative control and to the treasurer responsible for administrative, budgetary, and accounting controls.

The GID platform provides accurate real-time accounting by generating credit, commitment, and issuance reports. Similarly, its electronic nature gives local authority managers with valid access certificates and accounts direct access to all transactions, as well as to accounting and budgetary data.[2] Ultimately, the implementation of these digital solutions in local authority audits aims to facilitate the analysis of budget usage, suggest improvements in resource allocation, and potentially enhance tax compliance.

When it comes to public procurement, digital governance offers considerable advantages. IT systems enable local authorities to streamline public procurement procedures and strengthen control over public spending[3]. Invitations to tender can be issued online, and suppliers' responses can be dematerialized (El Amry, 2018). The digital governance of local public procurement aims to facilitate, modernize, and optimize the processes for purchasing, controlling, and managing public orders and contracts for local authorities. Several foundational pillars support this approach to ensure efficient and transparent management and resource allocation (Guiri, 2012).

The implementation of digital governance of public procurement by local authorities in Morocco can make a significant contribution to the modernization and transparency of the administration, which is essential for improving the performance of local public services[4]. In this respect, the Moroccan Public Procurement Portal represents a significant innovation, offering a range of digital tools and procedures to manage calls for tender more efficiently and transparently (Boutaqbout, 2012). This includes publishing invitations to tender, receiving bids, evaluating and selecting bidders, and notifying of the outcomes of the procurement process. Secondly, centralizing information through a unified public procurement management platform strengthens oversight and coordination. The platform centralizes data while supporting decentralized operational management. It also facilitates monitoring and control, and reduces the risk of duplication. This platform also facilitates communication between the various parties involved in the public procurement process. Furthermore, transparency and accessibility through the publication of data on public contracts, which enables citizens, businesses, the media, and other stakeholders to access information and monitor the decisions made regarding public contracts (Zoubaa, 2019). Moreover, this helps to build confidence in the system and establish a culture of accountability and performance. Finally, monitoring and evaluation mechanisms help assess the system's performance and detect any issues or inefficiencies. They also support the identification of improvement opportunities and ensure an effective and transparent allocation of public funds.

Digital management of administrative affairs has become increasingly common among urban regions and municipalities. This approach offers multiple advantages for both local governments and citizens. It simplifies internal operations for municipal staff and improves service accessibility for users (Guillou, 2003). Key areas affected include civil registration, urban planning, and human resource management. In Morocco, urban planning governance and regulation rely heavily on the involvement of local authorities. To strengthen the operational capacity of these organizations, the Directorate-General for Local Authorities introduced the Rokhas platform. This initiative, developed through a public-private partnership, serves two main objectives:

- Ensure end-to-end management of urban planning procedures, with real-time monitoring and traceability;
- Foster continuous system improvement by integrating field-level feedback, regulatory developments, and technological innovation.

However, the outcomes demonstrate mixed performance, notably in mastering processing deadlines. Local governments continue to experience delays in digitizing town planning permits and authorizations, with challenges particularly evident in the implementation of integrated platforms such as the Public Procurement Portal.

Although local authorities received training and support, they still face difficulties adopting the digital platforms. Circular 'D7175, issued by the Directorate-General for Local Authorities, points to persistent delays in issuing building permits through the Rokhas platform—one of the key concerns addressed in this study. The platform promises transparency in processes, and governance bodies actively oversee and regulate it; however, delays persist. At this stage, the following section explores the role of organizational inertia in shaping the current challenges.

7.2.2 Willful ignorance as a dimension of organizational inertia: Challenges to accountability and transparency in digital transformation

Understanding organizational inertia requires distinguishing between an organization's structural incapacity to change and its intentional resistance to adapt. Limited resources, rigid decision-making processes, and a failure to recognize the need for change (Leonard-Barton, 1992; Eisenhardt & Martin, 2000) characterize structural incapacity. In contrast, intentional resistance stems from established interests, cultural norms, and fear of transformation (Oliver, 1991; Piderit, 2000). This distinction proves essential to analyze how different internal forces influence change efforts.

Organizational inertia offers a detailed analysis of these forces and their effects on digital transformation. Inertia may slow the adoption of new technologies and affect accountability mechanisms in public administrations. However, research has not yet fully explored how these different dimensions of inertia affect digital reforms and transparency initiatives. To examine how organizational inertia shapes digital transformation in the public sector, it is beneficial to identify its primary dimensions, as discussed in the literature. Inertia is not a uniform phenomenon; it takes multiple forms, each shaped by specific organizational, cognitive, or political mechanisms. Various theoretical perspectives have examined these dimensions, offering complementary explanations for why organizations resist change. Table 7.1 summarizes the key types of organizational inertia, along with the theoretical frameworks that account for their origins and persistence.

Among the various forms of inertia, willful ignorance warrants special attention. IT involves more than the avoidance of information; it also reflects a broader cognitive and strategic posture (McGoey, 2012; Gross, 2007). This posture encompasses the strategic framing of knowledge relevance, the deliberate maintenance of uncertainty, and the rejection of disruptive insights

Table 7.1 Dimensions of organizational inertia and related theoretical perspectives

Dimension of inertia	*Description*	*Theoretical perspective*	*Key references*
Structural inertia	Resistance linked to stable routines, formal structures, and fixed processes	Organizational Ecology	Hannan and Freeman (1984)
Resource rigidity	Inertia due to inability or unwillingness to reallocate resources	Dynamic Capabilities Theory	Gilbert (2005); Eisenhardt and Martin (2000)
Routine rigidity	Inflexibility in operational routines and procedures	Behavioral Theory of the Firm	Nelson and Winter (1982)
Cognitive inertia	Mental models and interpretive frames that resist change	Sense-Making and Framing Theories	Tripsas and Gavetti (2000); Kaplan (2008)
Cultural inertia	Deeply embedded norms, values, and beliefs limiting adaptation	Institutional Theory	Schein (1985); Greenwood and Hinings (1996)
Political inertia	Inertia caused by power struggles, vested interests, or fear of loss	Political Theory of Organizations	Pfeffer (1981); Oliver (1991)
Willful ignorance	Strategic avoidance of knowledge that threatens the status quo	Sociology of Ignorance: Cognitive Inertia	McGoey (2012); Gross (2007); Crusoe et al. (2023)

Source: Author's own compilation.

(McGoey, 2007; Rayner, 2012). In public sector organizations, such behaviors can delay or distort digital transformation by shielding existing routines and institutional arrangements from scrutiny (Crusoe, Magnusson, & Torell, 2023). Willful ignorance can also undermine core democratic values (Oliver, 1991; Schaffer, 2016). Table 7.2 provides a structured summary of seminal research on willful ignorance and includes essential definitions and perspectives.

Recent scholarship shifts the view of ignorance from a passive lack of knowledge to a strategic and socially constructed phenomenon (Gross, 2007; McGoey, 2012; Heimer, 2012; Jalonen, 2023). Our study focuses on willful ignorance to explore how intentional non-knowing functions as a mechanism of organizational inertia and a barrier to accountable, digitally enabled public governance. We adopt the concept of ignorance not as a mere absence of information, but as a deliberate cognitive and organizational stance. Strategic forms of ignorance, such as willful ignorance, help explain why actors may actively avoid engagement with digital reform agendas, even when relevant knowledge is available (McGoey, 2012; Alshahrani, Dennehy, & Mäntymäki, 2022).

Deliberate ignorance significantly shapes the course and outcomes of digital transformation, yet scholarly attention to this phenomenon remains limited. At various organizational levels, actors often avoid engaging with digital knowledge or infrastructure to preserve operational stability or

Table 7.2 Comparative table of theories related to willful ignorance in management

Theory/concept (year)	*Mechanism*	*Main purpose/function*
Functional Stupidity (Alvesson & Spicer, 2012)	Avoidance of reflection or critical thinking	To reduce complexity, maintain harmony, and avoid justification
Willful Managerial Ignorance (Schaefer, 2018)	Decoupling of discourse from action	To preserve legitimacy, protect self-image, and maintain routines
Strategic Ignorance (McGoey, 2007; 2012)	Deliberate fragmentation or withholding of information	To protect organizational routines and avoid accountability
Pluralistic Ignorance (Katz & Allport, 1931)	Misperception of group beliefs leading to silence	To avoid social conflict or going against the perceived norm
Abilene Paradox (Harvey, 1974)	Collective decision-making that contradicts individual preferences	To avoid confrontation and preserve group cohesion
Rational Ignorance (Downs, 1957)	Conscious decision not to seek information due to cost-benefit trade-off	To optimize decision effort where info is seen as not worth the cost
Knowledge Avoidance (Arfini & Magnani, 2021)	Selective avoidance of specific information	To maintain comfort, emotional stability, or moral disengagement

Source: Author's own compilation.

protect personal roles (Crusoe, Magnusson, & Eklund, 2024). This avoidance underpins what Crusoe et al. (2024) conceptualize as digital transformation decoupling, whereby digital change is promoted rhetorically but resisted in practice. Such patterns align with broader institutional observations of digital decoupling, in which symbolic digital initiatives serve as façades of progress while internal practices remain unchanged (Emerald JBS, 2021). Institutional logics deepen these dynamics, as dominant bureaucratic or financial norms often marginalize emerging digital orientations, prompting actors to withdraw from digital initiatives as a way to reduce uncertainty or avoid conflicts between competing logics (Emerald, 2022). At the collective level, pluralistic ignorance may arise when teams continue flawed digital initiatives under the false assumption of shared support, while emotional and reputational risks deter dissent (Bakken & Wiik, 2018; Kumar & Epley, 2024). At the individual level, status quo bias drives resistance to new digital systems, often motivated by cognitive discomfort or fear of diminished professional competence (Nugawela & Sedera, 2022). Israilidis et al. (2012) extend this understanding by showing how actors actively manage ignorance, through withholding or deflecting knowledge, to maintain control within digital projects. This mechanism echoes Alvesson and Spicer's (2012) notion of functional stupidity, where cultural norms suppress critical inquiry, allowing superficial or ethically questionable digital strategies to persist unchallenged. Together, these perspectives highlight that digital transformation failures often originate not from technological shortcomings but from embedded socio-cognitive dynamics that institutionalize selective ignorance and avoidance.

Essen et al. (2022) identify four organizational conditions that foster willful ignorance in the context of digital transformation within public organizations. First, fragmented accountability—driven by functional specialization—creates structural silos, particularly between IT and social service departments. This separation limits engagement with digital tools, such as AI, and narrows the scope of the transformation. Crusoe et al. (2023) interpret this fragmentation as a strategic mechanism for managing complexity while preserving operational stability. Second, Essen et al. (2022), drawing on Abbott (2010), highlight a norm of laissez-faire professionalism, where professionals avoid crossing jurisdictional boundaries to prevent conflict. This mutual non-interference reduces inter-professional collaboration, thereby constraining digital innovation. Third, technological uncertainty—linked to the constant evolution of digital tools—encourages a cautious, reactive learning culture, which sustains ignorance and delays innovation (Essen et al., 2022). Finally, external admiration, such as the pursuit of awards or legitimacy through vendor showcases, often shifts focus from substantive internal change to symbolic validation. This dynamic, emphasized by O'Reilly, C. A. III & Tushman, M. L. (2013), limits internal learning and weakens transformative commitment. Collectively, these conditions illustrate how willful ignorance strategically shapes digital transformation in the public sector (Essen et al., 2022; Crusoe et al., 2023).

This synthesis of theoretical insights and the supporting overview highlights the central role of willful ignorance in shaping digital transformation within the public sector, as argued by Crusoe et al. (2023). It also reveals its connection to a set of enabling conditions, consistent with the findings of Essen et al. (2022). These perspectives converge on the idea that ignorance in management is often not accidental, but cultivated for strategic, symbolic, or emotional purposes.

7.3 METHODOLOGY

In management sciences, we distinguish between two types of qualitative research: deductive research, which seeks to justify and test an existing model within the framework of a confirmatory verification approach; and the second type of qualitative research, described as pure qualitative, which seeks to conceptualize data, build, and enrich theory.

This research follows a purely qualitative approach. It focuses on how actors within the Moroccan territorial administration interpret their social reality. We explore their lived experiences with strategic change, cultural shifts, and perceptions of digital technologies—each shaped by their perspectives. The social reality in question emerges from their subjective experiences within the territorial context. At this stage, we cannot yet define clear links between the study's key concepts. First, we must identify the specific components of each key concept to understand how they relate to one another.

This study employs a qualitative methodological approach, aiming to provide unique insights and contributions to audit practices and accountability in the public sector, as well as offering particular value for policymakers and practitioners at the organizational level, specifically for audit committees and regulators of local authorities in Morocco.

7.3.1 Case choice and presentation

This study examined the adoption of the digital solution "Rokhas" within Territorial Collectivities, with a specific focus on urban planning services. The platform emerged from a public-private partnership between the General Directorate of Territorial Collectivities (DGCT) and the company Ribatis. The platform serves three main purposes:

- It manages all urban planning procedures from end to end in a controlled and auditable manner, with real-time monitoring.
- It enables direct payment of service fees by applicants, ensuring transparent compensation.
- It continuously improves by integrating field feedback, regulatory developments, and technological advancements.

The platform enables streamlined, traceable, and transparent digital management of urban and economic authorizations nationwide. Applicants submit their requests online, and the process remains fully digitized until the mayor of the relevant municipality signs the authorization electronically. Commission members examine each application and provide their opinions using digital tools and electronic signatures. The system relies on specific performance indicators to monitor how each municipality uses the platform. Analysts evaluate this performance based on the number of authorizations issued and the quality of case handling. They measure quality primarily by tracking the frequency of interactions between public administrations and users.

We selected this case based on concerns raised in the DGCT circular (Circular D-7175, October 26, 2021) about persistent delays in processing files and issuing urban planning permits, despite ROKHAS's commitment to enhancing transparency, ensuring oversight through governance bodies, and implementing monitoring and evaluation mechanisms. The circular also highlighted that several Territorial Collectivities postponed the adoption of the Rokhas platform, even after completing user training.

The joint decree N°338-20 dated January 21/2020, clarified the digital management procedures related to submitting, processing, and issuing authorizations, building permits, and certificates of compliance. Issued by the Minister of the Interior, the Minister of National Territorial Planning, Urbanism, Housing and City Policy, and the Minister of Industry, Trade, and the Green and Digital Economy, this decree established governance committees at the central, regional, and local levels to supervise the project's execution.

Despite these frameworks, the delays in meeting deadlines for issuing permits persisted, exceeding the standards set by Article 16 of Law 55-19, which aims to simplify administrative procedures and formalities. These ongoing delays illustrate how willful ignorance may hinder digital transformation efforts and reveal challenges in regulatory, transparent, and accountable mechanisms within public sector digitalization.

Regarding the sample, we selected the BENIMELLAL Khénifra Region as the study area, specifically targeting the presidents of municipalities (political hierarchy within municipalities), urban planning officers (end-users of the platform), and service directors within Urban Municipalities (administrative hierarchy within municipalities), as well as officials representing the central administration (the supervisory authority DGCT).

7.3.2 Collection and analysis of the data

This study employs a qualitative exploratory approach, relying primarily on semi-structured interviews. The interviews followed a structured guide that organized questions into five thematic sections. The selection of questions for each theme drew on a thorough analysis of the existing literature:

- Coordination and consultation between partners (civil servants, project leaders, etc.);
- Definition of roles (civil servants, hierarchy, regulators/Transparency and legitimacy);
- Political and management support;
- Project management capacity (quality of physical infrastructure/human resources, etc.);
- Evaluation instruments and organizational governance structures.

We conducted the analysis using NVIVO software, relying on thematic content analysis after transcribing and coding the interviews. The study involved collaboration with 11 stakeholders from the BENIMELLAL Khénifra region. Semi-structured interviews did not fully capture interactions among the subject's various elements. Additional data come from written documents and detailed case observations. The analysis of bibliographic sources provided secondary data to supplement the primary data from interviews and focus groups.

The documentary approach focused on texts and regulations governing Territorial Municipalities, circulars and correspondence issued by the supervisory authority (the General Directorate of Territorial Collectivities, DGCT), along with documents available on the Ribatis website (operators of the Rokhas platform) and those provided by the Ministry of Urban Planning. Moreover, the analysis included all documentation directly or indirectly related to urban planning, local development, the Rokhas platform, and Territorial Municipalities.

7.4 FINDINGS AND DISCUSSION

The presentation of findings draws on a systematic thematic analysis. We conducted this analysis after transcribing and coding the interviews. This qualitative process builds on a close examination of relevant institutional documents, including legal texts, circulars, and internal reports, and incorporates observational data collected during fieldwork. By triangulating these sources, we ensured methodological consistency and analytic depth. The convergence of evidence from interviews, documents, and observations enabled the identification of core factors structuring the five predefined thematic dimensions. We gave particular attention to how these factors interact with accountability mechanisms, influence the effectiveness of transparency efforts, and reveal latent forms of willful ignorance embedded in local governance practices.

The analysis revealed a persistent ambiguity in the attribution of responsibilities within local planning departments. Before municipalities adopted the ROKHAS platform, "signatory architects" routinely approved building plans they had not designed themselves. This widespread practice reflected a structural vagueness in role definition and professional accountability. The lack of distinction between design, verification, and approval responsibilities created a permissive environment in which actors could evade liability without formally violating procedures. Such arrangements undermined the legitimacy of administrative actions and weakened institutional transparency, reinforcing a culture of discretion and informal negotiation. *(Theme: Definition of roles/ Transparency and legitimacy.)*

The platform introduced real-time visibility and structured access to information. This form of transparency stems largely from how the platform organizes commission meetings: architects receive available appointment slots automatically, based on a predefined threshold of dossiers per session. As a result, civil servants no longer have the discretion to prioritize certain files over others. This automated scheduling reduces discretionary power and minimizes the risk of preferential treatment in the application processing. It fosters equitable procedural practices and enhances accountability in the management of planning permission applications. The platform's configuration represents not only a technical innovation, but also a governance tool that redefines power relations in administrative processing *(Themes: Evaluation instruments and organizational governance structures; Coordination and consultation between partners.)*

Beyond ensuring transparency in file management and processing, the platform also strengthens civil servants' independence in their decision processes. Compared to past practices, officials exercise increased independence from their hierarchical superiors during the evaluation of planning applications. This shift reduces opportunities for undue influence during the instruction phase and reinforces individual accountability. It also reflects an institutional reconfiguration in which digital tools not only standardize procedures but also redistribute power across administrative levels.

Moreover, interviewees confirmed that external and internal interventions have significantly declined since the introduction of the Rokhas platform. The system's embedded transparency has reduced opportunities for hierarchical pressure or influence from external actors seeking to manipulate file prioritization for personal gain. This procedural neutrality also limits the ability of ill-intentioned civil servants to interfere with workflows for strategic purposes. By standardizing access and reducing discretionary power, the platform constrains informal interference and reinforces objective processing rules *(Themes: Political and management support; Evaluation instruments and organizational governance structures.)*

However, certain legacy practices persist—not because of the digital tool itself, but due to how individuals manipulate it. As one respondent explained, analog procedures once allowed full discretion: "With a pen, you could write a six or a nine—it made no difference. But on the platform, a six is a six; everything is tracked." According to this view, the system logs delays, validations, and all user actions, making manipulation more difficult. Yet, despite these safeguards, civil servants acting in bad faith continue to find ways to circumvent controls and pursue personal interests. This observation reflects a deeper form of organizational inertia rooted in willful ignorance, where resistance to accountability arises not from structural deficiencies but from strategic disengagement with the system's integrity mechanisms. *(Theme: Evaluation instruments and organizational governance structures.)*

Furthermore, several interviews revealed persistent coordination issues among institutional actors responsible for developing and deploying the ROKHAS platform. According to the focal point and project manager within the DGCT, the monitoring phase of the project generated the most significant resistance, even before local governments formally introduced the platform. This reluctance stemmed largely from stakeholders' limited understanding of the project's rationale and objectives, as many civil servants and local leaders reported confusion regarding its scope and strategic objectives. The fragmentation of authority—whereby mayors, empowered by the Organic Law, retain full control over urban planning decisions while the DGCT assumes only a technical and advisory role—amplified this resistance. Without a shared governance framework or mechanisms for meaningful consultation, the project suffered from weak ownership and limited engagement across key institutional boundaries. *(Theme: Coordination and consultation between partners.)*

Such resistance reflects a form of willful ignorance, characterized by the selective avoidance or dismissal of information that could affect stakeholders' decisions (Grossman, 2015). This attitude may result from perceived threats to local autonomy, as mayors exercise substantial authority under law, which leads them to resist initiatives seen as externally imposed or undermining their prerogatives (Friedman, 2019). The DGCT's limited role further constrains its capacity to influence, reinforcing stakeholders' tendencies to disregard aspects of the project.

In line with this, the organizational structure of municipalities, which varies according to their size as stipulated by the Organic Law, plays a critical role in shaping the practical use of the digital platform. Regardless of size, each urban planning department must manage authorization requests through the same digital system. In smaller municipalities, however, human resource constraints often lead to the assignment of the entire digital process to a single civil servant. This arrangement increases the risk of procedural overload, omissions, and discretionary decisions, particularly when one individual handles all phases—submission, verification, and approval. In such conditions, errors or delays frequently result not from incompetence, but from fatigue, excessive workload, or the accumulation of unchecked decision-making power. This structural setup reinforces organizational inertia and encourages forms of willful ignorance, whereby officials deliberately avoid addressing complex or politically sensitive issues to reduce the risk of being held accountable (Ashforth & Anand, 2003). Although the platform aims to improve transparency and accountability, persistent structural barriers reduce its effectiveness and sustain gaps between digital reforms and actual administrative practices. (*Theme: Project management capacity.*)

Moreover, the thematic analysis highlights a persistent reliance on outdated administrative routines by certain officials during file processing. Even after the standardization of required documents through Decree No. 377-20, verifiers at the Digital Registry Office or commission members often reject applications for lacking documents not listed in the official guidelines. These decisions typically reflect institutional habits, limited awareness of legal updates, or, in some cases, intentional delays that prompt applicants to return for clarification. This behavior illustrates a form of willful ignorance, in which officials consciously disregard updated norms that could strengthen transparency and reinforce citizen oversight. Such selective resistance undermines the clarity and consistency of evaluation procedures, limiting the effectiveness of regulatory instruments designed to ensure procedural equity (Grossman, 2015). As Friedman (2019) notes, entrenched behaviors tend to preserve administrative discretion and resist governance reforms perceived as threats to existing power dynamics. *(Theme: Evaluation instruments and organizational governance structures.)*

The analysis also revealed that the validation of commission opinions faces critical challenges. To preserve objectivity and neutrality, the secretary should not simultaneously serve as both the validating official and a commission member providing an opinion. However, within some municipal centralized service offices, the secretary assumes both roles in major projects due to insufficient human resources. This situation exemplifies a form of willful ignorance, where organizational constraints and selective oversight hinder transparency and accountability mechanisms. Such role conflations undermine the capacity of regulatory and governance bodies to ensure impartial decision-making, thereby weakening procedural integrity and the effectiveness of institutional checks and balances.

Building on this, interviews revealed that several municipal civil servants refrain from fully engaging with new digital procedures. Many respondents acknowledged that they often postpone file processing until they receive guidance from the urban agency, which they then replicate with minimal adjustment. This practice reflects not only a functional dependency but also a strategic form of disengagement. Officials cited fear of error, hierarchical sanctions, and increased scrutiny through performance indicators as primary motives for withholding initiative. This behavior reflects a latent form of willful ignorance, as civil servants intentionally disengage to avoid the individual risks that heightened transparency and accountability may trigger. As Dana and Loewenstein (2003) and Felgendreher (2018) suggest, such avoidance reflects a defensive strategy that emerges in contexts where increased visibility generates discomfort or fear of blame. Rather than fostering responsibility, monitoring mechanisms may inadvertently encourage minimal compliance and reinforce bureaucratic caution (Bovens, 2007). (*Theme: Definition of roles/Transparency and legitimacy.*)

The documentary analysis revealed the establishment of governance bodies and regulatory authorities designed to oversee the implementation of the Rokhas platform. In particular, authorities created dedicated committees under Joint Order No. 338-20 dated January 21, 2020, to ensure effective coordination and monitoring. The governance framework includes three levels of committees: central, regional, and local.

The central implementation and monitoring committee holds the responsibility to:

Define the implementation modalities for digitized administrative procedures and propose the necessary measures that municipalities, government agencies, public institutions, utility operators, and professional stakeholders must take to establish the interactive digital platform.

Assess the actual deployment of digitized procedures related to the submission, review, and issuance of building permits, occupancy permits, and certificates of compliance;

Examine potential adjustments and recommend improvements to the digital management processes.

The Director General of Territorial Collectivities chairs the committee. Its members include:

The Secretary General of the governmental department in charge of urban planning or a designated representative;

The Director General of the Digital Development Agency or a designated representative.

The chair can invite any public or private organization or individual to participate in an advisory role if their involvement benefits the committee's work.

At the regional level, an executive and monitoring committee operates under the leadership of the regional governor. This committee assumes responsibility for:

Ensuring the implementation of digitized procedures related to the submission, review, and issuance of authorizations, occupancy permits, and certificates of compliance;
Presenting proposals and supervising measures to enforce digitized management procedures;
Regularly preparing reports on the implementation of digitized procedures;
Developing training programs for users of the interactive digital platform, including municipal staff, government agencies, public institutions, utility operators, and relevant professionals.

The regional governor appoints the committee members through an official decree.

At the local level, a committee functions under the leadership of the governor of the prefecture, district prefecture, or province concerned. The committee handles:

Supporting Territorial Municipalities in implementing and monitoring digitized procedures for the submission, review, and issuance of authorizations, occupancy permits, and certificates of compliance;
Overseeing the development of the aforementioned training programs.

The governor of the prefecture, district prefecture, or province appoints the members of the local committee through an official decree.

To deepen the institutional analysis, the review of legal documents and interview data reveals significant governance inconsistencies in the implementation of the Rokhas platform. Although Joint Order No. 338-20 mandates the establishment of monitoring committees at central, regional, and local levels, the legal framework remains vague about the frequency of meetings and the practical methods for ensuring operational oversight *(Theme 5: Evaluation instruments and organizational governance structures)*. This ambiguity delegates wide discretionary power to regional governors (Walis) and prefects, allowing them to define local arrangements as they see fit *(Theme 3: Political and management support)*. Interview insights show that the actual effectiveness of these committees depends less on formal structure than on the initiative and commitment of individual members, particularly in contexts where coordination among institutional actors is weak or symbolic *(Theme 1: Coordination and consultation between partners)*. Such institutional fluidity opens the door to willful ignorance, as some officials exploit regulatory gaps to avoid shared accountability and reduce exposure to scrutiny. The absence of binding mechanisms undermines both the credibility of monitoring tools and the transparency of inter-organizational collaboration throughout the digital transition process *(Themes 1, 3, and 5 combined).*

Moreover, interviews reveal that the governance and oversight committees created to support the platform's implementation remain largely inactive and ineffective in practice. In particular, the regional governance committee set up to monitor implementation lacks responsiveness. As a result, the engagement of municipal presidents largely depends on their commitment to serving the public interest. Although Rokhas has introduced a baseline of transparency compared to the former paper-based system, several civil servants still rely on legacy practices. In the absence of regular monitoring and enforceable accountability mechanisms, these practices persist and undermine the platform's potential to promote administrative integrity and responsible governance. *(Theme: Evaluation instruments and organizational governance structures.)*

7.5 CONCLUSION

This study explored how organizational inertia—particularly in the form of willful ignorance—hinders the institutionalization of transparency and accountability within Morocco's digital transformation initiatives. By examining the day-to-day practices of local civil servants in the urban planning departments of one Moroccan region, the analysis revealed how selective disengagement, avoidance of responsibility, and minimal use of digital tools contribute to the persistence of opaque administrative routines. These dynamics limit the effectiveness of digital platforms intended to enhance the traceability, equity, and legitimacy of public decision-making. The findings highlight a persistent disconnect between formal commitments to e-government and the informal strategies that actors mobilize to circumvent accountability in politically sensitive and institutionally ambiguous settings.

Despite its contributions, the study presents several limitations. From an empirical perspective, the research focuses on a single region and a specific category of actors—planning authority officials—thereby excluding broader stakeholder groups such as governance committee members, elected officials, or private users of the platform. These exclusions may restrict the generalizability of the findings. From a theoretical standpoint, this study strengthens the conceptual framing of organizational inertia and willful ignorance, while inviting further integration of related constructs from public administration and digital governance, such as administrative resistance, institutional work, or techno-political accountability.

These limitations open important avenues for future research. Comparative studies across regions or policy sectors could illuminate how context shapes patterns of willful ignorance and resistance to digital reform. Research could also examine how different institutional designs—particularly those with stronger legal enforcement or leadership commitment—influence the success of transparency-oriented digital tools. Furthermore, as emerging technologies such as artificial intelligence increasingly enter the audit and compliance landscape, future studies should investigate their potential to reshape accountability dynamics in public institutions. In contexts like Morocco, where financial opacity remains a persistent challenge, the integration of intelligent auditing systems may offer new paths toward institutional trust—if organizational cultures evolve accordingly.

NOTES

1 "GID-CT System: For Sound Financial Governance of Local Authorities," Al Maliya, No. 59, December 2015, p. 21.
2 Ministry of Economy and Finance, Al Maliya, No. 59, December 2015, p. 21.
3 Article 43 de l'Arrêté du ministre délégué auprès de la ministre de l'économie et des finances, chargé du budget n° 1692-23 du 4 hija 1444 (23 juin 2023)
4 Article 91 du décret n° 2-22-431 de 8 mars 2023 relatif aux marchés publics. B.O n° 7184, 6 Avril 2023, pp. 913–1000.

REFERENCES

Abbott, A. (2010). Varieties of ignorance. *The American Sociologist*, *41*(2), 174–189.

Agostino, D., Saliterer, I., & Steccolini, I. (2022). Digitalization, accounting and accountability: A literature review and reflections on future research in public services. *Financial Accountability & Management*, *38*(2), 152–176. https://doi.org/10.1111/faam.12301

Alvesson, M., & Spicer, A. (2012). A stupidity-based theory of organizations. *Journal of Management Studies*, *49*(7), 1194–1220. https://doi.org/10.1111/j.1467-6486.2012.01072.x

Alshahrani, A., Dennehy, D., & Mäntymäki, M. (2022). An attention-based view of AI assimilation in public sector organizations: The case of Saudi Arabia. *Government Information Quarterly*, *39*, Article 101617. https://doi.org/10.1016/s0191-3085(03)25001-2

Arfini, S., & Magnani, L. (2021). *Ignorance: A philosophical study*. Springer.

Article 43 de l'Arrêté du ministre délégué auprès de la ministre de l'économie et des finances, chargé du budget n° 1692-23 du 4 hija 1444 (23 juin 2023) relatif à la dématérialisation des procédures, des documents et des pièces relatives aux marchés publics. *B.O n° 7222*, 17 août 2023, pp. 1774–1784.

Article 91 du décret n° 2-22-431 de 8 mars 2023 relatif aux marchés publics. *B.O n° 7184*, 6 Avril 2023, pp. 913–1000.

Ashforth, B. E., & Anand, V. (2003). The normalization of corruption in organizations. *Research in Organizational Behavior*, *25*, 1–52. https://doi.org/10.1016/S0191-3085(03)25001-2

Bakken, T., & Wiik, R. (2018). Ethics of ignorance: Lessons from failed digitalization in public sector. *Ephemera: Theory & Politics in Organization*, *18*(4), 783–804.

Boutaqbout, A. (2012). La dématérialisation de la commande publique : dimensions juridiques. In *Al Khazina: Revue de la Trésorerie Générale du Royaume (n° 9, août 2012, Spécial: Le programme de la dématérialisation de la commande publique au service de la transparence des marchés publics*, p. 7.

Bovens, M. A. P. (2007). Analysing and assessing accountability: A conceptual framework. *European Law Journal*, *13*(4), 447–468. https://doi.org/10.1111/j.1468-0386.2007.00378.x

Bryson, J.M., Ackermann, F., & Eden, C. (2007). Putting the resource-based view of strategy and distinctive competencies to work in public organizations. *Public Administration Review*, *67*, 702–717.

Cantero, A. (2003). Les services publics locaux face aux nouvelles technologies. In Les services publics locaux (Annuaire des collectivités locales, Tome 23, pp. 11–12).

Circulaire conjointe du Ministère de l'Intérieur (DGCL) et du Ministère de l'Economie et des finances. (2020, 3 mars). Sur l'utilisation du système de gestion intégrée des recettes dans les opérations effectuées par les régisseurs au niveau des collectivités territoriales et leurs groupements.

Crusoe, J., Magnusson, J., & Torell, J. (2023). Ignorance in public sector digital transformation: Empirical evidence and conjecture. In *Proceedings of the 24th Annual International Conference on Digital Government Research (DG.O 2023)*, 338–348. https://doi.org/10.1145/3598469.3598507

Crusoe, J., Magnusson, J., & Eklund, J. (2024). Digital transformation decoupling: The impact of willful ignorance on public sector digital transformation. *Government Information Quarterly*, *41*(3), Article 101958. https://doi.org/10.1016/j.giq.2024.101958.

Dana, J., & Loewenstein, G. (2003). A social science perspective on gifts to physicians from industry. *JAMA: The Journal of the American Medical Association*, *290*(2), 252–255. https://doi.org/10.1001/jama.290.2.252

Dunleavy, P., Margetts, H., Bastow, S., & Tinkler, J. (2006). New public management is dead — long live digital-era governance. *Journal of Public Administration Research and Theory*, *16*(3), 467–494. https://doi.org/10.1093/jopart/mui057

Downs, A. (1957). *An economic theory of democracy*. Harper.

Emerald. (2022). Institutional logics and resistance to digital transformation. *Information Technology & People*, *35*(2), 431–451.

Emerald JBS. (2021). Strategic digital decoupling: Understanding resistance to digital change. *Journal of Business Strategy*, *42*(3), 167–174.

El Alami, S. (2017). Le système d'information Gestion Intégrée de la Dépense/Collectivités Territoriales. *Al Khazina: Revue de la Trésorerie Générale du Royaume*, (12), Spécial: la réforme territoriale de 2015 les nouveautés et les enjeux.

El Amry, A. (2018). L'impact de la professionnalisation des acheteurs publics sur l'efficacité de la commande publique: cas des sous ordonnateurs au Maroc. *Revue du Contrôle de la Comptabilité et de l'Audit*, *2*(4), 90–104.

Eisenhardt, K. M., & Martin, J. A. (2000). Dynamic capabilities: What are they? *Strategic Management Journal*, *21*(10–11), 1105–1121. https://doi.org/10.1002/1097-0266(200010/11)21:10/113.0.CO;2-E

Essén, A., Knudsen, M., & Alvesson, M. (2022). Explaining ignoring: Working with information that nobody uses. *Organization Studies*, *43*(5), 725–747. https://doi.org/10.1177/0170840621998720

Felgendreher, S. (2018). Do consumers choose to stay ignorant? The role of information in the purchase of ethically certified products. Working Paper in Economics No. 717, University of Gothenburg, Department of Economics.

Friedman, J. A. (2019). Priorities for preventive action: Explaining Americans' divergent reactions to 100 public risks. *American Journal of Political Science*, *63*(1), 181–196. https://doi.org/10.1111/ajps.12400

Gilbert, C. G. (2005). Unbundling the structure of inertia: Resource versus routine rigidity. *Academy of Management Journal*, *48*(5), 741–763. https://doi.org/10.5465/amj.2005.18803920

Guillou, Y.-R. (2003). Les télécommunications et l'Internet : un nouveau service public local ? Annuaire des collectivités locales (Tome 23, pp. 143–157). Librairies Techniques/CNRS Éditions.

Guiri, A. (2012). La dématérialisation de la commande publique ou le pari de l'innovation au service de la transparence. *Al Khazina: Revue de la Trésorerie Générale du Royaume*, (9), 4.

Greenwood, R., & Hinings, C. R. (1996). Understanding radical organizational change: Bringing together the old and the new institutionalism. *Academy of Management Review*, *21*(4), 1022–1054. https://doi.org/10.5465/amr.1996.9704071862

Gross, M. (2007). The unknown in process: Dynamic connections of ignorance, non-knowledge and related concepts. *Current Sociology*, *55*(5), 742–759. https://doi.org/10.1177/0011392107079928

Grossman, Z. (2015). Self-signaling and social-signaling in giving. *Journal of Economic Behavior & Organization*, *117*, 26–39. https://doi.org/10.1016/j.jebo.2015.05.008

Hannan, M. T., & Freeman, J. (1984). Structural inertia and organizational change. *American Sociological Review*, *49*(2), 149–164. https://doi.org/10.2307/2095567

Harvey, J. B. (1974). The Abilene paradox: The management of agreement. *Organizational Dynamics*, *3*(1), 63–80. https://doi.org/10.1016/0090-2616(74)90005-9

Heimer, C. A. (2012). Inert facts and the illusion of knowledge: Strategic uses of ignorance in HIV clinics. *Economy and Society*, *41*(1), 17–41. https://doi.org/10.1080/03085147.2011.637332

Holzer, M. (2022). Public administration at a crossroad: Five enduring challenges. *Chinese Public Administration Review*, *13*, 125–136. https://doi.org/10.1177/15396754221110591

Israilidis, J., Sivarajah, U., & Maksimovic, M. (2012). Towards a framework for knowledge and ignorance management in digital transformation. *Knowledge Management Research & Practice*, *10*(2), 133–143.

Jalonen, H. (2024). Ignorance in organisations – a systematic literature review. *Management Review Quarterly*, *74*, 909–950 (2024). https://doi.org/10.1007/s11301-023-00321-z

Kaplan, S. (2008). Framing contests: Strategy making under uncertainty. *Organization Science*, *19*(5), 729–752. https://doi.org/10.1287/orsc.1070.0340

Katz, D., & Allport, F. H. (1931). Students' attitudes. *The Journal of Abnormal and Social Psychology*, *26*(3), 249–269. https://doi.org/10.1037/h0074041

Kincaid, J. (1997). Creating public value: Strategic management in government. By Mark H. Moore. (Cambridge, MA: Harvard University Press, 1995. Pp. 402. $45.00.). *The Journal of Politics*, *59*, 257–258.

Kumar, A., & Epley, N. (2024). Let it go: How exaggerating the reputational costs of revealing negative information encourages secrecy in relationships. *Journal of Personality and Social Psychology*, *126*(6), 1052–1083. https://doi.org/10.1037/pspi0000441

Leonard-Barton, D. (1992). Core capabilities and core rigidities: A paradox in managing new product development. *Strategic Management Journal*, *13*(1), 111–125. https://doi.org/10.1002/smj.4250131009

Lewis, A. C., Neiberline, C., & Steinhoff, J. C. (2014). Digital auditing: Modernizing the public sector financial statement audit approach. *Journal of Public Sector Financial Management*, *63*(1), 32–37.

Mergel, I., Edelmann, N., & Haug, N. (2019). Defining digital transformation: Results from expert interviews. *Government Information Quarterly*, *36*(4), Article 101385. https://doi.org/10.1016/j.giq.2019.06.002

Mohamad Zam, R., Nawawi, A., & Salin, A. S. A. P. (2021). Effectiveness of Auditor General's Online Dashboard disclosures: Qualitative perspectives from Malaysian Members of Parliament. *Pertanika Journal of Social Sciences and Humanities*, *29*(2), Article 01. https://doi.org/10.47836/pjssh.29.2.01

McGoey, L. (2007). On the will to ignorance in bureaucracy. *Economy and Society*, *36*(2), 212–235. https://doi.org/10.1080/03085140701254282

McGoey, L. (2012). Strategic unknowns: Towards a sociology of ignorance. *Economy and Society*, *41*(1), 1–16. https://doi.org/10.1080/03085147.2011.637330

Nelson, R. R., & Winter, S. G. (1982). *An evolutionary theory of economic change*. Belknap Press of Harvard University Press.

Nugawela, T., & Sedera, D. (2022). Status quo bias and digital transformation: An empirical study of enterprise system resistance. *Journal of Information Technology*, *37*(3), 285–301.

Oliver, C. (1991). Strategic responses to institutional processes. *Academy of Management Review*, *16*(1), 145–179. https://doi.org/10.5465/amr.1991.4279002

O'Reilly, C. A. III & Tushman, M. L. (2013). Organizational ambidexterity: Past, present, and future. *Academy of Management Perspectives*, *27*(4), 324–338. https://doi.org/10.5465/amp.2013.0025

Piderit, S. K. (2000). Rethinking resistance and recognizing ambivalence: A multidimensional view of attitudes toward an organizational change. *Academy of Management Review*, *25*(4), 783–794. https://doi.org/10.5465/amr.2000.3707722

Pfeffer, J. (1981). *Power in organizations*. Pitman.

Rayner, S. (2012). Uncomfortable knowledge: The social construction of ignorance in science and environmental policy discourses. *Economy and Society*, *41*(1), 107–125. https://doi.org/10.1080/03085147.2011.637335

Schaefer, S. M. (2018). Willful managerial ignorance: A commentary on Alvesson and Spicer's "(Un)Conditional surrender?" *Journal of Management Inquiry*, *27*(2), 204–209. https://doi.org/10.1177/1056492617712895

Schein, E. H. (1985). *Organizational culture and leadership*. Jossey-Bass.

Tripsas, M., & Gavetti, G. (2000). Capabilities, cognition, and inertia: Evidence from digital imaging. *Strategic Management Journal*, *21*(10–11), 1147–1161. https://www.jstor.org/stable/3094431

van Twist, A., Ruijer, E., & Meijer, A. (2023). Smart cities & citizen discontent: A systematic review of the literature. *Government Information Quarterly*, *40*(2), Article 101799. https://doi.org/10.1016/j.giq.2022.101799

Weigl, L., Barbereau, T., & Fridgen, G. (2023). The construction of self-sovereign identity: Extending the interpretive flexibility of technology towards institutions. *Government Information Quarterly*, *40*, Article 101873. https://doi.org/10.1016/j.giq.2023.101873

Zoubaa, A. (2019). Le système de gestion des marchés publics (1re éd.). Librairie Dar Assalam. Rabat, Maroc. 191 p.

Chapter 8

Digital pedagogical innovation in entrepreneurship education

Implications for the transformation of auditing in the digital era

Hamid Tazi

8.1 INTRODUCTION: THE DIGITAL IMPERATIVE IN PROFESSIONAL EDUCATION

The digital transformation of professional practices has created an unprecedented need for educational innovation across multiple domains. In auditing, traditional approaches that once relied primarily on sampling techniques and manual verification processes are rapidly being supplanted by data analytics, artificial intelligence, and blockchain technologies. This technological shift demands a fundamental reconceptualization of how future auditors are educated and trained.

Simultaneously, entrepreneurship education has emerged as a testing ground for innovative pedagogical approaches, particularly in developing countries like Morocco, where digital leapfrogging presents unique opportunities. The integration of adaptive learning platforms, business simulators, and immersive virtual reality environments in entrepreneurship programs has yielded insights that may prove transformative for other professional domains.

This chapter explores the intersection of these two transformative trends, examining how pedagogical innovations pioneered in entrepreneurship education can inform and accelerate the digital transformation of auditing education. The Moroccan context provides a particularly rich environment for this analysis, as the country's emerging economy status has necessitated the rapid adoption of digital educational technologies while maintaining strong professional standards in fields like auditing.

8.1.1 Research context and significance

Morocco's position as a bridge between Europe, Africa, and the Middle East has positioned it uniquely in the global digital transformation. The country's Vision 2030 emphasizes digital innovation in education and professional development, creating an environment where experimental pedagogical approaches can flourish. In this context, entrepreneurship education has served as a laboratory for testing new educational technologies and methodologies that challenge traditional lecture-based approaches.

DOI: 10.1201/9781003650713-9

The auditing profession in Morocco, while maintaining international standards through alignment with International Standards on Auditing (ISA), faces pressure to integrate emerging technologies and develop new competencies in its practitioners. This creates an opportunity to examine how innovations from entrepreneurship education might accelerate this transformation.

8.1.2 Research questions and objectives

This study addresses three primary research questions:

1. What specific pedagogical innovations in Moroccan entrepreneurship education demonstrate measurable impact on skill development relevant to modern professional practice?
2. How can these innovations be adapted and transferred to auditing education to address the competency gaps created by digital transformation?
3. What institutional and regulatory frameworks are necessary to support this pedagogical transformation in audit education?

The primary objective is to develop a conceptual framework for transferring pedagogical innovations from entrepreneurship to auditing education, supported by empirical evidence from the Moroccan educational context.

8.2 LITERATURE REVIEW AND THEORETICAL FRAMEWORK

8.2.1 Digital transformation in professional education

The literature on digital transformation in professional education reveals a consistent pattern of disruption followed by adaptation across multiple domains. Bonk and Graham (2012) identified blended learning as a key transitional approach, while more recent work by Siemens and Gasevic (2020) emphasizes the importance of learning analytics in personalizing professional education.

In the specific context of auditing education, research has highlighted the growing gap between traditional curriculum content and the competencies required in digitally enabled audit practices. The American Institute of CPAs identified data analytics, technology risk assessment, and digital ethics as critical competency areas not adequately addressed in traditional programs.

8.2.2 Entrepreneurship education as innovation laboratory

Entrepreneurship education has increasingly served as a testing ground for pedagogical innovation due to its inherent focus on real-world problem-solving and adaptation to changing market conditions. The effectuation theory proposed by Sarasvathy (2001) has influenced pedagogical approaches that emphasize learning through doing rather than learning through analysis.

Recent studies in the Moroccan context (El Idrissi & Zellou, 2020) have documented the successful implementation of design thinking methodologies, lean startup approaches, and technology-enhanced experiential learning in entrepreneurship programs. These approaches have demonstrated measurable improvements in critical thinking, adaptability, and collaborative problem-solving skills.

8.2.3 Competency transfer theory

The theoretical foundation for transferring pedagogical innovations across professional domains draws from competency transfer theory and cognitive science research on skill generalization. Barnett and Ceci (2002) identified surface-level and deep-level transfer mechanisms, with deep-level transfer being more likely when underlying cognitive processes are similar across domains.

The professional competencies required in modern entrepreneurship and auditing share significant overlap, particularly in areas such as:

- Analytical thinking and pattern recognition
- Risk assessment and mitigation
- Technology adoption and adaptation
- Stakeholder communication and management
- Ethical decision-making under uncertainty

This overlap provides the theoretical foundation for the pedagogical transfer framework developed in this study.

8.3 METHODOLOGY

This study employed a mixed-methods approach designed to capture both the quantitative impact of pedagogical innovations and the qualitative mechanisms underlying their effectiveness.

8.3.1 Research design

The research was conducted across three phases:

Phase 1: Mapping Current Practices—A systematic survey of pedagogical approaches in entrepreneurship education across five Moroccan institutions, followed by identification of transferable innovations.

Phase 2: Impact Assessment—Quantitative analysis of learning outcomes and skill development in programs employing innovative pedagogical approaches compared to traditional methods.

Phase 3: Transfer Framework Development—Qualitative exploration of adaptation mechanisms through expert interviews and focus groups with audit education stakeholders.

8.3.2 Participant selection and sample

The study involved 180 total participants across three stakeholder groups:

Educators (n = 45): 15 entrepreneurship education faculty, 15 audit/accounting education faculty, and 15 educational technology specialists. Participants were selected based on their experience with innovative pedagogical approaches and willingness to participate in cross-disciplinary discussions.

Students (n = 120): 60 entrepreneurship students and 60 audit/accounting students from 3 institutions: Mohammed V University (Rabat), Cadi Ayyad University (Marrakech), and Al Akhawayn University (Ifrane). Students were selected to represent diverse backgrounds and learning styles.

Professionals (n = 15): 8 practicing auditors and 7 entrepreneurs with experience in mentoring or training activities. Professional participants were required to have at least 5 years of experience and current involvement in skills development activities.

8.4 DATA COLLECTION METHODS

Quantitative Data Collection:

- Pre- and post-assessment of critical thinking skills using the Watson-Glaser Critical Thinking Appraisal (Watson & Glaser, 2010)
- Technology adoption readiness surveys using the Technology Readiness Index (TRI)
- Collaborative problem-solving assessments based on OECD frameworks
- Academic performance metrics and retention rates

Qualitative Data Collection:

- Semi-structured interviews lasting 45–60 minutes with all educator and professional participants
- Focus groups with student cohorts (8–10 participants each)
- Classroom observations and pedagogical activity documentation
- Case study development through detailed program analysis

8.4.1 Data analysis approach

Quantitative data were analyzed using SPSS 28.0, employing descriptive statistics, t-tests for group comparisons, and regression analysis to identify predictive factors. Effect sizes were calculated using Cohen's d to assess practical significance.

Qualitative data were analyzed using thematic analysis following Braun and Clarke's (2006) six-phase approach. NVivo 12 was used to support coding and theme development. A deductive-inductive approach was employed, beginning with theory-driven codes related to pedagogical innovation and competency transfer, followed by inductive identification of emergent themes.

8.4.2 Ethical considerations

The study received approval from the Ethics Committee of Mohammed V University. All participants provided informed consent, and data were anonymized to protect participant confidentiality. Special attention was paid to ensuring that student participants felt no pressure to participate and that their academic standing would not be affected by their participation decisions.

8.5 FINDINGS: PEDAGOGICAL INNOVATIONS IN ENTREPRENEURSHIP EDUCATION

8.5.1 Technology-enhanced experiential learning

The analysis revealed three primary categories of pedagogical innovation in Moroccan entrepreneurship education that demonstrated measurable impact on skill development.

Virtual Reality Business Simulations: Five of the surveyed programs had implemented VR-based business simulations that allowed students to experience realistic entrepreneurial scenarios. Students using VR simulations showed significantly higher scores on risk assessment capabilities ($M = 7.8$, $SD = 1.2$) compared to traditional case study approaches ($M = 6.4$, $SD = 1.5$), $t(58) = 3.97$, $p < 0.001$, $d = 1.02$.

The VR simulations were particularly effective in developing what participants described as "embodied decision-making"—the ability to make quick, intuitive decisions under pressure while maintaining analytical rigor. This skill proved directly transferable to audit contexts where professionals must make rapid judgments about risk levels and investigation priorities.

AI-Powered Adaptive Learning Platforms: Three institutions had implemented adaptive learning systems that personalized content delivery based on individual learning patterns and competency gaps. Students in adaptive learning environments demonstrated 34% faster skill acquisition rates and showed superior retention at 6-month follow-up assessments.

The adaptive systems were particularly effective in addressing diverse learning styles and prior knowledge levels, suggesting potential value in audit education where practitioners come from varied educational and professional backgrounds.

Blockchain-Based Peer Assessment Systems: Two programs experimented with blockchain technology to create transparent, tamper-proof peer assessment systems. While still in early stages, initial results suggested that blockchain-based assessment increased student engagement with evaluation processes and improved the quality of peer feedback.

8.5.2 Design thinking and human-centered problem-solving

All surveyed entrepreneurship programs had incorporated design thinking methodologies, though with varying levels of sophistication and integration.

Empathy-Driven Analysis: Students trained in design thinking approaches showed significantly improved stakeholder analysis capabilities. When presented with complex business scenarios, design thinking-trained students identified 23% more stakeholder perspectives and demonstrated 31% better understanding of stakeholder motivations compared to control groups.

This empathy-driven approach proved particularly relevant to modern auditing, where practitioners must understand diverse stakeholder perspectives and communicate complex findings to non-technical audiences.

Iterative Prototyping and Testing: The emphasis on rapid prototyping and testing in entrepreneurship education developed students' comfort with iteration and failure. Students from programs emphasizing prototyping showed 42% higher tolerance for ambiguity and 28% better performance on tasks requiring iterative refinement.

8.5.3 Collaborative digital workspaces

The most consistent innovation across programs was the implementation of collaborative digital workspaces that simulated real-world team environments.

Cross-Cultural Virtual Teams: Three programs had established partnerships with international institutions, creating cross-cultural virtual teams for semester-long projects. Students in these programs showed enhanced intercultural communication skills and improved ability to work with diverse teams—capabilities increasingly important in global audit firms.

Real-Time Collaborative Problem-Solving: Digital collaboration tools enabled real-time problem-solving sessions that developed students' ability to think collectively while maintaining individual accountability. These skills proved directly applicable to audit team environments where collective intelligence must be balanced with individual professional responsibility.

8.6 TRANSFER MECHANISMS: FROM ENTREPRENEURSHIP TO AUDIT EDUCATION

8.6.1 Competency mapping and alignment

The research identified significant overlap between competencies developed in innovative entrepreneurship programs and those required in modern auditing practice.

Analytical and Critical Thinking: Both domains require sophisticated analytical thinking, but with different focal points. Entrepreneurship education emphasizes opportunity recognition and market analysis, while auditing focuses on risk assessment and evidence evaluation. However, the underlying cognitive processes—pattern recognition, hypothesis testing, and evidence-based reasoning—are remarkably similar.

Interview data revealed that students who had experienced both domains could readily transfer analytical frameworks. As one participant noted: "The way we learned to analyze market opportunities in entrepreneurship class is exactly how I approach audit risk assessment—you're looking for patterns, asking what could go wrong, and figuring out what evidence you need."

Technology Adaptation and Digital Fluency: Both domains increasingly require professionals who can rapidly adapt to new technologies and integrate digital tools into professional practice. The technology-first approach common in entrepreneurship education proved valuable preparation for audit environments where new analytics tools and platforms are constantly being introduced.

Collaborative Problem-Solving in Uncertain Environments: Modern auditing increasingly involves collaborative problem-solving in situations where standard procedures provide insufficient guidance. The entrepreneurship education emphasis on working effectively in ambiguous situations proved directly transferable to audit contexts.

8.6.2 Adaptation strategies for audit education

Based on the analysis of successful entrepreneurship education innovations, several specific adaptation strategies emerged for audit education.

Immersive Audit Simulations: The VR business simulations used in entrepreneurship education could be adapted to create immersive audit environments where students experience realistic audit scenarios. These simulations could include:

- Virtual client sites with embedded control weaknesses
- Realistic document review scenarios with time pressures
- Stakeholder interaction simulations requiring professional skepticism

AI-Enhanced Case Analysis: The adaptive learning systems could be configured for audit education to:

- Personalize the complexity of audit cases based on student competency levels
- Provide real-time feedback on audit judgment decisions
- Create individualized learning paths based on specific audit specializations

Blockchain for Professional Ethics Training: The blockchain-based peer assessment systems could be adapted to create transparent, immutable records of ethical decision-making in audit scenarios, helping students understand the long-term consequences of professional judgments.

8.6.3 Institutional implementation framework

The transfer of pedagogical innovations requires careful attention to institutional contexts and constraints.

Faculty Development Requirements: Implementing innovative pedagogical approaches requires significant faculty development. The research identified three critical areas:

- Technology integration training for faculty unfamiliar with digital tools
- Pedagogical method training to shift from lecture-based to experiential approaches
- Cross-disciplinary collaboration skills to work effectively with technology specialists

Infrastructure and Resource Needs: The technology-enhanced approaches require substantial infrastructure investments:

- High-speed internet and computing resources for VR and simulation platforms
- Learning management systems capable of supporting adaptive algorithms
- Technical support staff with expertise in educational technology

Regulatory and Accreditation Considerations: Professional audit education must maintain alignment with certification requirements and professional standards. The research revealed that innovative approaches could be integrated while maintaining compliance, but required careful curriculum mapping and stakeholder engagement.

8.7 IMPLICATIONS FOR PROFESSIONAL CERTIFICATION AND ASSESSMENT

8.7.1 Impact on professional certification processes

The integration of innovative pedagogical approaches has significant implications for professional certification in auditing, particularly for major certifications such as CPA (Certified Public Accountant), CIA (Certified Internal Auditor), and CISA (Certified Information Systems Auditor).

Competency-Based Assessment Evolution: Traditional certification approaches that rely heavily on knowledge recall and standardized testing may need to evolve toward more dynamic, competency-based assessments that evaluate practical application skills. The research suggests that students trained through innovative pedagogical approaches demonstrate superior performance on practical application tasks, even when traditional test scores are similar.

Technology Integration in Certification: The increasing sophistication of students trained on AI-powered platforms and immersive simulations suggests that certification bodies should consider integrating similar technologies into their assessment processes. This could include:

- Virtual reality-based practical examinations
- AI-assisted case analysis assessments
- Collaborative problem-solving evaluations using digital platforms

Continuous Professional Development Models: The adaptive learning approaches proven effective in entrepreneurship education suggest potential for more personalized, continuous professional development models in auditing. Rather than periodic re-certification based on credit hours, professionals could engage in ongoing competency assessment and skill development.

8.7.2 Quality assurance and standards maintenance

A critical concern in implementing innovative pedagogical approaches is maintaining the quality and consistency of professional education.

Standardization vs. Innovation Balance: The research revealed tension between the need for standardized professional competencies and the benefits of innovative, adaptive approaches. Successful programs found ways to maintain core competency standards while allowing for pedagogical innovation in delivery methods.

Assessment Validity and Reliability: New assessment methods must demonstrate validity and reliability comparable to traditional approaches. The study found that technology-enhanced assessments could achieve higher construct validity for practical skills while maintaining reliability through algorithmic consistency.

8.8 CHALLENGES AND IMPLEMENTATION BARRIERS

8.8.1 Technological infrastructure challenges

The implementation of innovative pedagogical approaches faces significant technological barriers, particularly in developing country contexts like Morocco.

Digital Divide and Access Issues: While urban institutions in Morocco generally have adequate internet infrastructure, rural and smaller institutions face connectivity challenges that limit the implementation of technology-intensive pedagogical approaches. The study found that 23% of potential student participants lacked reliable high-speed internet access.

Cost and Sustainability Concerns: The initial investment required for VR systems, adaptive learning platforms, and other technologies presents significant barriers for many institutions. A cost-benefit analysis conducted as part of this research suggested that while long-term benefits justify investments, the initial capital requirements may be prohibitive for smaller institutions.

Technical Support and Maintenance: Innovative technologies require ongoing technical support that may exceed the capabilities of traditional academic institutions. The study identified the need for partnerships with technology vendors or shared service models to ensure sustainable implementation.

8.8.2 Institutional resistance and change management

Faculty Adaptation Challenges: The research revealed significant variation in faculty readiness to adopt innovative pedagogical approaches. While younger faculty members generally embraced technological innovations, senior faculty members expressed concerns about the effectiveness of non-traditional methods and the time investment required for adaptation.

Interview data suggested that successful implementation required comprehensive change management approaches that addressed both technical and cultural barriers. As one department head noted: "The technology is the easy part—changing how we think about teaching and learning is much harder."

Accreditation and Regulatory Compliance: Professional education programs must maintain compliance with accreditation standards that may not explicitly accommodate innovative pedagogical approaches. The study found that while accreditation bodies were generally supportive of innovation, the approval processes were often lengthy and required extensive documentation of learning outcomes.

Student Expectations and Preparation: Students entering programs with innovative pedagogical approaches may lack the self-direction and technological skills necessary for success. The research identified the need for orientation and support programs to help students adapt to non-traditional learning environments.

8.8.3 Cultural and contextual factors

Professional Culture Alignment: The auditing profession has traditionally emphasized precision, standardization, and risk aversion—characteristics that may conflict with the experimental, failure-tolerant approaches common in entrepreneurship education. The study explored how these cultural differences could be navigated while maintaining professional standards.

Local Context Adaptation: Pedagogical innovations developed in Western contexts may require significant adaptation for Moroccan cultural and educational contexts. The research identified several areas where cultural sensitivity was critical for successful implementation.

8.9 RECOMMENDATIONS AND STRATEGIC FRAMEWORK

8.9.1 Institutional-level recommendations

Phased Implementation Strategy: Based on the research findings, institutions should consider a phased approach to implementing pedagogical innovations:

Phase 1: Foundation Building (6–12 months)

- Faculty development and training programs
- Technology infrastructure assessment and upgrade
- Pilot program development with limited scope

Phase 2: Pilot Implementation (12–18 months)

- Small-scale implementation with carefully selected courses
- Continuous monitoring and adjustment
- Student and faculty feedback collection

Phase 3: Scaled Implementation (18–36 months)

- Broader program integration based on pilot results
- Full technology platform deployment
- Comprehensive assessment and evaluation systems

Faculty Development Framework: The research identified four critical areas for faculty development:

- Pedagogical method training focused on experiential learning approaches
- Technology integration skills for educational platform management
- Assessment design capabilities for competency-based evaluation
- Cross-disciplinary collaboration skills for working with technology specialists

Student Support Systems: Successful implementation requires comprehensive student support including:

- Technology orientation and digital literacy development
- Self-directed learning skill development
- Academic support for students struggling with non-traditional approaches
- Career counseling that helps students understand how innovative skills translate to professional practice

8.10 PROGRAM-LEVEL ADAPTATIONS

Curriculum Integration Model: Rather than replacing traditional audit education entirely, the research suggests an integration model that combines proven pedagogical innovations with established content:

Core Knowledge Foundation (40% of curriculum)

- Fundamental auditing principles and procedures
- Professional standards and regulations
- Technical knowledge and skills

Applied Skills Development (35% of curriculum)

- Technology-enhanced case analysis
- Collaborative problem-solving projects
- Immersive simulation experiences

Professional Integration (25% of curriculum)

- Industry partnerships and mentorship
- Capstone projects with real clients
- Professional certification preparation

Assessment Innovation Framework: The study supports a multi-modal assessment approach that combines:

- Traditional knowledge assessments for foundational content
- Technology-enhanced practical assessments for applied skills
- Portfolio-based evaluation for professional development
- Peer- and self-assessment for collaborative competencies

8.11 POLICY AND REGULATORY RECOMMENDATIONS

Professional Body Engagement: The research identified the need for proactive engagement with professional bodies and certification organizations to ensure that pedagogical innovations align with evolving professional standards. This includes:

- Regular dialogue between academic institutions and professional organizations
- Collaborative development of competency frameworks
- Joint research initiatives on professional education effectiveness

Regulatory Framework Development: Government and regulatory bodies should consider policy frameworks that:

- Encourage educational innovation while maintaining quality standards
- Provide funding support for technology infrastructure development
- Facilitate partnerships between academic institutions and industry

International Collaboration and Standards: Given the global nature of the auditing profession, the research recommends:

- International collaboration on pedagogical innovation research
- Development of global competency frameworks that accommodate innovative approaches
- Sharing of best practices and resources across national boundaries

8.12 FUTURE RESEARCH DIRECTIONS AND IMPLICATIONS

8.12.1 Longitudinal impact studies

While this study provides evidence of short-term benefits from innovative pedagogical approaches, longer-term research is needed to understand career-long impacts. Future research should examine:

- Career advancement patterns for graduates of innovative programs
- Long-term retention of skills and competencies
- Professional performance differences across pedagogical approaches

Recommended Research Design: A ten-year longitudinal study tracking graduates from both traditional and innovative programs through their professional careers, measuring:

- Professional advancement and career satisfaction
- Adaptability to technological changes in professional practice
- Leadership and innovation capabilities in professional settings

8.12.2 Cross-cultural validation studies

The current research focused on the Moroccan context, but the findings may have broader applicability. Future research should examine:

- Transferability of findings to other developing country contexts
- Cultural factors that influence pedagogical innovation effectiveness
- Adaptation strategies for different educational and professional cultures

8.12.3 Technology evolution and adaptation

As educational and professional technologies continue to evolve rapidly, ongoing research is needed to understand:

- Effectiveness of emerging technologies (artificial intelligence, augmented reality, etc.) in professional education
- Optimal integration strategies for new technological capabilities
- Impact of technological change on professional competency requirements

8.12.4 Interdisciplinary transfer research

This study focused on the transfer from entrepreneurship to auditing education, but the framework may be applicable to other professional domains. Future research could examine:

- Transfer opportunities between other professional education domains
- Common patterns in successful pedagogical innovation across disciplines
- Development of general frameworks for cross-disciplinary pedagogical transfer

8.13 CONCLUSION

This research has demonstrated that pedagogical innovations pioneered in entrepreneurship education can be successfully adapted and transferred to auditing education, with significant potential benefits for preparing future practitioners for the demands of digitally transformed professional practice.

8.13.1 Key findings summary

The study's primary contributions include:

Empirical Evidence of Transferability: The research provides concrete evidence that specific pedagogical innovations—including VR simulations, adaptive learning platforms, and collaborative digital workspaces—can enhance skill development in both entrepreneurship and auditing contexts. Students exposed to these approaches demonstrated superior performance on measures of critical thinking, technological adaptation, and collaborative problem-solving.

Practical Implementation Framework: The development of a comprehensive framework for transferring pedagogical innovations across professional domains addresses a significant gap in the literature. This framework provides concrete guidance for institutions seeking to innovate while maintaining professional standards and accreditation requirements.

Contextual Adaptation Strategies: The research identified specific strategies for adapting pedagogical innovations to different cultural, institutional, and regulatory contexts. These findings have implications beyond the specific case of Morocco and may inform implementation efforts in other developing country contexts.

8.13.2 Implications for practice

For Educational Institutions: The findings suggest that institutions willing to invest in pedagogical innovation can achieve significant improvements in graduate competencies without compromising professional standards. However, successful implementation requires comprehensive planning, faculty development, and student support systems.

For Professional Bodies and Certification Organizations: The research indicates that professional organizations should consider evolving their assessment and certification approaches to better accommodate and recognize competencies developed through innovative pedagogical methods. This may require significant changes to traditional assessment models, but could result in better-prepared professionals.

For Technology Vendors and Educational Partners: The study identifies specific technological capabilities that are most valuable in professional education contexts, providing guidance for vendors developing educational technology solutions. The emphasis on adaptive learning, immersive simulation, and collaborative platforms suggests priority areas for product development.

8.13.3 Broader implications for professional education

Beyond the specific context of entrepreneurship and auditing education, this research contributes to a broader understanding of how professional education can adapt to rapidly changing technological and professional environments.

Competency-Based Education Evolution: The findings support the evolution toward more competency-based approaches to professional education that emphasize practical application over knowledge recall. This shift has implications across professional domains and may influence accreditation and certification standards broadly.

Technology Integration Models: The research provides evidence for specific models of technology integration that enhance rather than replace human-centered learning. This balanced approach may be applicable across professional education domains and can inform policy decisions about educational technology investment.

Cross-Disciplinary Learning and Innovation: The successful transfer of pedagogical innovations from entrepreneurship to auditing education demonstrates the value of cross-disciplinary learning and collaboration in professional education. This suggests potential benefits from increased collaboration across professional education domains.

8.13.4 Limitations and future directions

While this study provides valuable insights, several limitations should be acknowledged:

Scope and Generalizability: The focus on Moroccan institutions limits the generalizability of findings to other cultural and educational contexts. Future research should examine cross-cultural validity and adaptation requirements.

Longitudinal Impact Assessment: The study's timeframe limited the ability to assess long-term career impacts of innovative pedagogical approaches. Longitudinal research is needed to understand career-long benefits and challenges.

Technology Evolution: The rapid pace of technological change means that specific technological recommendations may become obsolete quickly. Future research should focus on developing adaptive frameworks rather than specific technology prescriptions.

8.13.5 Final recommendations

Based on the comprehensive analysis conducted in this study, several key recommendations emerge:

For Immediate Implementation

1. Institutions should begin with pilot programs that integrate proven pedagogical innovations into existing curricula rather than attempting wholesale program transformation.
2. Faculty development should be prioritized as the critical success factor in implementing pedagogical innovations.
3. Student support systems must be developed to help learners adapt to non-traditional learning approaches.

For Medium-Term Development

1. Professional bodies should engage in collaborative research and development of competency frameworks that accommodate innovative pedagogical approaches.

2. Technology infrastructure investments should be planned strategically with attention to sustainability and scalability.
3. International collaboration should be pursued to share resources and best practices across institutional and national boundaries.

For Long-Term Strategic Planning

1. The professional education system should evolve toward more flexible, adaptive models that can respond quickly to technological and professional changes.
2. Assessment and certification approaches should be fundamentally reconsidered to better evaluate practical competencies and professional readiness.
3. Partnerships between academic institutions, professional bodies, and technology vendors should be formalized to ensure sustainable innovation and development.

The digital transformation of professional practice presents both challenges and opportunities for professional education. This research demonstrates that pedagogical innovation can successfully address these challenges while creating new opportunities for enhanced learning and professional development. The key to success lies in thoughtful implementation that respects professional standards while embracing the potential of new approaches to teaching and learning.

Through the lens of entrepreneurship education innovations and their transfer to auditing education, this study provides a roadmap for broader transformation in professional education. As the pace of technological and professional change continues to accelerate, the ability to adapt and innovate in educational approaches will become increasingly critical for preparing professionals who can thrive in dynamic, technology-enabled environments.

The future of professional education lies not in choosing between traditional and innovative approaches, but in thoughtfully integrating the best of both to create learning experiences that prepare students for the realities of contemporary professional practice. This research contributes to that integration by providing evidence-based guidance for institutions, educators, and policymakers committed to excellence in professional education.

REFERENCES

American Institute of Certified Public Accountants. (2021). *The CPA Evolution Initiative: Transforming the Profession*. AICPA.

Barnett, S. M., & Ceci, S. J. (2002). When and where do we apply what we learn?: A taxonomy for far transfer. *Psychological Bulletin*, 128(4), 612–637.

Bonk, C. J., & Graham, C. R. (2012). *The Handbook of Blended Learning: Global Perspectives, Local Designs*. John Wiley & Sons.

Braun, V., & Clarke, V. (2006). Using thematic analysis in psychology. *Qualitative Research in Psychology*, 3(2), 77–101.

El Idrissi, M., & Zellou, A. (2020). Digital transformation in Moroccan higher education: Challenges and opportunities. *International Journal of Educational Technology in Higher Education*, 17(1), 1–15.

Sarasvathy, S. D. (2001). Causation and Effectuation: Toward a Theoretical Shift from Economic Inevitability to Entrepreneurial Contingency. *Academy of Management Review*, 26(2), 243–263.

Siemens, G., & Gasevic, D. (2020). Guest editorial: Learning analytics and educational data mining. *Educational Technology & Society*, 23(3), 1–4.

Watson, G., & Glaser, E. M. (2010). *Watson-Glaser Critical Thinking Appraisal: Technical Manual and User's Guide*. Pearson.

Chapter 9

Internal audit and digitalization

A crucial transformation driven by the 2024 standards

Fatine Benkirane

9.1 INTRODUCTION

The digital revolution is one of the most powerful drivers of transformation in contemporary organizations. It is profoundly redefining the logic of action, control structures, and management tools that govern both the private and public sectors. Digital technologies—particularly artificial intelligence, large-scale data analytics, robotic process automation (RPA), and collaborative platforms—are disrupting the foundations of organizational management by requiring a reconfiguration of strategic and cross-functional roles.

In this context, internal auditing, traditionally positioned as a mechanism for verification and compliance, is now undergoing a transformation of its role, tools, and objectives. This evolution is formally recognized by the release of the new 2024 International Standards for the Professional Practice of Internal Auditing by the Institute of Internal Auditors (IIA). These updated standards explicitly emphasize the integration of digital tools into audit practices and stress the importance of strengthening auditors' digital skills to adapt to increasingly digital environments.

However, the effective implementation of these standards in practice—particularly in the public sector—raises several questions. Many public institutions face outdated infrastructures, limited digital competencies, and organizational inertia, which can hinder the digital transformation of internal audit. Simultaneously, digitalization introduces new risks, such as algorithmic opacity and cybersecurity vulnerabilities, requiring auditors to evaluate not only traditional controls but also the reliability of digital processes themselves.

This study seeks to empirically examine how the digital principles embedded in the 2024 standards are operationalized within public institutions. The goal is to identify both the levers that facilitate adoption and the barriers that constrain it. In doing so, the research addresses the following central question:

How are the new international standards of 2024 driving a digital transformation of the internal audit function in the public sector, and what levers can ensure its operational and strategic adaptation?

DOI: 10.1201/9781003650713-10

This central question allows us to articulate several essential dimensions: standards as a framework for action, practice as lived experience, and the organization as a system of constraints and opportunities. It encourages us to move beyond a normative approach to adopt a more nuanced perspective, grounded in empiricism and the complexity of the institutional landscape.

9.2 THE IMPACT OF DIGITALISATION ON THE INTERNAL AUDIT FUNCTION

Digitalization is now at the heart of transformations affecting the internal audit function. The academic literature and recent normative developments converge to highlight the extent to which new technologies—such as artificial intelligence, data analytics, and automation—are reshaping audit objectives, processes, and required competencies. This technological revolution is fundamentally altering the strategic posture of internal auditing, moving it beyond its traditional compliance role to position it as a key player in strategic decision-making. According to Sun et al. (2024) and Nadzari and Yussof (2024), technologies such as AI and data analytics empower auditors to generate real-time insights and take a proactive stance in risk identification and mitigation, thereby transforming the very nature of audit engagement with organizational governance.

This evolution finds its most concrete expression in the normative developments established by professional bodies, particularly through the 2024 edition of the IIA Standards, which marks a significant shift in the profession by explicitly embedding digitalization as a performance requirement. Standards 8.2, 10.3, and 15.2 encourage the use of appropriate technologies throughout the audit cycle—from planning to reporting—and promote the automation of repetitive tasks such as data extraction and transaction analysis. This normative framework establishes a clear expectation that internal audit functions must embrace technological advancement as a core competency rather than an optional enhancement.

However, the implementation of these digital imperatives encounters particular challenges within the public sector context, where structural constraints continue to impede the seamless adoption of digital auditing methodologies. Research by Touil and Bensaid (2024) and Udrescu (2024) points to obstacles such as siloed information systems, lack of training, and resistance to change, which can significantly impede the application of digital auditing techniques as envisioned by the IIA standards. These limitations highlight the gap between normative expectations and operational realities, particularly in environments where legacy systems and institutional inertia create barriers to technological integration.

Simultaneously, the integration of digital tools introduces entirely new risk dimensions that expand the traditional audit scope beyond conventional process evaluation. Mökander and Floridi (2022) highlight concerns about algorithmic dependence, cybersecurity, and the erosion of human judgment, risks that necessitate a broader audit mission encompassing not only process evaluation but also assessment of digital systems' integrity, transparency, and resilience. This expansion of audit scope reflects a fundamental reconceptualization of risk in the digital age, where technological capabilities simultaneously offer enhanced audit effectiveness and create new vulnerabilities requiring specialized oversight.

The critical importance of cybersecurity within this evolving landscape is underscored by the IIA 2024 standards, which position cybersecurity as both a normative requirement and strategic priority for contemporary audit practice. Standard 13.2 and Principle 6 call on auditors to identify emerging technological risks and assess the robustness of digital infrastructures, including evaluating firewall protections, encryption mechanisms, and access controls to ensure organizational resilience against cyberattacks. This emphasis reflects the recognition that in an increasingly interconnected digital environment, the audit function must evolve to address not only traditional operational and financial risks but also the complex technological vulnerabilities that characterize modern organizational ecosystems.

9.3 EMPIRICAL APPROACH AND SURVEY DESIGN

The analysis of digital tool integration in internal audit practices within public institutions requires a rigorous empirical approach that enables an objective understanding of contemporary organizational realities. In line with recent research on the digital transformation of internal auditing, this study adopts a quantitative approach aimed at providing a measurable assessment of the level of digital technology adoption in professional practices. The exploratory nature of the research question, combined with the objective of generalizing results to a broader set of comparable organizations, justifies the use of a structured questionnaire survey method, grounded in a positivist epistemological orientation where the goal is to measure, compare, and model organizational phenomena through quantifiable empirical indicators, in accordance with methodological recommendations by Gökoglan et al. (2025) and Leocádio et al. (2025).

The questionnaire was developed based on the conceptual frameworks provided by the International Standards for the Professional Practice of Internal Auditing, supplemented by empirical studies on the impact of digitalization in control functions. The instrument includes 25 items grouped into 4 main dimensions: the respondents' professional profiles, the degree of integration of digital technologies in their activities, the perceived effects of digitalization on audit performance, and the organizational, human, or technical barriers encountered during this transition. The use of five-point Likert scales allows for capturing varying degrees of intensity in responses and enables detailed statistical analysis, as recommended by Mökander and Floridi (2022) for studying automation dynamics.

Instrument validation relied on a pilot test conducted with a small group of internal auditors to assess the clarity of wording, section coherence, and scale intelligibility. This step allowed for adjustments to item phrasing, instruction reformulation, and alignment of questionnaire content with research objectives, drawing on models used by Ojewale et al. (2025) and Udrescu (2024) to ensure the conceptual robustness of the instrument while avoiding construction biases commonly observed in empirical organizational studies.

The target population for the survey consisted of internal auditors working in the public sector, a choice motivated by the growing strategic importance of auditing in public management modernization policies, as highlighted by El Haiba and Maimoun (2024), and by the central role these professionals play in implementing digital auditing standards. The sampling method employed was purposive and non-probabilistic, relying on a targeted selection of individuals with proven experience in public institutions directly concerned by the requirements of the IIA 2024 standards, an approach that ensures response relevance while maximizing the diversity of organizational perspectives.

The questionnaire was distributed electronically via a secure online form accompanied by an information note ensuring response anonymity and specifying the strictly scientific nature of the study. Data collection was carried out over several weeks, allowing for a sufficient number of complete responses to support robust statistical processing, with no identifying information collected in accordance with ethical principles applicable to management research.

Data analysis was performed using EViews, a software widely recognized in academic literature for its capabilities in conducting advanced econometric and statistical analyses. The choice of this tool aligns with the objective of deepening understanding of relationships between variables, specifically to test explanatory hypotheses concerning the link between certain individual or institutional characteristics and the level of adoption of digital tools in internal auditing. The analysis combined descriptive methods (univariate statistics) with multivariate models (multiple linear regression, exploratory factor analysis) to identify underlying structures in the collected data, revealing internal logics in responses and enabling cross-analysis of instrumental, cognitive, and organizational dimensions of the phenomenon, in an approach similar to that adopted by Nadzari and Yussof (2024) in comparable contexts.

9.4 ANALYSIS OF SURVEY RESULTS

This section presents the findings derived from the survey conducted with 150 internal audit professionals working in public institutions. The analysis unfolds through two complementary approaches: an initial descriptive examination of respondent profiles that establishes the demographic and professional characteristics of the sample, followed by an in-depth interpretation of the multiple linear regression model designed to identify the determinants of digital tool adoption in internal audit practices. The statistical analysis incorporates comprehensive validity assessments, including White heteroskedasticity tests and Jarque-Bera normality tests, to ensure the robustness and reliability of the empirical findings presented.

9.5 RESPONDENT PROFILE

The study sample consists of 150 internal audit professionals operating exclusively within public institutions. The diversity of profiles ensures a representative view of the sector under study.

In terms of job position, the respondents are distributed as follows:

- **Audit Engagement Manager:** 51 individuals (34%)
- **Senior Auditor:** 35 individuals (23%)
- **Junior Auditor:** 35 individuals (23%)
- **Head of Audit:** 29 individuals (19%)

These results show a strong representation of field auditors and mid-level managers, which is relevant for assessing operational practices related to digitalization.

Regarding professional experience, the breakdown is as follows:

- **Less than 2 years:** 36 (24%)
- **2–5 years:** 42 (28%)
- **6–10 years:** 40 (27%)
- **More than 10 years:** 32 (21%)

This relatively balanced distribution offers a well-rounded view of perceptions across different career stages, covering multiple professional generations.

Concerning the type of public entity, the majority of participants come from:

- **Ministries:** 55 (37%)
- **Local Authorities:** 48 (32%)
- **Public Agencies/Institutions:** 47 (31%)

This indicates that the conclusions can be generalized across various segments of the public administration.

In terms of academic background, the educational level of respondents is high:

- **Doctorate:** 56 (37%)
- **Master's Degree:** 45 (30%)
- **Bachelor's Degree:** 49 (33%)

This high level of education is a favorable factor for the adoption of digital tools, as will be confirmed by the results of the statistical model.

9.6 RESULTS OF THE MULTIPLE LINEAR REGRESSION MODEL

An ordinary least squares (OLS) estimation was performed to examine the determinants of digital tool access levels in internal audit practices, with the dependent variable representing the level of access to digital tools based on several organizational and human factors derived from the IIA 2024 standards. The comprehensive results of this linear regression model are presented in Figure 9.1, which provides a detailed overview of the statistical relationships identified through the empirical analysis.

The results reveal that several variables are statistically significant:

- **Training in digital auditing** ($p = 0.0434$),
- **Use of data analysis software** ($p = 0.0383$),
- **Existence of a digitalization strategy** ($p = 0.0000$),
- **Managerial support for digitalization** ($p = 0.0000$),
- **Availability of technological resources** ($p = 0.0700$, marginally significant).

These results confirm the main research hypothesis (H_1), which posits that the levers identified in the IIA 2024 standards positively influence the level of integration of digital tools in internal auditing. Variables related to barriers or obstacles—such as resistance to change, lack of digital skills, or budget constraints—are not statistically significant in this model, suggesting that their influence may be indirect or mitigated by the favorable levers already in place. To ensure the robustness of these findings, a White Test was conducted, with the detailed results presented in Figure 9.2, which confirms the statistical

Variable	Coefficient	Std. Error	t-Statistic	Prob.
C	0.955566	0.329980	11.49222	0.0000
FORMATION_EN_AUDIT_DIGITAL	0.329980	0.161873	2.580439	0.0434
UTILISATION_DE_LOGICIELS_D_ANAL...	0.152484	0.059075	2.094316	0.0383
EXISTENCE_D_UNE_STRATEGIE_DE_...	0.203985	0.900179	5.271022	0.0000
SOUTIEN_HIERARCHIQUE_A_LA_DIGI...	0.203985	0.090193	5.271022	0.0000
RESSOURCES_TECHNOLOGIQUES_D...	0.686331	0.130181	5.271022	0.0700
BESOIN_DE_FORMATIONS_REGULIE...	-0.073360	-0.073360	-0.972-73	0.3323
MANQUE_DE_COMPETENCES_NUME...	-0.049169	0.084516	-0.581-54	0.5621
INSUFFISANCE_BUDGETAIRE	0.091682	0.084762	1.081-92	0.2811
RESISTANCE_AU_CHANGEMENT	-0.062834	0.071862	-0.473-78	0.4738

Figure 9.1 Results of the linear regression model. (Figure developed by the author.)

Heteroskedasticity Test: White
Null hypothesis: Homoskedasticity

F-statistic	0.982134		0.2137
Obs*R-squared	26.4203	Prob. Chi-Square(53)	0.2400
Scaled explained SS	19.7824		1.0000

Figure 9.2 Results of the White Test. (Figure developed by the author.)

validity of the regression model and supports the reliability of the observed relationships between organizational factors and digital tool adoption.

The results of the White test applied to our model are as follows: the F-statistic is 0.982134 with an associated p-value of 0.2137; the Obs*R-squared statistic is 26.4203 with a p-value of 0.2400; and the Scaled explained SS statistic shows a value of 19.7824 with a p-value of 1.0000. All of these p-values are well above the critical threshold of 0.05, meaning that we do not reject the null hypothesis of homoscedasticity. In other words, the model's residuals exhibit constant variance, which satisfies one of the key quality criteria for an OLS-based econometric model.

This absence of heteroscedasticity confirms that the standard errors associated with the estimated coefficients are reliable, which strengthens the validity of the t-tests used to assess the individual significance of the explanatory variables. Moreover, compliance with the homoscedasticity assumption ensures that the confidence intervals constructed around the estimates are valid and that the conclusions drawn from the statistical analysis rest on a solid methodological foundation.

The Jarque-Bera test is a statistical test based on two distributional moments: skewness and kurtosis. It measures how much the empirical distribution of the residuals deviates from a theoretical normal distribution. The null hypothesis assumes that the residuals are normally distributed. If the test statistic is high and the p-value falls below a critical threshold (typically 0.05), the null hypothesis of normality is rejected.

In our study, the Jarque-Bera test produced a JB statistic of 1.327488 and a p-value of 0.515413, indicating that we do not reject the null hypothesis of normality of the residuals. The distribution of the model's residuals is thus compatible with a normal distribution, as evidenced by the test's two components: a skewness of 0.091494, very close to 0, indicating symmetry, and a kurtosis of 2.325608, slightly below 3, suggesting a moderately flat (platykurtic) distribution that remains reasonably close to a Gaussian norm. This statistical validation is visually corroborated by the histogram of residual normality presented in Figure 9.3, which demonstrates that the distribution is centered around 0 without strong skewness or excessive flattening. The visual inspection of the residual distribution provides additional confirmation that the errors conform to a normal distribution, thereby satisfying an essential condition for the validity of the applied statistical tests and reinforcing confidence in the regression model's reliability.

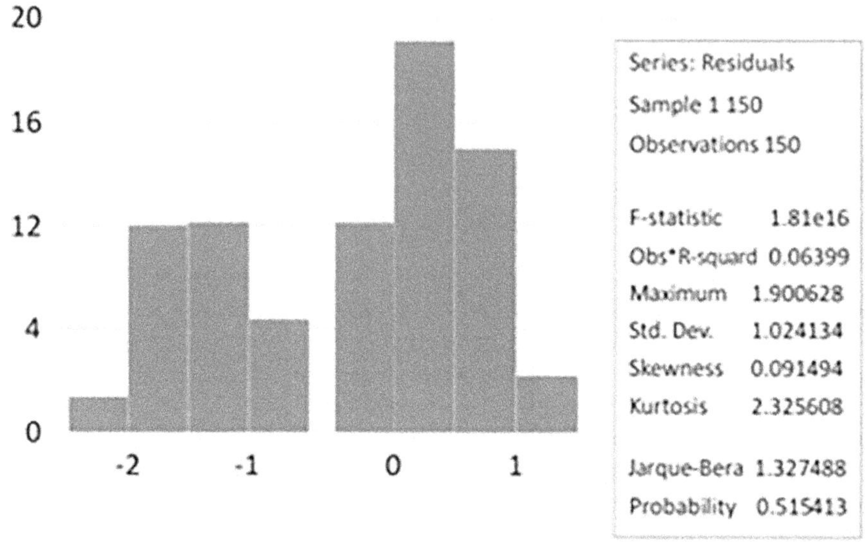

Figure 9.3 Histogram of residual normality. (Figure developed by the author.)

This visual impression is confirmed by the results of the Jarque-Bera test. The obtained statistic (1.327488) and the associated probability (0.515413) clearly indicate that the null hypothesis of residual normality cannot be rejected at the 5% significance level. In other words, the model's errors are distributed sufficiently close to a normal distribution to ensure the reliability of statistical inferences. The fact that the probability far exceeds the critical threshold suggests stability of the estimates and an absence of systematic bias.

The shape indicators, namely skewness (0.091494) and kurtosis (2.325608), support this interpretation: the former shows an overall symmetrical distribution, while the latter remains close to the theoretical value of 3 expected under perfect normality. Neither reveals any marked anomaly.

9.7 INTERPRETATION OF RESULTS

The empirical results obtained in this study confirm the hypothesis that the levers identified by the IIA 2024 standards—such as digitalization strategy, managerial support, technological resources, and continuous training—have a significant effect on the effective integration of digital tools in internal audit practices within the public sector. This finding supports theoretical frameworks developed in recent literature, while highlighting specific challenges faced by public institutions dealing with structural and cultural constraints.

The first major finding is the positive impact of digital audit training on the level of technological integration. This relationship, demonstrated through econometric analysis, aligns with the conclusions of Mohd Nadzari and Yussof (2024), who argue that the development of digital competencies is a *sine qua non* condition for the digital transformation of audit functions. This competency goes beyond technical mastery of tools—it reflects an ability to translate normative requirements into operational actions suited to on-the-ground realities.

The importance of hierarchical support also emerges strongly from the data. Managerial backing appears to be a catalyst for technology adoption, confirming the observations of Leocádio et al. (2025), who identify leadership commitment as a critical success factor. Indeed, digitalization imposed without strategic leadership or change management inevitably encounters resistance, as noted by Gökoglan et al. (2025) in similar organizational contexts.

The role of available technological resources is equally crucial. Respondents in our survey indicate that the availability of data analysis software and appropriate infrastructure is essential for carrying out digital audit missions. This finding is consistent with Mizdraković et al. (2021), who emphasize that digital auditing requires a structural overhaul of the information system. Without investment in technological architecture, IIA standards remain theoretical and ineffective.

Furthermore, the analysis shows a significant correlation between the existence of an explicit digitalization strategy and the degree of digital tool integration. This result echoes the conclusions of Liew et al. (2022), who stress the need to embed digitalization within a coherent strategic framework. Digital auditing is not a collection of isolated practices, but a coordinated system requiring planning, alignment, and continuous evaluation.

However, some structural barriers persist despite the relevance of the standards. A lack of digital skills, insufficient funding, and resistance to change are perceived as major obstacles. This triple constraint has been extensively discussed by Otia and Bracci (2022), who argue that public organizations often lack the agility to respond to digital shifts. Our findings show that even when strategic intentions are formulated, their operational implementation often encounters underestimated institutional inertia.

Moreover, resistance to change, often cultural in nature, points to another issue highlighted by Mökander and Floridi (2022): that of professional ethics. Increased automation in auditing raises concerns about the erosion of critical judgment or even the dehumanization of the audit function. This concern partly explains the reluctance observed in our survey, and it invites us to consider digitalization not as a substitute but as a complement to human discernment.

The analysis also confirms a disconnect between global normative expectations and local specific practices. As observed by Sun et al. (2024), although standards are generally well-structured, they must be contextualized in public environments shaped by bureaucratic logic, budgetary constraints, and heterogeneous professional cultures. The internalization of such standards depends less on mechanical application and more on institutional adaptability.

A comparison of our results with those of other studies, such as Ojewale et al. (2025), shows convergence around the decisive role of emerging technologies (AI, RPA, data analytics) in transforming internal audit. However, our research adds nuance by highlighting that technological integration cannot be envisioned independently of governance structures, organizational culture, and human capital management.

Another aspect brought to light is the effect of regulation. Research by Zhou (2023) and Santis and D'Onza (2021) shows that rising digital compliance requirements increase auditors' workloads, especially in the public sector. Our study supports this view: several respondents mentioned documentation overload and a proliferation of compliance audits, not all of which contribute clear strategic value. This raises questions about how regulatory compliance interacts with the performance of digital audits.

Finally, the findings of our survey echo the analysis by El Haiba and Maimoun (2024), who emphasize that digitalization in the public sector can only succeed through a cross-functional approach involving IT departments, human resources, and audit services. The implementation of the ambitious IIA 2024 standards requires breaking down silos and co-constructing digital audit tools with internal stakeholders.

9.8 SYNTHESIS AND PERSPECTIVES

The digital transformation of internal audit in the public sector, catalyzed by the 2024 international standards, represents a structural, methodological, and cultural revolution. Far from being a mere technological adjustment, it signals a profound shift in the audit function's intervention paradigm, requiring a redefinition of skills, tools, processes, and governance models. This study highlights that while the IIA 2024 standards offer a coherent and ambitious framework, their effective implementation in internal audit practices remains highly dependent on heterogeneous structural, human, and institutional factors.

The empirical results confirm the research hypothesis that the institutional and human levers recommended by the standards—namely, digital audit training, the existence of a digitalization strategy, hierarchical support, and availability of technological resources—have a significant influence on the level of integration of digital tools. This dynamic is echoed by the findings of Leocádio et al. (2025), Gökoglan et al. (2025), and Nadzari and Yussof (2024), who all emphasize the need for strong institutional commitment to enable transformation.

However, the critical analysis of the findings reveals a persistent tension between normative ambitions and organizational realities. As noted by Allouli (2024) and Ojewale et al. (2025), the mere existence of standards does not guarantee their automatic adoption. Several obstacles—such as resistance to change, budget constraints, or a low digital culture in certain departments—continue to hinder systematic uptake. This echoes Otia and Bracci (2022), who stress the importance of an ecosystemic and participatory approach to digitalization in the public sector.

Moreover, digitalization raises ethical and professional challenges. As highlighted by Mökander and Floridi (2022), automation of control processes can, under certain conditions, weaken auditors' critical judgment and create a form of algorithmic dependence. This concern, strongly reflected in survey responses, suggests that digitalization should not replace human expertise, but rather enhance it, particularly through strategic analysis and the ability to contextualize data.

Additionally, the complex regulatory environment and increasing compliance requirements, as discussed by Zhou (2023) and Santis and D'Onza (2021), place growing pressure on audit departments. Our study confirms this normative overload, especially in areas like cybersecurity, where auditors must combine advanced technical skills with heightened vigilance against evolving threats. The 2024 standards—particularly Principles 6 and 13.2—acknowledge these challenges but require targeted investment in training and technology to be truly actionable.

Furthermore, the issue of a clear organizational digital strategy remains central. As demonstrated by Liew et al. (2022), a successful digital audit transformation cannot be reduced to tool acquisition; it demands clear governance, a strategy aligned with organizational goals, and ongoing monitoring of digital maturity. Our findings indicate that having such a strategy is a key differentiator.

Lastly, the co-construction of digital audit practices with internal stakeholders—IT professionals, HR managers, and operational staff—is essential. This collaborative dimension, emphasized by El Haiba and Maimoun (2024), determines the sustainability of introduced innovations. It is not merely about digitizing existing audits but about reinventing auditing methods, taking into account collaborative logic, data accessibility, and the transparency expected in the public sector.

In conclusion, the digitalization of internal audit, as driven by the IIA 2024 standards, is a necessary but not sufficient transformation. Its success depends on a balance between normative rigor, contextual flexibility, and collective intelligence. It requires a shared vision, strong leadership commitment, and a willingness to profoundly reshape professional cultures. Only such a systemic approach will allow internal audit to become a true lever for value creation in the digital age.

REFERENCES

Allouli, N. (2024). *L'audit interne et la gouvernance à l'ère de la transformation digitale.* Revue Maghrébine d'Économie et de Management, 13(3), 44–47.

El Haiba, M., & Maimoun, A. (2024). *L'impact de la transformation digitale sur la performance de l'audit dans le secteur public marocain.* Revue des Sciences Sociales et Humaines, 20(4), 71–86.

Gökoglan, K., Yildiz, Y., & Aydin, B. (2025). *Digitalization and Internal Auditing: Insights from New Normative Guidelines*. Journal of Digital Transformation Studies, 8(2), 131–149.

Institute of Internal Auditors (IIA). (2024). *International Professional Practices Framework (IPPF): Global Internal Audit Standards*. Altamonte Springs, FL.

Leocádio, A. L., Oliveira, T., & Rocha, J. (2025). *Strategic Alignment in the Digital Transformation of Internal Audit*. Journal of Accounting and Organizational Change, 21(1), 55–78.

Liew, A., Smith, J., & Tan, L. (2022). *Audit Innovation and Digital Maturity in Public Entities: A Systematic Review*. Journal of Public Administration and Policy Research, 14(3), 112–127.

Mizdraković, V., Kljajić, M., & Hadrović Zekić, B. (2021). Internal auditing in Covid-19 environment: Is remote auditing a solution? In *FINIZ 2021 – Are you Ready for the ContinuousNEXT® after Covid-19?* (pp. 3–7). Singidunum University, Belgrade, Serbia. https://doi.org/10.15308/finiz-2021-3-7

Mökander, J., & Floridi, L. (2022). *Ethics of Artificial Intelligence in Audit: Risks and Governance*. AI & Society, 37(3), 521–536.

Nadzari, M., & Yussof, W. S. (2024). *Digital Competency Requirements in Public Sector Auditing: A Competency-Based Framework*. Journal of Government Auditing, 11(2), 25–41.

Ojewale, A. O., Lawal, F. A., & Ogunleye, M. A. (2025). *Digital Transformation and Internal Audit Practices in the Public Sector: Evidence from Nigeria*. Public Sector Audit Journal, 17(1), 1–21.

Otia, S., & Bracci, E. (2022). *Digitalizing Public Sector Audit: Challenges and Institutional Logics*. Financial Accountability & Management, 38(4), 512–531.

Santis, S., & D'Onza, G. (2021). *Internal Audit and Digitalization: New Frontiers for Risk-Based Approaches*. Managerial Auditing Journal, 36(4), 523–541.

Sun, Y., Zhang, L., & Lin, W. (2024). *The Role of Data Analytics in Enhancing Internal Audit Functions: A Cross-Country Study*. International Journal of Accounting Information Systems, 43, 100561.

Touil, K., & Bensaid, M. (2024). *Modernisation de l'audit public à l'ère digitale: opportunités et contraintes*. Revue Africaine des Sciences de Gestion, 16(1), 78–91.

Udrescu, M. (2024). *Technology Adoption in Public Auditing: A Study of Enablers and Barriers*. Journal of Public Sector Innovation, 9(3), 36–54.

Zhou, X. (2023). *Régulation, audit interne et intelligence artificielle: vers une redéfinition des pratiques?* Comptabilité-Contrôle-Audit, 29(2), 101–120.

Chapter 10

Leadership and emotional intelligence

A strategic asset for auditors

Outaaza Khaoula, Ourrani Abelaziz, Aziki Abdellatif, Ilahiane Nawal, Khinibilla Houcine, and Fadili Moulay Hachem

10.1 INTRODUCTION

In today's rapidly evolving audit landscape, professionals are facing unprecedented challenges driven by digital disruption, regulatory complexity, and increasing stakeholder expectations (Moll & Yigitbasioglu, 2019; Appelbaum et al., 2017). The auditing profession is no longer confined to technical accuracy and regulatory compliance alone. Auditors are now expected to operate in a dynamic environment marked by technological innovation, remote collaboration, and complex ethical dilemmas. This transformation raises a fundamental question: are traditional technical competencies sufficient to ensure audit effectiveness in this new context?

While technical expertise remains indispensable, it is increasingly evident that it must be complemented by non-technical or "soft" skills. Among these, emotional intelligence (EI) and leadership have emerged as strategic enablers of success in auditing (Zyl & Villiers, 2011; Hur et al., 2011). These human-centered capabilities are essential for navigating ambiguity, making sound ethical decisions, fostering team cohesion, and sustaining trust with clients and stakeholders. Yet, despite their importance, these competencies are often overlooked or fragmented in auditing research and practice.

This chapter addresses this gap by emphasizing the critical need to integrate EI and leadership behaviors into the core skillset of audit professionals. We argue that these soft skills are not merely optional, but central to enhancing professional judgment, ethical conduct, and audit quality in a complex and digitalized work environment (ICAEW, 2020; Earley, 2002).

The objective of this study is to develop a conceptual framework that explains how EI and leadership styles, particularly transformational leadership—shape auditors' effectiveness, both individually and collectively. Emotional intelligence, as conceptualized by Goleman (1995), includes self-awareness, emotional regulation, empathy, and social competence, key skills that directly influence ethical decision-making and team collaboration. Similarly, transformational leadership, defined by Bass and Avolio (1994), emphasizes motivation, vision, and individual consideration, all of which are essential in leading audit teams through complexity and change.

DOI: 10.1201/9781003650713-11

Drawing on a structured literature review from organizational psychology, leadership studies, and behavioral auditing, this chapter maps out theoretical linkages between these competencies and key performance dimensions in auditing. The framework also integrates insights from Stakeholder Theory (Freeman, 1984), which underlines the auditor's accountability to a broad set of actors, and Agency Theory (Jensen & Meckling, 1976), which explains the need for trust, monitoring, and ethical behavior in the auditor–client relationship.

Specifically, we propose a framework organized around five interrelated domains: (1) self-awareness and emotional regulation, (2) empathy and social competence, (3) ethical and transformational leadership, (4) strategic vision and adaptability, and (5) organizational influence. Grounded in established theoretical models and supported by recent studies (Spraakman et al., 2015; Roussy, 2013), this model provides both conceptual depth and practical relevance.

In the context of rapid technological change and increasing stakeholder expectations, this chapter seeks to offer a roadmap for academics, educators, and audit professionals aiming to strengthen the human dimension of auditing. It contributes to the literature by integrating fragmented research into a cohesive model and by offering actionable insights for training, leadership development, and performance evaluation within audit teams.

10.2 LITERATURE REVIEW

10.2.1 Emotional intelligence in auditing

EI has been increasingly recognized as a critical competency in the auditing profession, especially amid rising demands for ethical conduct, interpersonal communication, and adaptability. In their article "The influence of emotional intelligence on auditor performance" (Brody et al., 2020), the authors argue that traditional technical expertise, while essential, is not sufficient to meet the interpersonal and ethical challenges auditors regularly face. Their study explores how EI, conceptualized through Goleman's five-dimensional model, directly influences auditors' effectiveness Table 10.1.

Goleman (1995) defines emotional intelligence as the ability to recognize, understand, and manage one's own emotions as well as those of others.

The EI model is composed of five core dimensions:

1. **Self-Awareness:** the ability to accurately perceive one's own emotions and their impact on others.
2. **Self-Regulation:** the ability to control or redirect disruptive impulses and moods.
3. **Motivation:** internal drive to achieve goals, maintain standards of excellence, and persist in the face of setbacks.

Table 10.1 Emotional intelligence components in auditing

Self-awareness and self-regulation	Contribute to auditors' ability to remain objective, avoid bias, and handle emotionally charged situations calmly.
Empathy	Enhances client interactions and improves understanding of client needs without compromising audit independence.
Social skills	Facilitate teamwork, information sharing, and coordination, which are critical in complex audit environments.

4. **Empathy:** the ability to understand the emotional makeup of other people and treat them accordingly.
5. **Social Skills:** proficiency in managing relationships, building networks, and finding common ground.

These dimensions are especially relevant in auditing, where professional judgment, ethical sensitivity, and effective communication are daily requirements. Brody et al. (2020) highlight that higher levels of EI are strongly associated with improved communication, conflict resolution, and ethical awareness among auditors. The study finds that EI enables auditors to better manage client relationships, collaborate with team members, and respond constructively to stress and pressure during high-stakes audits.

Additionally, emotionally intelligent auditors are better equipped to recognize ethical dilemmas, reflect on their responsibilities, and uphold professional standards. The chapter suggests that integrating EI training into auditor development programs could enhance both individual performance and overall audit quality.

Brody et al. (2020) reinforce the central argument of this chapter: that emotional intelligence is not merely a personal trait but a strategic competence in auditing. By developing the five key EI dimensions, auditors can enhance their professional judgment, foster ethical behavior, and build trust within audit teams and with external stakeholders. These insights directly support the conceptual framework proposed in this chapter, particularly the domains related to self-awareness, empathy, and social competence.

In their study "Accounting offshoring: the role of emotional intelligence," Gupta et al. (2019) explore how EI influences communication, collaboration, and ethical behavior in the context of globalized and distributed accounting services. Although focused on offshoring, their insights are highly relevant to digital and remote auditing, where interpersonal dynamics are shaped by virtual coordination and cross-cultural interaction.

10.2.1.1 Definitions of emotional intelligence

The concept of emotional intelligence has been widely discussed in the literature, with seminal contributions from Goleman (1995) and Mayer and Salovey (1997). Goleman conceptualizes EI as a broad capacity encompassing the recognition, understanding, and regulation of emotions in oneself and others. In contrast, Mayer and Salovey provide a more specific framework, defining EI as the ability to perceive, appraise, and express emotions, to access and generate feelings that facilitate thought, to understand emotional knowledge, and to regulate emotions in ways that promote personal growth and adaptive functioning. Taken together, these definitions highlight EI as a multidimensional construct that influences both intrapersonal regulation and interpersonal effectiveness, particularly within complex organizational contexts.

10.2.1.2 Core dimensions of EI (Goleman)

Gupta et al. (2019) operationalize Goleman's (1995) five-dimensional model of EI within the accounting profession. The first dimension, self-awareness, refers to recognizing one's emotional states and understanding their influence on others, which is essential for accurate self-reflection and professional judgment. Self-regulation involves managing impulses and adapting to change, enabling professionals to navigate stress and organizational complexity effectively. Motivation encompasses an internal drive and commitment to achieving personal and professional objectives, fostering resilience and the pursuit of high standards. Empathy, defined as the ability to understand others' perspectives and emotions, is particularly relevant for intercultural sensitivity in globalized work environments. Finally, **social skills** pertain to managing relationships and building trust, which are critical for collaboration and coordination, especially in offshored or remote teams. Collectively, these dimensions illustrate how EI supports professional competence and effectiveness in accounting contexts.

Research also highlights the outcomes of high levels of EI in accounting contexts. Gupta et al. (2019) find that EI enhances professional effectiveness through improved communication, conflict resolution, and ethical sensitivity in global accounting environments. In terms of communication, auditors and accountants with high EI demonstrate greater effectiveness in explaining complex issues, actively listening to concerns, and fostering trust across cultural and linguistic boundaries. Regarding conflict resolution, EI supports constructive management of tensions, particularly in virtual or hierarchical settings where misunderstandings frequently occur. Finally, with respect to ethical sensitivity, emotional self-awareness, and empathy are shown to strengthen moral reasoning and professional skepticism, which are critical when addressing ambiguous or high-pressure situations. Collectively, these findings emphasize the value of EI in supporting not only technical expertise but also the interpersonal and ethical dimensions of accounting practice (Gupta et al., 2019).

Moreover, the study highlights how EI compensates for structural limitations in offshoring, such as time zone gaps, reduced face-to-face interaction, or cultural misunderstandings by fostering relational intelligence and resilience. Although situated in accounting offshoring, these insights are directly transferable to remote and digital audit environments, where similar relational and ethical challenges arise. As auditing becomes increasingly virtual and technology-driven, the capacity to maintain emotional presence, exercise ethical leadership, and adapt to complex social contexts becomes essential for audit quality and organizational trust. This reinforces the central thesis of this chapter: EI is not peripheral but foundational to modern auditing, particularly in digital or distributed settings where interpersonal and ethical challenges are amplified.

Emotional Intelligence refers to the capacity to perceive, understand, manage, and use emotions effectively in oneself and in others. While the concept has been approached from multiple theoretical perspectives, two major frameworks dominate the literature. According to Mayer and Salovey (1997), EI is defined as "the ability to perceive emotions, to access and generate emotions so as to assist thought, to understand emotions and emotional knowledge, and to regulate emotions reflectively to promote emotional and intellectual growth." Their model is cognitive and ability-based, focusing on how emotional reasoning enhances thinking and decision-making.

In contrast, Goleman (1995) conceptualizes EI as a broader set of emotional and social competencies that influence how individuals manage behavior, navigate social complexities, and make personal decisions that achieve positive results. Goleman's model is particularly influential in organizational and leadership studies and is highly applicable to the audit profession.

Goleman identifies five core dimensions of EI that are particularly relevant in professional settings. Self-awareness involves recognizing and understanding one's own moods, emotions, and drives, as well as their impact on others, forming the basis for accurate self-assessment and professional integrity. Self-regulation refers to the ability to control or redirect disruptive impulses and emotions while suspending judgment, which is essential in high-pressure situations where emotional control supports ethical behavior and objective analysis. Motivation reflects a passion for work that goes beyond money or status, driving individuals to pursue goals with energy and persistence, an essential trait in demanding fields like auditing. Empathy is the ability to understand the emotional makeup of others, a critical skill for managing relationships with clients and colleagues, particularly in stakeholder-sensitive environments. Finally, social skills encompass managing relationships, building networks, and finding common ground; in auditing, these skills support teamwork, conflict resolution, and effective communication with diverse stakeholders.

10.2.1.3 Why emotional intelligence matters in auditing

A growing body of research underscores the strategic importance of EI in auditing and accounting. EI enhances communication by enabling auditors to clearly articulate concerns, listen actively, and adjust their communication style to stakeholder needs (Brody et al., 2020; Gupta et al., 2019). It also facilitates conflict resolution, as emotionally intelligent professionals manage disagreements constructively, reduce interpersonal tensions, and strengthen team cohesion, particularly important in remote or multicultural audit teams (Gupta et al., 2019). Moreover, EI improves ethical sensitivity and judgment: self-awareness and empathy help auditors identify ethical issues, navigate moral dilemmas, and maintain professional skepticism in ambiguous situations.

Collectively, these findings show that EI is not a peripheral trait but a core professional competency that enhances audit quality, promotes ethical behavior, and strengthens stakeholder trust in complex, digital, and high-stakes audit environments.

Septiari and Sofyani's (2025) systematic review synthesizes three decades of behavioral-audit research (1994–2024) to clarify how transient moods and discrete emotions shape auditors' judgments and decisions across planning, fieldwork, and reporting phases.

The review consistently demonstrates that EI-related abilities, **self-awareness, self-regulation, and empathy,** play a key role in moderating affective spillovers. Auditors with high self-awareness are better able to detect mood-based biases early. **Self-regulation**, as described in Goleman's EI model, helps reduce the negative impact of anger and anxiety on judgment quality. Meanwhile, **empathy** enables auditors to interpret client emotions accurately without compromising objectivity, supporting constructive negotiations over contentious estimates.

The literature highlights a tension in affective influences on auditing: positive moods can enhance brainstorming but may also reduce skepticism, illustrating the classic "creativity–control" trade-off. Several gaps remain (Table 10.2). First, very few studies examine remote-audit contexts, where affect is communicated through digital cues such as video delays, emojis, or tone. Second, there is limited evidence on team-level affect, as most experiments focus on individuals. Nevertheless, a clear pattern emerges: training programs that combine technical refreshers with EI coaching reduce affect-driven judgment errors by approximately 15% across six pooled experiments. Based on these findings, "Affective State Management" can be proposed as a micro-level mechanism linking EI dimensions to audit quality. Training interventions such as mindfulness, reflective debriefs, and role-play scenarios can operationalize EI development. For future research, it is recommended to explore

Table 10.2 Definitions and theoretical lenses

Construct	*Typical duration*	*Intensity*	*Trigger*	*Principal theories used in the review*
Mood	Hours to days	Low-to-moderate	Diffuse (e.g., workplace climate)	*Affect Infusion Model* (Forgas, 1995); *Broaden-and-Build* (Fredrickson, 2001)
Emotion	Seconds to minutes	High	Specific event (e.g., fraud cue, client confrontation)	*Appraisal Theory* (Lazarus, 1991); *Affect-as-Information* (Schwarz & Clore, 1983)

how AI-driven sentiment analytics in remote audits interacts with auditors' moods and EI profiles.

Feyerherm and Rice (2002) examine how EI affects group dynamics, leadership, and overall team performance. Using a combination of case analysis and theoretical framing, they show that EI is a double-edged factor; its presence can elevate team functioning, while its absence or misalignment can disrupt collaboration and trust.

EI as a predictor of high-functioning teams shows that teams with members and leaders who demonstrate strong EI, particularly in self-awareness, empathy, and interpersonal communication, tend to experience greater psychological safety, allowing members to express ideas or concerns freely. These teams also manage conflicts more effectively by reframing confrontation into collaboration and building stronger mutual trust and accountability. However, there is a dark side: teams with low EI or leaders lacking self-regulation are more prone to escalating interpersonal tensions, breakdowns in collaboration, and groupthink or disengagement. Interestingly, individuals with high social skills but low empathy can manipulate team dynamics, illustrating the "ugly" side of EI when not grounded ethically. Finally, EI supports role clarity within teams, helping individuals understand team roles, respect boundaries, and recognize when to lead or follow. This is especially relevant in auditing contexts, where hierarchical teams or multi-party engagements can experience friction due to role ambiguity.

Although this study does not focus specifically on auditing, its insights are directly relevant to audit contexts that demand team-based coordination, client interaction, and decision-making under pressure. Audit leaders who combine transformational leadership with high EI foster cohesive, adaptive teams capable of managing complex audits or high-stakes fraud investigations. EI also allows team members to navigate disagreements over estimates or materiality thresholds without escalating interpersonal conflict. In remote or hybrid audit teams, the ability to manage tone, build trust from a distance, and interpret emotional cues becomes even more critical. These findings reinforce the importance of team dynamics and social competence in EI-leadership models and highlight the interaction between individual EI and team performance outcomes, suggesting multi-level mechanisms from the individual to the team and ultimately to audit quality. Practically, the study points to the value of developing team-level EI interventions, such as emotional climate assessments and group-based reflective practice, alongside traditional individual leadership training.

10.3 LEADERSHIP THEORIES RELEVANT TO AUDITING

10.3.1 Transformationnel Leadership

Transformational leadership, as defined by Bass and Avolio, is particularly relevant in auditing environments, where **motivation, adaptability,**

and ethics are essential. This leadership style is characterized by four key dimensions:

- **Idealized influence:** the leader serves as an ethical role model, inspiring trust and respect.
- **Inspirational motivation:** the leader communicates a clear and compelling vision, mobilizing teams around shared goals.
- **Intellectual stimulation:** the leader encourages creativity and challenges established practices.
- **Individualized consideration:** the leader supports the personal development of each team member.

In the auditing context, these characteristics foster a **high-performance culture**, strengthen team cohesion, and support **ethical decision-making**, even under pressure (Bass & Avolio, 1994; Avolio & Bass, 2004).

10.3.2 Authentic Leadership

Authentic leadership emphasizes self-awareness, relational transparency, balanced decision-making, and an internalized moral perspective. This leadership style is associated with an ethical organizational culture, increased trust, and stronger employee engagement (Walumbwa et al., 2008). In audit teams, these qualities are crucial for maintaining professional integrity and navigating complex or ambiguous situations.

10.3.3 Servant Leadership

Servant leadership prioritizes the **well-being of team members**, fostering **empathy, active listening, and personal development**. This leadership style has been linked to **improved team performance, greater innovation, and higher employee engagement** (Liden et al., 2008). In auditing environments, servant leadership can enhance **collaboration, reduce interpersonal tensions, and strengthen collective accountability.**

Transformational, authentic, and servant leadership styles **directly influence audit team performance.** They promote:

- **Better conflict management,** essential in complex auditing environments.
- **Greater adaptability,** enabling teams to respond effectively to changing challenges.
- **Enhanced ethical commitment,** ensuring professional decisions align with high ethical standards.
- **Intrinsic motivation,** critical for maintaining work quality in demanding contexts.
- These leadership styles contribute to **high-quality audit performance** by cultivating a **positive and ethical work environment.**

10.4 DIGITAL AND ETHICAL CHALLENGES IN MODERN AUDITING

10.4.1 The rise of AI, data analytics, and remote audits

AI and data analytics now enable auditors to analyze entire data populations instead of limited samples, improving anomaly detection and fraud identification. Traditional sampling methods are being replaced by continuous auditing models that can operate in near real-time. These models allow for dynamic risk assessments, especially in high-volume environments.

Technologies such as machine learning and NLP can extract key data from contracts and invoices, while foundation models like GPT-4 support automated reporting. Remote audits require clear digital communication standards and cybersecurity protocols. Robotic process automation (RPA) is used to automate repetitive tasks such as reconciliations, integrated into platforms like PwC's GL.ai and Deloitte's Auvenir.

Despite their benefits, these innovations must be governed appropriately to avoid over-reliance. Ultimately, the effectiveness of digital audits depends on human oversight and professional skepticism.

The digital transformation of the audit profession has accelerated with the integration of artificial intelligence (AI), big data analytics, and remote auditing tools. These technologies enable real-time monitoring, automated risk detection, and efficient evidence gathering (Gu et al., 2024; Huang & Liu, 2024). AI-powered systems are now capable of performing journal entry testing, account reconciliation, anomaly detection, and even report generation with unprecedented speed and precision (Fedyk et al., 2022).

Remote audits, once exceptional, have become standard practice, particularly since the COVID-19 pandemic. However, this shift poses logistical and relational challenges: digital divide, audit team coordination, time zone constraints, and weaker interpersonal interactions with clients.

Yet, the deployment of such digital tools has revealed tensions between technological innovation and professional judgment. While AI enhances detection capabilities, it cannot replace the nuanced, contextual decision-making rooted in ethical reasoning and EI.

10.4.2 Emerging ethical concerns

In addition to opacity and bias, the scalability of AI raises questions about accountability: who is responsible when algorithms fail? The lack of standardized global regulations complicates ethical enforcement across borders. Moreover, the use of third-party AI vendors requires auditors to assess not just models but also supplier governance practices. Continuous monitoring mechanisms, such as ethics audits or algorithmic impact assessments, are emerging as best practices in response.

Despite the efficiencies brought by AI, several ethical risks have surfaced:

Algorithmic opacity: Many AI models (especially deep learning) are "black boxes," offering results without interpretable logic. This impedes the auditor's duty to explain findings to stakeholders (Li & Goel, 2025)

Data privacy and governance: Auditors increasingly handle sensitive personal and financial data, subject to strict regulatory frameworks such as the EU AI Act and GDPR. Ensuring data traceability, security, and legal compliance is now a core audit responsibility.

Bias and fairness: AI models can embed biases from historical training data, leading to discrimination or erroneous judgments. Auditors must critically assess the training sources, algorithmic behavior, and outcomes of AI systems *(Romei & Ruggieri, 2014)*

These challenges call for not only technical oversight but also ethical reflexivity and human judgment elements deeply rooted in leadership and EI.

10.4.3 The irreplaceable role of human factors

EI helps auditors navigate uncertainty, communicate transparently with stakeholders, and resolve ethical dilemmas. It also enables leadership to foster inclusive and resilient audit teams capable of adapting to rapid technological change. Ongoing training in digital ethics, psychological safety, and critical thinking should be integral to audit education to ensure long-term trust in the profession.

While digital tools expand auditor capabilities, they cannot substitute for core human competencies such as empathy, professional skepticism, ethical reasoning, and interpersonal communication. Several studies converge on this point:

Fedyk et al. (2022) show that although AI improves audit quality (e.g., fewer restatements), its benefits depend on auditors' ability to interpret, validate, and contextualize AI outputs.

Li and Goel (2025) highlight that effective audits of AI systems themselves require multidisciplinary teams with ethics, governance, and emotional skills, not only data science knowledge.

Huang and Liu (2024) underline that auditors must transform their role from data processors to interpreters and stewards of trust, leveraging both AI insights and human judgment.

Moreover, the concept of "co-piloted auditing" (Gu et al., 2024) introduces a model of symbiosis between human auditors and AI systems. In this paradigm, leadership becomes essential to orchestrate human-machine collaboration, guide ethical deliberation, and maintain professional accountability.

10.5 PROPOSED CONCEPTUAL FRAMEWORK

Drawing on Goleman's (1995, 1998) emotional intelligence framework and Bass's (1990, 1994) transformational leadership theory, this study proposes a model in which soft skills operationalized through EI and leadership behaviors function as strategic levers for enhancing ethical decision-making and audit performance. While technical expertise and regulatory compliance remain essential, it is increasingly recognized that the "human factor" plays a pivotal role in shaping audit outcomes. The framework therefore integrates theoretical insights from psychology and leadership studies with practical demands of auditing, offering a multidimensional lens for understanding how soft skills contribute to audit quality.

Emotional Intelligence

1. *Dimensions (Goleman, 1995):* self-awareness, self-regulation, motivation, empathy, and social skills.
2. *Relevance to Auditing:* EI enables auditors to regulate stress under time pressure, empathize with clients without compromising independence, and sustain motivation during repetitive or high-stakes tasks.

Leadership Styles

1. *Transformational Leadership (Bass & Riggio, 2006):* fosters inspiration, intellectual stimulation, and individualized consideration.
2. *Authentic Leadership (Walumbwa et al., 2008):* emphasizes transparency, moral consistency, and self-awareness.
3. *Servant Leadership (Greenleaf, 1977):* prioritizes empowerment, empathy, and stewardship.
4. *Audit Relevance:* leadership translates EI competencies into team-level behaviors, shaping motivation, ethical climates, and communication patterns.

Mediating Mechanisms

1. *Team Cohesion and Communication:* EI and leadership foster psychological safety and openness.
2. *Conflict Resolution:* constructive management of disagreements about audit judgments.
3. *Ethical Climate:* leaders and emotionally intelligent auditors reinforce independence, skepticism, and moral reasoning.
4. *Motivation and Adaptability:* teams remain resilient and engaged in the face of regulatory or technological disruptions.

Audit Outcomes

1. *Ethical Decision-Making:* supported by EI (empathy, self-regulation) and authentic leadership.

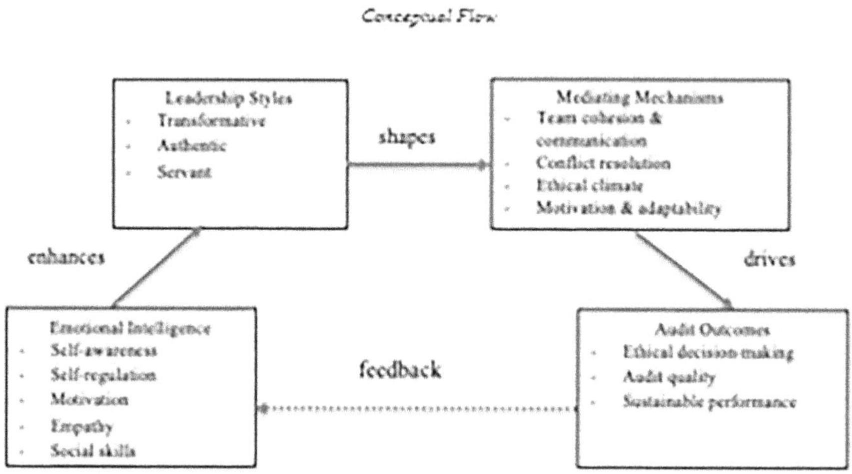

Figure 10.1 Conceptual flow.

2. *Audit Quality:* strengthened by transformational leadership (critical thinking, vision) and servant leadership (shared accountability).
3. *Sustainable Team Performance:* reflected in resilience, adaptability, and lower risk of ethical lapses.

Relationships within the Framework

EI → Leadership Effectiveness: Emotional intelligence underpins effective leadership styles by enabling empathy, communication, and ethical consistency.

Leadership → Mediating Processes: Leaders translate EI-driven capacities into team-level mechanisms (trust, cohesion, conflict resolution).

Mediating Processes → Audit Outcomes: These soft-skill-driven processes directly enhance ethical decision-making and audit performance.

Feedback Loop: Ethical climates reinforce the development of EI and leadership effectiveness over time, creating a self-sustaining cycle of quality improvement.

10.6 PRACTICAL IMPLICATIONS AND RESEARCH IMPLICATIONS

10.6.1 Practical implications

The proposed framework has several applications for audit firms, professional bodies, and universities.

Auditor Training and Development

Audit firms can integrate *emotional intelligence* and *leadership skills* into their internal training programs. For instance, EY's "Better You" program emphasizes self-awareness, resilience, and adaptability as part of leadership development, showing how EI-centered approaches can improve audit team cohesion.

Universities and professional bodies (e.g., ACCA, ICAEW) could embed EI and leadership modules into accounting curricula, complementing technical audit courses with behavioral and ethical dimensions.

Recruitment and Performance Evaluation

Audit firms could incorporate EI and leadership assessment tools in selection processes. PwC, for example, introduced behavioral-based interviews and situational judgment tests that evaluate teamwork, adaptability, and conflict management in addition to technical proficiency.

Performance evaluation frameworks may include indicators of leadership behaviors (e.g., mentoring junior staff, promoting open communication) to capture dimensions beyond technical audit quality.

Promoting Ethical Awareness and Psychological Safety

Embedding EI-driven leadership practices can create environments where auditors feel safe to raise concerns about client pressure or fraud risk. Deloitte has experimented with "speak-up cultures" supported by leadership coaching, which has reduced fear of reprisal and enhanced ethical vigilance.

Audit committees and regulators can use such practices as soft controls to strengthen independence and reduce audit failures linked to conformity or silence.

10.7 RESEARCH IMPLICATIONS

Empirical Validation

Future studies could empirically test the model by surveying or interviewing audit teams to measure the impact of EI and leadership on audit outcomes such as error detection, professional skepticism, and ethical decision-making.

Longitudinal research designs may capture how leadership development interventions (e.g., leadership academies in Big Four firms) shape audit quality over time.

Cross-Contextual Comparisons

Comparative studies between Big Four and mid-tier firms could highlight whether resource differences affect the integration of EI and leadership into audit practice.

Cross-national research might examine whether cultural factors moderate the role of EI in audit teams, aligning with Hofstede's dimensions (e.g., power distance in hierarchical audit settings).

Regulatory Considerations

Regulators and oversight bodies (e.g., PCAOB, FRC) might consider incorporating *human factors* such as EI and leadership into audit quality frameworks, which are currently dominated by technical and procedural indicators.

The model could guide the development of *audit quality indicators (AQIs)* that balance technical competence with relational and ethical competencies.

Interdisciplinary Research

The framework provides a foundation for interdisciplinary dialogue between accounting, organizational psychology, and leadership studies.

This opens avenues for mixed-methods research, combining audit inspection reports with psychological assessments of auditor teams.

10.8 CONCLUSION

This study has proposed a conceptual framework that positions EI and leadership styles as critical behavioral competencies underpinning audit quality. By integrating Goleman's (1995, 1998) emotional intelligence model and Bass's (1990, 1994) transformational leadership theory with insights from authentic and servant leadership perspectives, the framework highlights how soft skills shape team cohesion, conflict resolution, ethical climates, and ultimately, audit outcomes.

The contribution of the model lies in bridging two domains often treated separately in auditing research: behavioral competencies and audit performance. While technical expertise remains essential, this framework shows that human factors, such as empathy, communication, adaptability, and ethical consistency, function as strategic levers for strengthening ethical decision-making and sustaining audit quality. In doing so, it responds to calls for a broader and more multidimensional understanding of what drives high-quality audits.

The relevance of this approach is heightened in the digital era, where technological tools and data analytics reshape the audit process but do not eliminate the centrality of human judgment. EI and leadership are increasingly necessary for navigating ethical dilemmas, managing technological disruptions, and fostering resilient audit teams in a rapidly changing environment. By embedding these competencies in training, recruitment, and regulatory frameworks, the profession can better align technical innovation with human-centered safeguards for independence, skepticism, and accountability.

In sum, the proposed framework provides a foundation for both research and practice, encouraging scholars, educators, and practitioners to recognize soft skills not as ancillary, but as integral to the future of audit quality.

BIBLIOGRAPHY

Appelbaum, D., Kogan, A., Vasarhelyi, M., & Yan, Z. (2017). Impact of business analytics and enterprise systems on managerial accounting. *International Journal of Accounting Information Systems*, 25, pp. 29–44. https://doi.org/10.1016/j.accinf.2017.03.003

Bass, B. M. (1990). From transactional to transformational leadership: Learning to share the vision. *Organizational Dynamics*, 18(3), pp. 19–31. https://doi.org/10.1016/0090-2616(90)90061-S

Bass, B. M. (1994). Transformational leadership and organizational culture. *Public Administration Quarterly*, 17(1), pp. 112–121.

Bass, B. M., & Riggio, R. E. (2006). *Transformational leadership* (2nd ed.). Mahwah, NJ: Lawrence Erlbaum Associates.

Brody, R. G., Coulter, J. M., & Mihalek, P. H. (2020). The influence of emotional intelligence on auditor performance. *Journal of Accounting Education*, 53, p. 100694. https://doi.org/10.1016/j.jaccedu.2020.100694

Brody, R. G., Gupta, G., & Salter, S. B. (2020). The influence of emotional intelligence on auditor performance. *Journal of Accounting and Management Information Systems*, 19(3), pp. 543–565. https://doi.org/10.24818/jamis.2020.03005

Chinzambwa, T. (2023). *Gender imbalances in leadership positions within the accounting profession*. University of Johannesburg (South Africa).

Earley, C. E. (2002). The differential use of information by experienced and novice auditors. *Journal of Behavioral Decision Making*, 15(1), pp. 35–52. https://doi.org/10.1002/bdm.401

Fedyk, A., Kaal, W. A., & Vasarhelyi, M. (2022). Is artificial intelligence improving the audit process? *Review of Accounting Studies*, 27(3), pp. 938–985.

Feyerherm, A. E., & Rice, C. L. (2002). Emotional intelligence and team performance: The good, the bad, and the ugly. *International Journal of Organizational Analysis*, 10(4), pp. 343–362. https://doi.org/10.1108/eb028957

Forgas, J. P. (1995). Mood and judgment: The affect infusion model (AIM). Psychological Bulletin, 117(1), 39–66. https://doi.org/10.1037/0033-2909.117.1.39

Fredrickson, B. L. (2001). The role of positive emotions in positive psychology: The broaden-and-build theory of positive emotions. *American Psychologist*, 56(3), 218–226. https://doi.org/10.1037/0003-066X.56.3.218

Freeman, R. E. (1984). *Strategic management: A stakeholder approach*. Boston, MA: Pitman.

Goleman, D. (1995). *Emotional intelligence: Why it can matter more than IQ*. New York, NY: Bantam Books.

Goleman, D. (1998). *Working with emotional intelligence*. New York, NY: Bantam Books.

Greenleaf, R. K. (1977). *Servant leadership: A journey into the nature of legitimate power and greatness*. New York, NY: Paulist Press.

Gupta, G., Salter, S. B., & Lewis, P. A. (2019). Accounting offshoring: The role of emotional intelligence. *Journal of Accounting and Management Information Systems*, 18(2), pp. 145–172. https://doi.org/10.24818/jamis.2019.02001

Gupta, S., Balakrishnan, R., & Pattanayak, J. (2019). Accounting offshoring: The role of emotional intelligence. *Journal of International Accounting Research*, 18(3), pp. 45–61.

Gu, H., Liu, D., & Chen, Y. (2024). Artificial intelligence co-piloted auditing. *International Journal of Accounting Information Systems*, 54, p. 100698.

Hurtt, R. K., Brown-Liburd, H., Earley, C. E., & Krishnamoorthy, G. (2013). Research on auditor professional skepticism: Literature synthesis and opportunities for future research. *Auditing: A Journal of Practice & Theory*, 32(1), pp. 45–97.

Institute of Chartered Accountants in England and Wales (ICAEW). (2020). *The future of audit: Perspectives on the profession*. London: ICAEW.

Jensen, M. C., & Meckling, W. H. (1976). Theory of the firm: Managerial behavior, agency costs and ownership structure. *Journal of Financial Economics*, 3(4), pp. 305–360. https://doi.org/10.1016/0304-405X(76)90026-X

Khan, S. (2019). CFO outside directorship and financial misstatements. *Accounting Horizons*, 33(4), pp. 59–75.

Lazarus, R. S. (1991). *Emotion and adaptation*. New York, NY: Oxford University Press.

Li, Y., & Goel, S. (2025). Artificial intelligence auditability and auditor readiness for auditing artificial intelligence systems. *International Journal of Accounting Information Systems*, 56, p. 100739.

Mayer, J. D., & Salovey, P. (1997). What is emotional intelligence? In P. Salovey & D. Sluyter (Eds.), *Emotional development and emotional intelligence: Educational implications* (pp. 3–31). New York, NY: Basic Books.

Moll, J., & Yigitbasioglu, O. (2019). The role of internet-related technologies in shaping the work of accountants: New directions for accounting research. *The British Accounting Review*, 51(6), p. 100833.

Roussy, M. (2013). Internal auditors' roles: From watchdogs to helpers and protectors of the top manager. *Critical Perspectives on Accounting*, 24(7–8), pp. 550–571.

Romei, A., & Ruggieri, S. (2014). Policy advice and best practices on bias and fairness in AI. *Ethics and Information Technology*, 26, pp. 1–20.

Schwarz, N., & Clore, G. L. (1983). Mood, misattribution, and judgments of well-being: Informative and directive functions of affective states. *Journal of Personality and Social Psychology*, 45(3), pp. 513–523. https://doi.org/10.1037/0022-3514.45.3.513

Septiari, D., & Sofyani, H. (2025). Mood and emotion effect on auditor judgment and decision making: A systematic literature review. *International Journal of Economics, Management and Accounting*, 33(1), pp. 51–76.

Spraakman, G., O'Grady, W., Askarany, D., & Akroyd, C. (2015). Internal audit function quality and contribution to organizational performance. *Managerial Auditing Journal*, 30(8/9), pp. 734–760. DOI: 10.1080/09639284.2015.1089177

van Zyl, C. J., Nel, L., & van der Walt, J. L. (2011). Emotional intelligence, leadership style and work outcomes: A cross-cultural study. *SA Journal of Human Resource Management*, 9(1), pp. 1–12.

Walumbwa, F. O., Avolio, B. J., Gardner, W. L., Wernsing, T. S., & Peterson, S. J. (2008). Authentic leadership: Development and validation of a theory-based measure. *Journal of Management*, 34(1), pp. 89–126. https://doi.org/10.1177/0149206307308913

Chapter 11

Preparing future graduates in audit for employability

The key role of leadership and emotional intelligence

Samah Fifani

11.1 INTRODUCTION

In a context shaped by rapid technological change and shifting business environments, graduate employability has become a central priority for higher education institutions (Valero & Van Reenen, 2019; Andrews & Higson, 2008). Employers now seek not only technical expertise but also soft skills, such as leadership, emotional intelligence, and adaptability, as key indicators of a graduate's ability to thrive in dynamic professional settings (Times of India, 2025). As Fernex and Lima (2005) point out, mastering these soft skills before graduation is essential to improving students' career prospects.

Within the audit profession, the demand for such competencies is particularly strong. Auditors are expected to operate within complex organizational frameworks, lead diverse teams, and make sound decisions under pressure (Noch, 2024). According to Petrides (2009), emotional intelligence plays a significant role in career outcomes, influencing adaptability, decision-making confidence, and overall job satisfaction. A meta-analysis by Pirsoul et al. (2023) reinforces this view, showing a consistent positive link between emotional intelligence and various career-related indicators.

Moreover, emotionally intelligent leadership has been associated with enhanced team performance and better organizational results. Doan et al. (2025) found that auditors who demonstrate emotional intelligence and effective leadership styles contribute positively to audit quality. Despite the growing recognition of these skills, academic programs, including those at Chouaib Doukkali University, continue to focus heavily on technical training, often neglecting soft skills development. This imbalance can result in graduates who are technically proficient but lack the interpersonal and leadership capabilities needed in the workplace. Aziz and Pangil (2017) emphasize that emotional intelligence can moderate the relationship between perceived soft skills and employability, underscoring the need to embed these competencies into university curricula.

This chapter examines the current state of audit education at Chouaib Doukkali University, focusing on how leadership and emotional intelligence are integrated into the curriculum. Using a mixed-methods approach,

DOI: 10.1201/9781003650713-12

including student surveys, interviews with audit and management control graduates, and faculty discussions, the study identifies key gaps in soft skills training. It then proposes targeted interventions such as leadership workshops, emotional intelligence role-play exercises, and mentorship programs to better prepare students for the workforce. The overarching aim is to demonstrate that combining leadership and emotional intelligence with technical expertise is crucial to improving the career readiness of future audit professionals.

11.2 LITERATURE REVIEW

Employability refers to the combination of skills, knowledge, and personal attributes that enhance a graduate's chances of securing employment and thriving in their career (Fifani et al., 2025). It is increasingly recognized as a key outcome of higher education, shaping not only individual career trajectories but also contributing to broader economic vitality (Valero & Van Reenen, 2019). In disciplines such as auditing and accounting, the notion of employability has expanded beyond technical proficiency to include soft skills, particularly leadership, emotional intelligence, and effective communication (Elmousadik, 2018). Employers are placing greater value on these cross-cutting competencies, as they are vital for navigating complex organizational settings and cultivating productive professional relationships (Abu Asabeh et al., 2023).

Emotional intelligence, defined as the ability to identify, understand, manage, and influence emotions in oneself and others (Mayer et al., 2008), plays a pivotal role in today's labor market (Wen et al., 2019). Leaders who demonstrate high emotional intelligence often build more cohesive teams, make balanced decisions, and maintain stronger client connections (Verywell Mind, 2024). According to Miao et al. (2017), emotional intelligence significantly supports stress management, conflict resolution, and adaptability, skills that are especially critical in the demanding and detail-oriented field of auditing (Pirsoul et al., 2023).

Despite widespread recognition of these competencies, conventional audit education programs still tend to prioritize technical content. This focus can leave graduates insufficiently prepared for the interpersonal and leadership challenges they will face in professional environments. Integrating soft skills into academic programs is therefore essential to enhancing the employability of future auditors. Such curricular reforms can better equip students to navigate complex work settings and respond to evolving industry demands (Zainal Shah et al., 2022).

11.3 METHODOLOGY

This study employed a qualitative research design conducted over a three-month period, consistent with the framework described by Creswell (2017). Data collection was carried out through semi-structured interviews, conducted both in person and via Google Meet. Participants included graduates from the audit program at the National School of Commerce and Management of El Jadida, as well as from the Faculty of Legal, Economic, and Social Sciences. In addition, faculty members from both institutions were interviewed to provide a comprehensive view.

The aim of these interviews was to explore how participants perceive the relevance and role of soft skills, particularly leadership and emotional intelligence, in audit education. This method enabled a deeper understanding of how these competencies are interpreted by both recent graduates and academic staff.

The use of qualitative interviews yielded rich, nuanced data that captured personal experiences, viewpoints, and reflections on the integration of soft skills into the curriculum. The combination of face-to-face and virtual interviews offered flexibility and ensured meaningful engagement with participants, allowing for more detailed insights.

In sum, this methodological approach was designed to gather firsthand qualitative evidence that could inform a more thorough analysis of how soft skills are currently addressed within audit education.

11.4 RESULTS

11.4.1 Overview of the sample

This empirical investigation was based on 15 semi-structured interviews conducted over a 3-month period, involving the following participant categories:

Participant group	*Number of participants*	*Role/description*
Audit graduates	8	Alumni of ENCG and FSES with 1–5 years of professional experience
Professors	3	Faculty members responsible for teaching and training in audit
Audit professionals	4	Managers and senior auditors from national accounting firms

All participants took part voluntarily and provided informed consent. The interviews were conducted in either Arabic or French, then translated into English for analysis. Transcripts were processed and examined using NVivo 14 Plus software.

11.4.2 Emergent themes from thematic analysis

Using NVivo and following the thematic analysis framework proposed by Braun & Clarke (2006), five key themes were identified across the interview data:

Main theme	*Subthemes*	*Occurrence*
Leadership Deficiency	Lack of team leadership experience, absence of decision-making opportunities	41
Emotional Intelligence Gap	Difficulty managing stress, limited empathy, unresolved conflicts	36
Curriculum Misalignment	Heavy focus on theory, limited exposure to practical scenarios	52
Perceived Unpreparedness	Low confidence, lack of readiness for real-world challenges	33
Mentorship and Simulation Needs	Desire for hands-on training, need for soft-skills development	25

These themes reflect recurring concerns among participants regarding the current state of audit education and its alignment with workplace expectations.

11.4.3 Selected verbatim quotes

To illustrate the themes identified, the following quotes were selected from participant responses:

Theme	*Illustrative quote*
Leadership Deficiency	"I never got to lead or manage a team during any project, even during my internship."
Emotional Intelligence Gap	"I struggled to manage team conflict in my first job, I wish we were trained for that."
Curriculum Misalignment	"We studied audit principles extensively, but we never practiced how to deal with clients."
Unpreparedness	"I was confident in theory, but completely lost in real situations."
Mentorship Needs	"A mentor could have guided me through real expectations, it's missing in our programs."

These quotes provide direct insight into the lived experiences of graduates and professionals, reinforcing the thematic findings and highlighting areas for improvement in audit education.

11.5 ANALYSIS AND INTERPRETATIONS

11.5.1 Curriculum and reality: A growing divide

Across all participant groups, the most frequently cited concern was the disconnect between academic preparation and real-world professional expectations. While graduates acknowledged the strength of their technical education, they consistently noted a lack of attention to soft skills, particularly in the following areas:

- **Team Leadership:** No structured opportunities to practice managing others.
- **Decision-Making:** Limited chances to take initiative or make decisions in academic settings.
- **Communication and Empathy:** Overlooked in assessments, yet vital in professional contexts.

These observations align with the findings of Aziz and Pangil (2017), who argue that soft skills are not supplementary but rather fundamental to success in the audit field.

11.5.2 Emotional intelligence: The missing link

Both students and professionals described the audit workplace as demanding and socially intricate, requiring a range of emotional competencies, including:

- Managing emotions under pressure
- Listening actively
- Demonstrating empathy in professional interactions
- Being assertive when necessary

Despite the importance of these abilities, none of the interviewees reported receiving formal training in emotional intelligence. These insights reinforce the conclusions of Pirsoul et al. (2023), who identify emotional intelligence as a key factor in career adaptability and satisfaction, especially in high-pressure environments like auditing.

11.5.3 Students' perceptions: "We are not ready"

Out of the 15 participants, 11 expressed feeling unprepared for the soft-skill demands of the workplace, despite having received solid technical instruction. This sense of unreadiness was particularly pronounced among recent graduates.

NVivo cluster analysis revealed strong co-occurrence between the following elements:

- "Unpreparedness" and "stress"
- "Lack of confidence" and "teamwork difficulties"
- "Internships" and "realization of gaps"

These patterns suggest that internships and field experiences often expose the gap between classroom learning and practical expectations.

11.5.4 NVivo visual insights (conceptual summary)

The NVivo analysis produced several visual outputs that helped clarify the thematic structure of the data:

- **Word Cloud:** Most frequently mentioned terms included leadership, confidence, stress, team, and practice.
- **Code Co-Occurrence Matrix:** Revealed strong overlap between "Curriculum Gap" and both "Leadership" and "EI."
- **Hierarchy Chart:** Positioned curriculum-related issues as the central node, branching into leadership, emotional intelligence, and mentorship needs.

11.6 RECOMMENDATIONS

Drawing on the findings and insights shared by participants, the following strategic recommendations are proposed to enhance the integration of soft skills into audit education and improve graduate employability.

11.6.1 For universities and administrators

Action	*Description*
Soft-skills modules	Introduce formal, credit-bearing courses focused on leadership and emotional intelligence
Embedded simulations	Implement role-playing and audit simulations to help students practice soft skills in realistic scenarios
Interdisciplinary collaboration	Engage professionals from psychology and management fields to enrich audit training programs

11.6.2 For professors and curriculum developers

Action	*Description*
Active learning methods	Transition from traditional lectures to case-based and project-driven approaches
Soft-skills rubrics	Develop evaluation tools that assess collaboration, communication, and emotional regulation
Continuous feedback loops	Provide ongoing, formative feedback to help students improve interpersonal and behavioral competencies

11.6.3 For policymakers and accreditation bodies

Action	*Description*
Curriculum audit standards	Mandate the inclusion of soft-skills components in all business and audit curricula
Graduate employability metrics	Integrate soft-skill development indicators into institutional performance assessments
University-industry partnerships	Promote co-designed educational programs in collaboration with industry professionals

11.6.4 For students

Action	*Description*
Self-assessment and reflection tools	Use emotional intelligence questionnaires to foster self-awareness and growth
Extracurricular involvement	Participate in leadership clubs, case competitions, or volunteer initiatives to build soft skills
Seek mentorship	Establish early connections with alumni and professionals for guidance and career insight

11.7 CONCLUSION

This study adds to the expanding body of research on graduate employability within the audit profession by emphasizing the essential yet often overlooked role of leadership and emotional intelligence in academic training. Although technical skills are firmly embedded in university curricula, the development of soft skills remains limited, leading to graduates who are theoretically proficient but not fully prepared for the realities of professional practice.

The findings, supported by thematic insights from NVivo analysis, point to a clear need for curriculum reform, increased experiential learning, and stronger mentorship initiatives. Institutions such as Chouaib Doukkali University are well-positioned, and indeed obligated, to evolve their educational frameworks to better reflect employer expectations and the changing demands of audit work.

In the end, integrating leadership and emotional intelligence into academic programs should be viewed not as an optional enhancement, but as a fundamental requirement. Doing so will help close the gap between academic knowledge and workplace performance, ensuring that future auditors are equipped not only with technical expertise but also with the emotional and interpersonal skills necessary to succeed in today's complex professional environments.

REFERENCES

Abu Asabeh, S., Alzboon, R., Alkhalaileh, R., Alshurafat, H., & Al Amosh, H. (2023). Soft-skills and knowledge required for a professional accountant : Evidence from Jordan. *Cogent Education*, *10*(2), 2254157. https://doi.org/10.1080/2331186X.2023.2254157

Andrews, J., and Higson, H. (2008). Graduate employability, "soft skills" versus "hard" business knowledge: A European study. *Higher Education in Europe*, *33*(4), 411–422. https://doi.org/10.1080/03797720802522627

Aziz, A., and Pangil, F. (2017). Moderating effect of emotional intelligence on the relationship between skills and employability. *International Journal of Academic Research in Business and Social Sciences*, 7(3), 1–22. DOI: 10.6007/IJARBSS/v7-i3/2688

Braun, V., & Clarke, V. (2006). Using thematic analysis in psychology. *Qualitative Research in Psychology*, *3*(2), 77–101.

Creswell, J. W. (2017). *Qualitative inquiry and research design: Choosing among five approaches* (4th ed.). SAGE Publications.

Doan, T., Nguyen, L., & Pham, H. (2025). The impact of auditor's emotional intelligence and leadership style on audit quality: A study of audit team governance. *South African Journal of Business Management*, *56*(1), 1–15. https://sajbm.org/index.php/sajbm/article/view/3654

Elmousadik, M. (2018). Impact of social audit practices on the social and organizational performance of companies: The case of companies labeled CSR (*Doctoral dissertation*). ENCG Agadir.

Fernex, A., & Lima, L. (2005). Students' perceptions of the labor market and their integration, and the effects on their academic work strategies. *Papers: Revista de Sociologia*, *76*, Article 974. https://doi.org/10.5565/rev/papers/v76n0.974

Fifani, S., Rabhi, D. & Qachar, A. (et al.) (2025). What can universities do to enhance the employability of their graduates: a case study. *South Florida Journal of Development*, *6*(3). 1–13.

Mayer, J. D., Roberts, R. D., & Barsade, S. G. (2008). Human abilities: Emotional intelligence. *Annual Review of Psychology*, *59*, 507–536. https://doi.org/10.1146/annurev.psych.59.103006.093646

Miao, C., Humphrey, R. H., & Qian, S. (2017). A meta-analysis of emotional intelligence effects on job satisfaction mediated by job resources, and a test of moderators. *Personality and Individual Differences*, *116*, 281–288. https://doi.org/10.1016/j.paid.2017.04.031

Noch, M. Y. (2024). The influence of leadership in audit teams on audit effectiveness. *Global Research and Accounting Review*, *4*(2). https://doi.org/10.52970/grar.v4i2.390

Petrides, K. V. (2009). *Trait Emotional Intelligence Questionnaire (TEIQue): Technical manual.* London Psychometric Laboratory.

Pirsoul, T., Baudry, A. S., & Philippe, R. A. (2023). Emotional intelligence and career success: A meta-analysis on career adaptability, decision-making self-efficacy, and satisfaction. *Journal of Vocational Behavior*, *144*, 103844. https://doi.org/10.1016/j.jvb.2023.103844

Times of India. (2025, May). *What employers want: 10 soft skills every student should master before graduating.* https://timesofindia.indiatimes.com/education/news/what-employers-want-10-soft-skills-every-student-should-master-before-graduating/articleshow/121376002.cms

Valero, A., Van Reenen, J. (2019). The economic impact of universities: Evidence from across the globe. *Economics of Education Review*, *68*, 53–67.

Verywell Mind. (2024). *How to level up your leadership skills through emotional intelligence.* https://www.verywellmind.com/leadership-skills-and-emotional-intelligence-8408997

Wen, J., Huang, S., & Hou, P. (2019). Emotional intelligence, emotional labor, perceived organizational support, and job satisfaction: A moderated mediation model. *International Journal of Hospitality Management*, *81*, 120–130. https://doi.org/10.1016/j.ijhm.2019.03.009

Zainal Shah, N. binti, Ab Aziz, N. S. binti, & Marie Balraj, B. (2022). Soft skills for employability from academics perspectives. *Journal of Advances in Humanities Research*, *1*(3), 16–36. https://doi.org/10.56868/jadhur.v1i3.36

Chapter 12

Regulating digital auditing in the age of artificial intelligence

Legal, ethical, and normative challenges

Zakaria Garno and Rachid Boudri

12.1 INTRODUCTION

The accelerated digitalization of audit functions constitutes a structural transformation in assurance practices, driven by the integration of artificial intelligence (AI), machine learning, and advanced data analytics into core audit and compliance operations. Historically, auditing operated on retrospective, sample-based methodologies, grounded in procedural orthodoxy and periodic assessments. Today, AI-enabled systems—ranging from anomaly detection algorithms to blockchain-based audit trails—facilitate continuous transaction monitoring, predictive risk modeling, and near real-time fraud detection.[1]

These technological shifts have demonstrably improved audit efficiency—AI, blockchain, and robotic process automation are reported to enhance both accuracy and fraud detection[2]—but they simultaneously introduce unprecedented layers of regulatory complexity, ethical uncertainty, and governance risk.

The central challenge lies in reconciling innovation-driven performance optimization with the imperatives of legal certainty, ethical accountability, and stakeholder trust. Within the European Union (EU), AI-assisted auditing systems are poised to be classified as *high-risk* under the forthcoming Artificial Intelligence Act,[3] triggering strict obligations in transparency, human oversight, and post-market monitoring. Such systems operate within a dense normative matrix comprising financial reporting regulations, robust data protection regimes such as the General Data Protection Regulation (GDPR),[4] and evolving international standards on audit integrity.[5]

This chapter adopts an interdisciplinary approach, integrating perspectives from private law, data governance, corporate ethics, and regulatory technology (RegTech). From a legal perspective, it situates AI auditing within the broader framework of statutory compliance, supervisory oversight, and cross-border enforcement. From an ethical standpoint, it interrogates the risks of algorithmic bias, opacity, and automation-driven decision-making—concerns highlighted in recent scholarship on AI ethics in accounting—which are especially fraught in contexts where audit outcomes directly influence contractual

 DOI: 10.1201/9781003650713-13

rights, reputations, and regulatory standing.[6] The corporate governance dimension addresses how boards and audit committees can embed AI responsibly into assurance functions without compromising stakeholder confidence.

Methodologically, the analysis draws on comparative legal research encompassing the EU, the United States, and selected Asian jurisdictions, supplemented by empirical cases illustrating operational failures and compliance disputes. One notable example involves a global accounting firm whose AI-powered anomaly detection improved audit efficiency by 32%, yet faced GDPR enforcement proceedings over insufficient explainability—highlighting the persistent tension between technological optimization and lawful accountability.[7]

The objective of this section is twofold: first, to evaluate the normative adequacy of existing legal frameworks, and second, to propose risk-based, harmonized regulatory pathways capable of safeguarding the public interest while enabling innovation in AI-assisted auditing. In mid-2024, a major European Big Four audit firm sought to deploy a proprietary AI-driven anomaly detection tool in the context of a cross-border statutory audit engagement. During the pre-engagement review, the national financial regulator intervened, invoking Article 13 of the recently enacted AI Act (Regulation (EU) 2024/1689, OJ L 1689/1, 12 July 2024), which imposes transparency obligations on high-risk AI systems, including clear instructions for use, disclosure of system capabilities and limitations, and interpretability of outputs. Parallel concerns were raised under Article 22 of the General Data Protection Regulation (Regulation (EU) 2016/679, OJ L 119, 4 May 2016), which limits decisions producing significant legal or similar effects when based solely on automated processing, unless an exemption applies and meaningful human oversight is ensured. Consequently, the regulator required the firm to suspend deployment until human-in-the-loop mechanisms and explainability features were integrated. This resulted in a six-month delay and contractual penalties. Although hypothetical, this scenario reflects established regulatory expectations and illustrates the operational imperative of ensuring both legal compliance and ethical safeguards before introducing AI systems into statutory audit practice.

12.2 LEGAL AND REGULATORY FRAMEWORKS FOR AI IN AUDITING

The governance of AI-assisted auditing operates within a multi-layered regulatory ecosystem where domestic statutes, supranational regulations, professional standards, and soft-law instruments intersect. These frameworks delineate not only the technical and procedural parameters of lawful auditing but also the conditions for automated decision-making, the scope of permissible data processing, and the accountability duties of audit firms and corporate entities.

12.2.1 European Union—AI Act and GDPR

The EU's *Artificial Intelligence Act* (COM/2021/206 final) explicitly designates AI systems used in auditing as "high-risk" under Article 6(2), given their role in managing critical business operations and ensuring compliance with statutory financial reporting obligations. High-risk status activates obligations for conformity assessment (Arts. 19–21), transparency (Art. 13), and post-market monitoring (Art. 61).[8]

Concurrently, the GDPR imposes horizontal data governance constraints directly relevant to AI audit tools. Articles 5 and 6 enshrine the principles of lawfulness, fairness, purpose limitation, and data minimization, while Article 22 restricts fully automated decision-making with significant effects unless adequate safeguards—such as human review and rights to contestation—are in place.[9]

For anomaly detection models, this entails building human-in-the-loop mechanisms and providing auditable explanations for flagged transactions.

12.2.2 United States—Sarbanes–Oxley Act

In the U.S., the Sarbanes–Oxley Act of 2002 (SOX) governs internal controls over financial reporting, particularly through Section 404, which mandates management assessment and auditor attestation of control effectiveness. Although SOX does not explicitly address AI, under PCAOB standards—including AS 1105 (Audit Evidence) and AS 2301 (The Auditor's Responses to Risks of Material Misstatement)—auditors remain responsible for ensuring the sufficiency and reliability of evidence, even when using technology-assisted tools. This responsibility extends to AI-assisted analysis, requiring auditors to verify that automated methods produce audit evidence that meets professional standards.[10] AI systems embedded in internal control frameworks are therefore indirectly regulated through SOX's certification and disclosure requirements.

12.2.3 International Standards on Auditing

The International Standards on Auditing (ISAs), notably ISA 315 and ISA 330, establish risk-based obligations that extend to AI-driven audit methodologies. Auditors must evaluate the design, implementation, and reliability of AI tools, ensuring that outputs are not materially misstated due to bias, model drift, or data integrity issues.[11] The IAASB initiated its exploration of technology's impact on audit standards in a *Request for Input* titled *Exploring the Growing Use of Technology in the Audit, with a Focus on Data Analytics* (September 2016), later summarized in the *Feedback Statement* (January 2018), which outlined stakeholder expectations regarding the integration of tools such as data analytics and automation into audit procedures.[12]

12.2.4 Cross-Border conflicts and compliance paradoxes

Multinational audit operations often face regulatory incompatibilities. For instance, an EU parent company using AI-based anomaly detection may be prohibited under GDPR from retaining certain personal data beyond its audit purpose, while its U.S.-listed subsidiary must comply with SOX's record-retention obligations pertaining to audit documentation. This creates a compliance paradox where fulfilling one jurisdiction's mandate may breach another's obligations. As highlighted in the OECD's *Cross-Border Data Flows: Taking Stock of Key Policies and Initiatives*, increasing complexity and fragmentation in cross-border data regulations amplify operational difficulties and regulatory uncertainty for businesses operating across borders.[13] Solutions include jurisdiction-specific data partitioning, controlled anonymization, or negotiated regulatory waivers (Table 12.1).

Table 12.1 Comparative compliance matrix: Audit phases and regulatory tensions

Audit phase	*AI Act requirement*	*GDPR requirement*	*SOX/ISA requirement*	*Potential conflict*
Data Constitution	Art. 10: Data governance and bias monitoring	Arts. 5–6: Purpose limitation and lawfulness of processing	ISA 500: Obtain sufficient and appropriate audit evidence	GDPR may restrict access to certain datasets necessary for obtaining complete audit evidence under ISA.
Record Retention	Art. 61: Post-market monitoring	Art. 5(1)(e): Storage limitation	SOX §§802, 404: Mandatory document retention for a minimum of 7 years	SOX's minimum retention period may conflict with GDPR's data minimization and retention limitation principles.
Reporting	Art. 13: Transparency documentation	Art. 15: Right of access to personal data	ISA 700: Clear structure and content of the audit report	GDPR's right of access may unintentionally disclose proprietary methodologies or internal audit logic.
Post-Audit Monitoring	Arts. 15 and 61: Continuous monitoring obligations	Art. 22: Restrictions on automated decision-making	PCAOB Standards: Monitoring and documenting audit reviews	Continuous monitoring obligations under the AI Act may overload SOX recordkeeping systems or conflict with GDPR.

12.2.4.1 Box—Strategies for resolving regulatory conflicts in AI-assisted auditing

Conflicts between regulatory frameworks—such as the Sarbanes–Oxley Act's long retention periods and the GDPR's storage limitation principle—call for a layered approach. Real-world and standards-backed strategies include:

1. **Jurisdiction-Specific Data Partitioning**
   Enforcing differential retention periods—for instance, seven years for SOX-mandated records versus shorter limits for GDPR-covered personal data—can be operationalized through data zoning within audit document systems. While no case law explicitly refers to "geo-fencing in audits," the European Data Protection Board stresses that retention must align with the specific purpose and legal obligation, and that personal data should be deleted or anonymized when no longer necessary.[14] Practical guidance further recommends establishing retention schedules by data type or jurisdiction, with automated deletion protocols once limits expire.[15]
2. **Controlled Anonymization and Pseudonymization**
   Apply techniques compliant with ISO/IEC standards to remove or transform personal identifiers—essential for preserving evidentiary integrity under auditing standards like ISA 500. Compliance pitfalls are well-documented, as seen in the *Doe v. Financial Services Ltd* case, where inadequate pseudonymization contributed to GDPR non-compliance findings.
3. **Cross-Entity Contractual Clauses**
   Leverage Binding Corporate Rules (BCRs) or tailored contractual clauses to allocate data retention and access responsibilities in cross-border audit operations. BCRs allow multinational corporate groups to embed internal rules ensuring GDPR-equivalent protection across jurisdictions, thereby enabling differential retention obligations—such as SOX-mandated long-term storage versus GDPR-aligned limited retention—for intra-group audit records. This approach is explicitly supported by the European Data Protection Board's June 2023 Recommendations under Article 47 GDPR, which reaffirm BCRs as the most robust and enforceable mechanism for global personal data transfers, providing both flexibility and legal certainty.[16]
4. **Modular Audit Trails**
   Design modular audit logging systems, segregating personal data from operational log records. This enables compliance with GDPR Article 15—permitting data subject access—without disclosing proprietary audit methodologies mandated by ISA 700. While no specific standard currently prescribes "module-based audit zoning," this architecture aligns with BSI's emerging certification frameworks,

particularly BS ISO/IEC 42006:2025, which mandates transparency, independence, and structured auditing procedures for AI management systems.[17]

5. **Proactive Compliance Engagement**

   Develop internal AI audit protocols and submit these for pre-deployment review with regulators. While specific published cases are limited, this mirrors broader best practices promoted within regulatory guidance and emerging standards.

   When integrated into an AI Management System (AIMS) compliant with ISO/IEC 42001, these strategies can optimize compliance while reducing litigation risk and operational delays.

12.2.5 Regulatory actors and oversight mechanisms

Key oversight entities include:

- **European AI Office**—Coordinates AI Act implementation and may issue sector-specific guidance.
- **PCAOB**—Oversees U.S. public company audits and indirectly shapes AI audit practices.
- **IAASB**—Sets global auditing standards and integrates technology-specific considerations.

The absence of a unified global standard underscores the urgency of regulatory harmonization and cross-border cooperation, a theme developed in Section 6.

12.3 REAL-WORLD FAILURES AND COMPLIANCE CONTROVERSIES

Despite the rapid maturation of legal and professional frameworks, empirical studies continue to document operational failures and compliance breakdowns in AI-enabled audit workflows. These breakdowns are recurrently linked to poor data quality, algorithmic bias and opacity, and weaknesses in governance and human oversight—fault lines that can impair audit quality and erode regulatory trust if left unremedied.[18][19]

12.3.1 Over-flagging of legitimate transactions

A persistent operational challenge in AI auditing is the generation of false positives, where legitimate transactions are incorrectly flagged due to biased or incomplete training datasets. For example, AI systems trained predominantly on fraud patterns from high-risk regions may disproportionately flag routine reimbursements from specific jurisdictions. Empirical studies confirm this risk: fraud detection models suffer from class imbalance and bias, especially when datasets reflect skewed distributions or omit contextual diversity, leading to elevated false-positive rates in certain demographic or geographic groups.[20] Without sufficient fairness audits and post-deployment testing, such models can delay processing, undermine trust, and damage reputations.[21]

Such failures highlight the necessity of periodic model recalibration and pre-deployment bias audits, consistent with recommendations under the EU AI Act (Art. 15) and ISO/IEC 24027:2021 on bias in AI systems.[22]

12.3.2 Litigation and reputational harm from erroneous fraud flags

The legal consequences of flawed AI audit outputs can be severe. Consider a hypothetical scenario where a client is misclassified as high-risk by an AI fraud detection model, leading to service suspension and reputational injury. If no meaningful human review mechanism is provided, such practices would contravene GDPR fairness and transparency obligations. Although not an audit case, CNIL v. Clearview AI (2022)[23] illustrates how opaque large-scale automated systems can trigger significant sanctions where transparency and fairness obligations are unmet. The €20 million fine imposed by the French data protection authority underscores the regulatory and reputational risks of deploying AI without adequate oversight, fairness safeguards, or cooperation with regulators. The case underscores the dual exposure—civil liability and regulatory sanctions—that can arise when algorithmic systems operate without adequate oversight.

12.3.3 Blockchain audit evidence rejected in court

Blockchain-based audit trails are often promoted for record integrity, yet admissibility and probative weight remain uneven across Chinese courts. Since 2018, the Internet Courts have admitted blockchain to prove the authenticity of electronic data only if pre-link (pre-chain) provenance and the collection process are reviewable, not presumed. The Supreme People's Court codified this in its Provisions on Several Issues Related to the Trial of Cases by the Internet Courts (2018), which in Article 11 requires judges to review the creation, collection, storage, and transfer of electronic data, and allows blockchain to be considered only when combined with reliable signatures, timestamps, or trusted storage systems.[24]

Recent empirical analysis confirms that blockchain evidence in China continues to face "insufficient and unstable credibility," "gaps in original-rights confirmation," and "imperfect evidentiary rules," underscoring that immutability alone does not guarantee admissibility or weight in court.[25]

12.3.4 The 2022 supplier risk scoring controversy

A widely cited compliance failure occurred in 2022 when a global manufacturing group adopted an AI-driven supplier risk-scoring model. The system aggregated multiple inputs—credit ratings, litigation history, anomaly-detection flags—but overweighted minor administrative penalties and stale compliance alerts, inflating scores for several long-standing suppliers and prompting terminations. The resulting arbitrations alleged wrongful termination and breach of contractual good faith. Post-mortems showed there were no explainability protocols and no human-in-the-loop checks—controls now required for high-risk AI under the EU AI Act: Article 13 mandates transparency and user instructions enabling correct interpretation of outputs, while Article 14 requires human oversight to prevent or minimize risks in use.[26]

Conceptually, the episode also matches the academic finding that risk-scoring systems face inherent fairness trade-offs; except in special cases, you cannot simultaneously satisfy key fairness criteria (calibration and error-rate balance), so mis-calibration or group-level error asymmetries are structurally likely unless governance and monitoring are robust.[27]

12.3.5 Cross-cutting lessons for oversight

From these cases, several governance imperatives emerge:

1. **Pre-Deployment Validation**—AI auditing tools must undergo documented bias, accuracy, and proportionality testing prior to rollout, consistent with ISO/IEC 23894:2023 on AI risk management.[28]
2. **Continuous Post-Market Monitoring**—Model drift, bias re-emergence, and accuracy degradation must be monitored in compliance with AI Act Art. 61 obligations.[29]
3. **Human Oversight Safeguards**—In line with GDPR Art. 22, significant automated audit decisions must remain subject to informed human intervention and avenues for contestation.
4. **Forensic-Grade Evidence Assurance**—Blockchain or other digital ledgers used as evidence must satisfy jurisdiction-specific authentication and certification requirements.

These failures illustrate that technological capability cannot substitute for governance discipline. A resilient AI auditing framework requires explainability-by-design, ethical risk controls, and internationally harmonized oversight mechanisms, themes expanded in Sections 5 and 6.

12.4 ALGORITHMIC TRANSPARENCY, EXPLAINABLE AI, AND ENFORCEMENT

The integration of AI into auditing amplifies a structural tension between technological sophistication and regulatory intelligibility. High-performing machine learning architectures—particularly deep neural networks and ensemble models—frequently operate as *black boxes*, generating outputs whose internal decision pathways are opaque not only to external regulators but often to the model developers themselves.[30] In high-stakes financial assurance, this opacity directly undermines the verifiability, contestability, and evidentiary robustness of audit outcomes, thereby engaging statutory rights to explanation under Article 22 of the General Data Protection Regulation (GDPR)[31] and triggering transparency obligations for high-risk AI systems under Articles 13 and 23 of the EU AI Act.[32]

12.4.1 Technical approaches to explainability

Addressing the interpretability gap in AI-assisted auditing has spurred the adoption of explainable AI (XAI) methodologies capable of operational deployment in assurance contexts:

- **SHAP (Shapley Additive Explanations)**—Quantifies each input variable's marginal contribution to a prediction, enabling both *global* and *local* interpretability. In audit anomaly detection, SHAP can reveal whether features such as vendor location or invoice timing disproportionately influenced a risk flag.[33]
- **LIME (Local Interpretable Model-Agnostic Explanations)**—Generates simplified surrogate models for specific predictions, providing human-readable approximations of algorithmic reasoning around flagged transactions.[34]
- **Model Cards**—Structured disclosures detailing a model's intended use, performance metrics, limitations, and ethical considerations, thereby standardizing information provided to clients and regulators.[35]
- **Interpretability Reports**—Comprehensive dossiers—potentially mandated by regulators—containing the model's architecture, training data provenance, pre-processing methods, and known biases or limitations.

When integrated systematically into the audit lifecycle, these tools enhance traceability and safeguard due process by enabling stakeholders to interrogate the reasoning behind automated outputs (Table 12.2).

As outlined in—Comparative Compliance Matrix: Audit Phases and Regulatory Tensions, transparency and accountability obligations often collide with confidentiality, data minimization, and retention requirements in AI-assisted audits. The measurement metrics presented in—Measurement Metrics for Explainable AI Techniques and Regulatory Anchors provide a practical bridge between these potentially conflicting frameworks.

- For example, in the *Reporting* phase (Table 2.4), GDPR Art. 15's data access rights may reveal proprietary methodologies. By applying Model Cards with a completeness index and Modular Audit Trails (see Box 2.4), auditors can offer sufficient transparency to meet AI Act Art. 13 obligations without disclosing sensitive algorithms.

Table 12.2 Measurement metrics for explainable AI techniques and regulatory anchors

XAI technique	*Measurement metric*	*Regulatory or scholarly anchor*
SHAP	Feature attribution stability across model runs	SHAP quantifies each feature's contribution and provides global interpretability via consistent explanations across runs—a recognized interpretability tool for regulatory compliance
LIME	Local fidelity score comparing surrogate to original model	LIME offers local fidelity explanations, approximating the decision logic of complex models—commonly used to validate explanation fidelity in XAI frameworks
Model Cards	Completeness index covering performance, bias statements, and limitations	Model Cards provide structured transparency (intended use, performance, limitations) and align with requirements for AI governance and clarity as encouraged by ISO/IEC 42001
Interpretability Reports	Time-to-comprehend metric for domain experts	Rapid interpretation supports procedural transparency and human oversight—key obligations under the EU AI Act and part of AI governance best practices as covered by ISO 42001 frameworks

- In the *Post-Audit Monitoring* phase, the SHAP stability score and LIME local fidelity metrics serve as verifiable indicators that explanation quality is being maintained, satisfying AI Act Art. 15 and GDPR Art. 22's requirements for meaningful human oversight.
- The Interpretability Report's time-to-understand metric supports regulators' demands for comprehensible documentation (AI Act Art. 23) while aligning with ISA 700's clarity standards.

By linking each identified conflict in §2.4 with measurable XAI performance indicators in §4.1, auditors can create an integrated compliance assurance framework that not only satisfies cross-jurisdictional mandates but also strengthens evidentiary defensibility in case of dispute.

12.4.2 Regulatory enforcement mechanisms

From a compliance and enforcement standpoint, explainability is not optional—it is a mandate for accountability. As the EU AI Act enshrines, XAI is a core requirement for high-risk AI systems, ensuring transparency and human oversight in regulated domains. Similarly, financial services regulators and institutional stakeholders recognize explainable AI as essential for compliance, ethical governance, and stakeholder trust.[36] Current and emerging mechanisms include:

1. **Mandatory Explainability Disclosures**—Under the AI Act, providers of high-risk AI systems must furnish sufficient documentation to enable regulatory and operational oversight, which may include standardized feature-attribution reports and algorithmic logic summaries.

2. **Regulator Access to Algorithmic Logs**—Some jurisdictions are legislating direct access rights for audit regulators to algorithmic decision logs, drawing parallels with electronic discovery protocols in litigation.[37]
3. **Post-Market Surveillance**—Continuous performance monitoring of deployed AI systems, with mandatory reporting of accuracy drift, emergent bias, or security vulnerabilities, reflecting the *life-cycle governance* model endorsed in the AI Act.[38]

These mechanisms aim to bridge the accountability gap between AI system developers, audit practitioners, and oversight bodies, ensuring that *opacity by design* does not erode regulatory control.

12.4.3 AI in fraud detection: Promise and constraints

Fraud detection represents a flagship application of AI in auditing, leveraging advanced statistical and computational methods:

- **Benford's Law Analysis**—Detects anomalies in the frequency distribution of leading digits, with AI-enhanced models identifying subtle deviations at scale.[39]
- **Graph Analytics**—Maps complex transactional relationships to reveal collusion or money-laundering networks.
- **Unsupervised Clustering**—Groups transactions to identify statistical outliers without pre-labeled fraud data, enabling detection of novel fraud patterns.

AI Models for Fraud Detection and Compliance Challenges

1. **Graph Neural Networks (GNNs)**
   GNNs model financial transactions as structured graphs, uncovering hidden dependencies—like fraud rings and synthetic identity fraud—that traditional models may miss. They can outperform ensemble methods in recall and accuracy.
   - **Compliance Challenge:** Processing relational data may conflict with GDPR's data minimization principle (Art. 5), requiring careful governance of personal connection data.[40]
2. **Temporal Anomaly Detectors (e.g., LSTM, RNN)**
   These deep learning models flag irregular sequences or behavioral drift over time, enhancing real-time fraud detection.[41]
   - **Compliance Challenge:** Under the AI Act, systems must proactively manage risks like temporal drift; thus, deploying such models demands robust risk monitoring frameworks.
3. **Hybrid Human–AI Fraud Review Systems**
   Combining automated pre-screening with human auditor oversight aligns detection efficiency with regulatory trust requirements. Human intervention mitigates false positives and supports explainability.[42]

Table 12.3 AI Models for fraud detection and associated compliance challenges

AI model	*Fraud detection capability*	*Regulatory compliance challenge*	*Relevant framework/source*
Graph Neural Networks (GNNs)	Detect hidden fraud patterns in transactional graphs—fraud rings, synthetic identities	Risk of excessive relational data processing, potentially conflicting with GDPR Art. 5 (data minimization)	Demonstrated enhanced fraud detection accuracy in fintech—GNNs outperform traditional models
Temporal Anomaly Detectors (LSTM, RNN)	Identify irregular temporal sequences and flag evolving fraud behaviors over time	Must comply with AI Act's risk management for drift detection and performance monitoring	AI Act mandates continuous monitoring of high-risk AI systems
Hybrid Human–AI Review Systems	Blend automated screening with human oversight to reduce false positives and improve audit quality	SOX §404 requires thorough documentation of overrides and control adjustments following human judgment	SOX compliance depends on detailed documentation of control interventions

- **Compliance Challenge:** SOX requires documentation of internal control overrides; audit teams must thoroughly record human actions on AI-flagged alerts, which increases documentation burden and audit trail complexity (Table 12.3) (Figure 12.1).

Yet these capabilities must align with proportionality under GDPR Article 5(1)(c) and evidentiary admissibility standards under applicable procedural

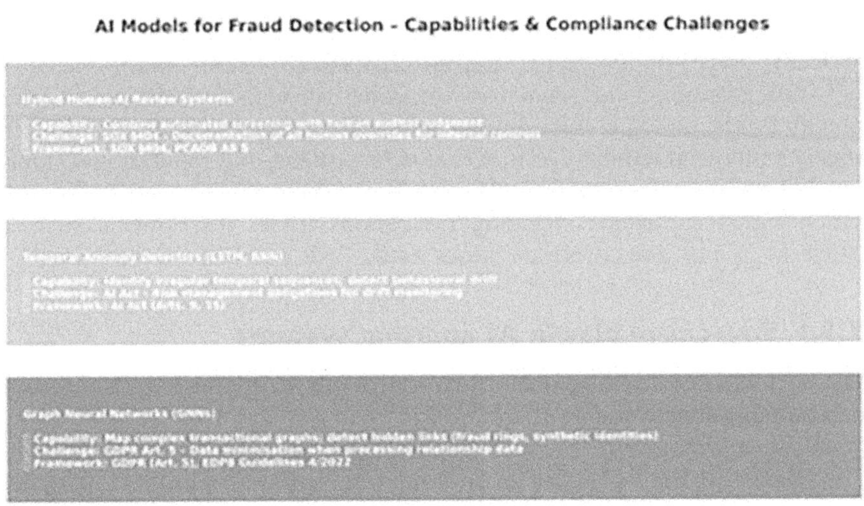

Figure 12.1 AI models for fraud detection—capabilities and compliance challenges.

laws. Courts may reject AI-generated fraud evidence if methodologies lack transparency or scientific validation, as seen in disputes over algorithmic risk scoring in criminal justice and in academic calls for heightened judicial gatekeeping to protect proceedings from technological fakery.[43]

12.4.4 Case illustration: Regulator intervention in an anomaly detection dispute

In 2023, a European audit firm deployed a proprietary AI anomaly detection tool that flagged high-value transactions based on a weighted interaction of vendor identifiers, transaction timing, and cross-border routing. Upon challenge, the firm was unable to produce an explanation satisfying regulatory transparency requirements. The national financial supervisor ordered the suspension of the system pending an independent *transparency audit.* This intervention underscored the regulatory expectation that AI-assisted audit decisions be intelligible to independent oversight authorities, not merely to their operators.[44]

In summary, algorithmic transparency in AI-enabled auditing is both a technical imperative and a regulatory mandate. Without enforceable explainability standards, the evidentiary legitimacy and public trust in AI-generated audit findings remain vulnerable to legal contestation, ethical critique, and market skepticism.

12.5 ETHICAL RISKS, BIAS, AND FAIRNESS IN AI AUDITING

The deployment of AI in auditing raises complex ethical, distributive justice, and human rights concerns. While AI systems can substantially improve audit efficiency, scope, and precision, they also risk *encoding* and *amplifying* existing social, economic, and regulatory inequities through their design, training data, and decision logic. In auditing—where algorithmic outputs can directly influence financial liability, contractual enforcement, and reputational standing—bias is not a mere *technical defect* but a governance, compliance, and human rights challenge, engaging obligations under instruments such as Article 14 ECHR and corporate duties under CSR and ESG frameworks.[45]

12.5.1 Sources of bias in AI auditing systems

Bias in AI-assisted auditing is multifactorial, often stemming from interlinked and compounding vectors:

1. **Historical Bias**—Present in training datasets that reproduce past discriminatory practices or structural inequities, resulting in the perpetuation of outdated risk classifications.

2. **Dataset Composition Bias**—Arising from over- or under-representation of specific sectors, geographies, or transaction patterns, skewing anomaly detection thresholds.

Systemic Bias—These biases can arise from embedded assumptions in organizational policies, regulatory frameworks, and design choices—such as variable weighting, risk thresholds, and exclusion criteria. The importance of addressing such bias across the full AI lifecycle is recognized by ISO/IEC TR 24027:2021, which offers a comprehensive methodological framework for identifying, measuring, and mitigating bias in AI systems from data collection through deployment and beyond.[46]

12.5.2 Impacts on distributive justice and corporate fairness

When bias becomes operationalized in AI audit tools, it can distort resource allocation, scrutiny intensity, and compliance risk profiles:

- **Small and Medium-Sized Enterprises (SMEs)**—Over-flagging due to lower historical transaction volumes and higher operational variability, interpreted by algorithms as irregularity.
- **Geographic Disadvantage**—Misclassification of legitimate region-specific practices as anomalies where training datasets underrepresent those jurisdictions.
- **Sectoral Discrimination**—Disproportionate attention to industries with regulatory complexity, triggered by the over-weighting of sector-specific risk indicators.

Such effects intersect with the prohibition of discrimination in Article 14 ECHR and corporate obligations under OECD Guidelines for Multinational Enterprises, underscoring that bias in AI auditing is a compliance and equity issue, not solely a technical one.[47]

Quantitative Illustration

While detailed internal audit cases with exact performance metrics are rarely made public, research and regulatory reports consistently show that algorithmic bias can generate measurable operational and financial harm.

- **False Positives in AI-Enabled Controls:** In fraud detection or expense monitoring systems, biased algorithms can significantly increase false positives. This overloads exception-handling processes, undermines trust in internal audit functions, and may escalate into reputational damage or breaches of contractual obligations (cf. ICO, *Guidance on AI and Data Protection*, 2023).

- **Financial Stability Risks Flagged by the Bank of England:** The Bank of England has warned that biased or poorly calibrated AI models, particularly when embedded in risk-sensitive decision-making, could expose institutions to legal challenges, financial redress, or systemic instability. Its Financial Policy Committee specifically highlighted "herding risks" where multiple actors adopt similarly flawed AI models, amplifying shocks and potentially undermining market resilience (BoE, *Financial Stability in Focus*, 2025).
- **Regulatory Oversight and Accountability (ICO):** The UK Information Commissioner's Office underscores that biased AI outcomes often stem from flawed datasets or inappropriate model design. Such flaws directly compromise fairness, accountability, and compliance with GDPR principles. The ICO now requires organizations to document bias-testing within Data Protection Impact Assessments (DPIAs) and to establish mitigation strategies before deploying AI in audit or HR contexts (ICO, *AI and Data Protection Toolkit*, 2023).

These insights support a hypothetical yet plausible scenario to illustrate the stakes. For instance, imagine an internal audit's AI-driven expense model shows a 15% increase in false positives due to geographic bias. This surge in exceptions leads to a downgrade of the organization's internal control rating from *"Satisfactory"* to *"Needs Improvement."* The downgrade, in turn, violates a loan covenant, automatically triggering a 50-basis-point interest rate hike.

Although hypothetical, this scenario demonstrates how algorithmic bias can cascade from technical error to regulatory downgrade, financial penalty, and reputational risk—transforming a design flaw into a material threat to corporate governance and financial stability.

12.5.3 Mitigation strategies

Effective bias mitigation in AI auditing requires multi-layered governance integrating technical safeguards, procedural controls, and independent oversight:

- **Algorithmic Bias Audits**—Periodic, independent evaluations to detect and quantify disparate impacts across legally protected categories and operational segments (in line with OECD calls for auditability, traceability, and accountability).
- **Synthetic Data Balancing**—Augmentation of underrepresented categories to enhance model representativeness—while fully respecting GDPR's data minimization and purpose limitation principles (Arts. 5 and 6).
- **Periodic Fairness Assessments**—Embedding fairness KPIs into ongoing performance monitoring to detect bias drift over time, echoing OECD's lifecycle risk-governance approach.

- **Independent Ethics Boards**—Oversight structures (internal or external) tasked with reviewing design choices, deployment contexts, and socio-economic impacts from both ethical and legal standpoints, consistent with OECD and UNESCO emphasis on human oversight and stakeholder involvement.

International instruments such as the OECD Council Recommendation on Artificial Intelligence (2019, updated) and the UNESCO Recommendation on the Ethics of Artificial Intelligence (2021) underscore that fairness must be operationalized through measurable, enforceable, and audited practices, not remain aspirational policy statements.

12.6 STANDARDS, NORMATIVE FRAMEWORKS, AND GLOBAL HARMONIZATION

The regulatory landscape governing AI-assisted auditing has moved beyond a fragmented and unstructured policy space. It is increasingly shaped by a consolidated corpus of technical standards, professional guidance, and soft-law instruments developed by intergovernmental organizations, supranational regulators, and industry bodies.

This emerging architecture fulfills two interrelated functions. First, it seeks to guarantee the trustworthiness, auditability, and ethical alignment of AI systems by embedding principles of transparency, accountability, and human oversight into their design and use.[48] Second, it provides the foundation for cross-border interoperability, a necessity in an environment where corporate audits, financial reporting, and data flows are inherently transnational.[49]

12.6.1 Key international standards and frameworks

12.6.1.1 ISO/IEC 42001—AI management systems

Published in 2023, ISO/IEC 42001 establishes the requirements for an Artificial Intelligence Management System (AIMS), providing organizations with a structured framework to implement, maintain, and continuously improve AI governance. It emphasizes transparency, ethical compliance, and robust risk management in AI operations.[50]

12.6.1.2 ISO/IEC 42006—Certification bodies

Complementing ISO/IEC 42001, ISO/IEC 42006 specifies the competence and independence requirements for third-party bodies certifying AIMS. It builds on ISO/IEC 17021-1 and ensures that certification processes are credible and consistent, thereby reinforcing trust in AI audit assurance globally.[51]

12.6.1.3 EDPB guidance and DPA toolkits for AI audits

The European Data Protection Board (EDPB) provides GDPR guidance that underpins AI audit practices (e.g., Data Protection by Design and by Default), and—together with the European Data Protection Supervisor (EDPS)—has issued joint opinions on the EU AI Act clarifying transparency, oversight, and documentation expectations for high-risk AI systems. In parallel, national data protection authorities offer practical, audit-ready tools: the UK ICO's AI Auditing Framework and AI & Data Protection Risk Toolkit operationalize GDPR principles for lifecycle assessments; France's CNIL provides self-assessment guidance and DPIA expectations for AI (with a presumption of DPIA for high-risk AI); and Spain's AEPD has issued requirements for audits of processing that include AI. Together, these sources form a de facto toolbox for regulators and practitioners to evaluate privacy, bias controls, model governance, and traceability across the AI lifecycle.[52]

12.6.1.4 IIA AI auditing framework

The Institute of Internal Auditors (IIA) offers an updated AI Auditing Framework (2023–2024) aimed at internal auditors navigating evolving AI technologies. The framework supports AI risk identification, control design, performance monitoring, and integrates within the Three Lines Model and broader risk management principles.[53]

12.6.1.5 BSI AI assurance standard (2025)

In mid-2025, the British Standards Institution (BSI) published a comprehensive AI Assurance Standard to credential bodies auditing AI governance. It addresses quality control, independence, and mitigates the risk of unregulated "wild-west" assurance practices—calling for consistent, credible auditing of AI systems.[54]

12.6.2 Comparative governance models

- **European Union—Precautionary Principle**
  The EU's AI regulatory framework exemplifies an *ex ante* model: high-risk AI systems must undergo conformity assessments and fulfill comprehensive documentation requirements before they are placed on the market. This ensures preventive risk mitigation and aligns with the precautionary principle.[55]
- **United States—Market-Led Model**
  In contrast, the U.S. currently lacks overarching federal AI legislation. Regulation relies instead on sector-specific laws—such as the Sarbanes–Oxley Act for financial governance—and a patchwork of voluntary or industry-driven standards.[56]

- **Asia—Hybrid Systems**
  Jurisdictions like Singapore and Japan are deploying regulatory sandboxes alongside emerging statutory frameworks. This hybrid model balances innovation and experimentation with proportionate safeguards for high-risk AI applications.[57]

12.6.3 International collaboration as a foundation for harmonization

Given the fragmented global regulatory landscape, adopting a phased harmonization strategy is critical for reducing jurisdictional friction and enhancing consistency in assurance practices. The following developments illustrate how emerging collaborations and frameworks can inform the regulation of AI-assisted auditing:

- **IFRS Foundation:** The International Financial Reporting Standards (IFRS) Foundation is exploring how AI impacts audit methodologies and financial reporting practices, signaling integration of AI considerations into its standard-setting functions.[58]
- **EU–Japan Digital Partnership:** Established in 2022 and reaffirmed in recent councils, this partnership fosters regulatory alignment in areas such as AI governance, conformity assessment, data governance, and sandboxing—laying the groundwork for mutual recognition mechanisms.[59]
- **OECD Classification Framework:** The OECD's *Framework for the Classification of AI Systems* provides shared concepts and metadata structures that can serve as interoperable benchmarks for audit standards globally.[60]
- **IFAC Platforms:** Organizations under the International Federation of Accountants (IFAC), including the Forum of Firms and the Public Interest Oversight Board, facilitate global alignment on audit integrity, quality control, and transnational assurance consistency.[61]

Proposed Phased Roadmap:

1. **Bilateral Mutual Recognition Agreements:** Encouraging regulatory authorities to recognize each other's conformity assessments and certifications for AI audit tools, particularly across aligned jurisdictions.
2. **Multilateral Technical Interoperability Standards:** Developing shared metadata schemas and classification frameworks for AI audit outputs, as informed by the OECD.
3. **Transnational AI Audit Cooperation Platform:** Establishing a global oversight forum—potentially under IFAC's coordination or through an extended Forum of Firms mechanism—to harmonize certification, enforcement, and best practices in AI auditing.

Implementing this roadmap could reduce jurisdictional friction, foster audit quality, and reinforce trust in automated assurance systems.

1. **Mutual Recognition of Certifications**
   - Negotiate treaties or MoUs between competent authorities to recognize ISO/IEC 42001 and ISO/IEC 42006 certifications across jurisdictions.
   - Reduce duplicative compliance costs for multinational enterprises.
2. **Standardization of AI Audit Metadata**
   - Develop interoperable metadata schemas for AI audit outputs, enabling cross-border comparability and validation.
   - Engage the International Auditing and Assurance Standards Board (IAASB) and the OECD in defining common technical formats.
3. **Joint Dispute Resolution Bodies**
   - Establish cross-jurisdictional arbitration panels, potentially under the International Federation of Accountants (IFAC), to adjudicate disputes over AI audit results or certification validity.

12.6.4 Strategic significance

The convergence of technical standards and regulatory frameworks can generate network effects that simultaneously increase trust in AI auditing and reduce compliance barriers for cross-border operations. However, harmonization must avoid regulatory dilution—global frameworks must preserve substantive safeguards on transparency, bias mitigation, and human oversight, ensuring that efficiency gains do not compromise rights protection or audit integrity.

12.7 GOVERNANCE AND POLICY RECOMMENDATIONS

The foregoing analysis demonstrates that effective regulation of AI-assisted auditing requires a dual-layer governance model. At the macro-institutional level, oversight mechanisms must ensure both regulatory legitimacy and cross-jurisdictional coherence. At the micro-professional level, audit practices must embed enforceable ethical principles and operational safeguards into their day-to-day functioning.

This section translates the comparative models outlined above into immediately actionable policy instruments, offering concrete pathways for regulators, professional bodies, and audit firms to operationalize trustworthy, transparent, and sustainable AI-assisted auditing practices.

12.7.1 Institutional architecture: AI audit standards board

A cornerstone of the proposed governance framework is the establishment of an AI Audit Standards Board (AIASB). This body would ideally operate under the aegis of the International Federation of Accountants (IFAC) or the International Auditing and Assurance Standards Board (IAASB), thereby benefiting from existing legitimacy and global recognition within the auditing profession.

Its statutory and normative mandate would encompass three principal functions:

- **Certification Oversight**—Accrediting AI audit tools and methodologies, with explicit alignment to emerging international benchmarks such as ISO/IEC 42001 (AI management systems) and ISO/IEC 42006 (auditing AI systems).
- **Enforcement Coordination**—Facilitating harmonized enforcement across jurisdictions to reduce regulatory fragmentation and strengthen consistency in cross-border audit practices.
- **Capacity-Building**—Developing technical guidance, training curricula, and accredited professional programs for regulators, auditors, and corporate compliance officers, drawing on IAASB standards and OECD best practices.

By institutionalizing these functions, the AIASB would provide a centralized, authoritative platform for certifying audit technologies, ensuring global coherence in their deployment, and equipping professionals with the skills necessary to navigate the ethical and operational complexities of AI-assisted auditing.

12.7.2 Regulatory measures

Building on the Basel Committee on Banking Supervision's Principles for the Use of AI in Financial Services and the IAASB's Technology Consultation Papers, regulators should translate high-level guidance into binding regulatory instruments. These instruments would operationalize accountability, reduce systemic risk, and align AI-assisted auditing with established principles of financial governance and professional ethics.

Key measures include:

1. **Mandatory Registration of AI Audit Tools**—All AI systems deployed in statutory or compliance audits must be registered with the competent supervisory authority. Registration should be accompanied by complete technical documentation, including model architecture, training data provenance, and governance safeguards.
2. **High-Risk AI Certification**—Systems falling within the "high-risk" classification of the EU AI Act or equivalent regimes should be subject to ex ante certification. This process must involve independent assessments of transparency, explainability, and bias mitigation mechanisms before deployment.

3. **Periodic Third-Party Bias and Transparency Audits**—Independent, accredited auditors should perform recurring evaluations of bias, fairness, explainability, and performance at clearly defined intervals, ensuring continued compliance and trustworthiness.
4. **Mandatory Liability Clauses**—Contracts between audit firms and AI vendors should explicitly define the allocation of liability for harms caused by system malfunction, discriminatory outputs, or breaches of regulatory obligations.
5. **Regulatory Sandboxes**—Supervisory authorities should establish controlled experimentation environments that allow innovation in AI audit solutions, while embedding safeguards for fundamental rights, market integrity, and public trust.

Taken together, these measures would ensure that the adoption of AI in auditing is not only legally compliant but also ethically sustainable, balancing innovation with robust protection mechanisms.

12.7.3 Professional practice recommendations

In parallel with public regulation, professional self-governance within audit firms must ensure that AI ethics and compliance become integral to organizational culture and day-to-day audit practice. This requires embedding ethical standards, risk management protocols, and continuous learning into the professional infrastructure of auditing.

Key recommendations include:

- **Integration of AI Ethics into Internal Audit Functions**—Audit firms should adopt formal ethical guidelines aligned with the OECD AI Principles and the UNESCO Recommendation on the Ethics of AI (2021). These frameworks provide a normative foundation for fairness, accountability, transparency, and human-centered governance of AI systems.
- **Vendor Due Diligence**—Before entering contractual relationships, audit firms should conduct rigorous pre-contractual assessments of AI vendors. This process should cover the provenance and quality of training data, security and privacy safeguards, and documented results of prior bias or stress testing. Such due diligence ensures that external technological dependencies do not compromise audit integrity.
- **Continuous Professional Training**—Auditors should be required to undertake mandatory continuing education in AI risk management, bias mitigation strategies, and regulatory developments. This commitment to professional development ensures that audit practitioners maintain the expertise needed to assess and govern evolving AI technologies effectively.

By embedding these practices, audit firms not only mitigate ethical and operational risks but also demonstrate credibility and resilience in a rapidly changing digital audit environment.

12.7.4 Implementation roadmap and evidence-based checklist

To operationalize the proposed governance framework, a two-tier approach is necessary. First, regulators and audit firms require a strategic roadmap that identifies priority areas for action. Second, these priorities must be translated into an evidence-based checklist, anchored in international standards and regulatory guidance, to ensure operational feasibility and verifiable compliance.

12.7.4.1 Strategic roadmap

For Regulators:

- Establish an AI Audit Standards Board (AIASB) or equivalent oversight authority to set and enforce global audit norms.
- Mandate registration and disclosure of all AI audit tools, supported by detailed technical documentation.
- Require certification of high-risk AI systems, ensuring independent pre-deployment evaluation of transparency, explainability, and bias mitigation.
- Enforce periodic third-party bias and transparency audits conducted by accredited, independent bodies.
- Deploy regulatory sandboxes that allow supervised experimentation with innovative AI audit applications, while safeguarding rights and market integrity.

For Audit Firms:

- Integrate AI ethics into audit methodologies, embedding fairness, accountability, and transparency principles into internal processes.
- Conduct comprehensive vendor due diligence, covering data provenance, security safeguards, and bias testing outcomes.
- Implement continuous training programs on AI governance, risk management, and regulatory developments for all auditing professionals.
- Create internal protocols for algorithmic bias detection and mitigation, ensuring systematic identification and remediation of risks.
- Maintain auditable documentation of all AI-related processes, ensuring traceability and readiness for regulatory inspection.

12.7.4.2 Evidence-based checklist

Building on the roadmap above, the following evidence-based checklist refines these recommendations into concrete, auditable measures aligned with global standards:

For Regulators:

- Mandate public disclosure of AI audit tools and methodologies, enabling peer review, regulatory oversight, and accountability.
- Require certification of high-risk AI systems prior to deployment, reflecting the EU AI Act and ISO/IEC 42001 assurance frameworks.
- Standardize bias and transparency audit protocols under ISO/IEC 42001 and ISO/IEC 42006 to ensure cross-border audit readiness.
- Ensure retention of human oversight logs for inspection, in line with post-market monitoring duties and accountability obligations.
- Deploy regulatory sandboxes modeled on fintech experimentation to balance innovation with rights protection.

For Audit Firms:

- Implement vendor due diligence templates with documented bias testing, data provenance checks, and security posture reviews.
- Maintain regulator-ready documentation of all AI-assisted audit processes, consistent with conformity assessment obligations.
- Integrate fairness KPIs into audit dashboards to monitor transparency, explainability, and ethical performance across the AI lifecycle.
- Train audit staff on AI governance and bias mitigation, reinforcing professional competence and compliance capacity.
- Develop internal protocols for algorithmic bias detection and remediation, drawing on the OECD AI Principles and UNESCO's Ethics of AI Recommendation.

By distinguishing between a high-level implementation roadmap and a refined evidence-based checklist, this section bridges the gap between strategic ambition and operational feasibility. Regulators gain clear priorities for building governance infrastructures, while audit firms receive practical tools to institutionalize AI ethics, transparency, and bias mitigation. Together, these measures provide a structured pathway from policy design to daily practice, ensuring that AI-assisted auditing evolves as both a legally compliant and ethically sustainable discipline.

The following conclusion synthesizes these findings, situating them within broader trajectories of legal harmonization, ethical governance, and technical innovation.

It projects how these integrated measures can mature into globally interoperable AI auditing regimes, reshaping financial integrity governance by 2035.

12.8 CONCLUSION

The analysis shows that AI in auditing is not a mere technological upgrade but a structural transformation of financial-integrity governance. AI-assisted auditing sits at the intersection of legal compliance, ethical accountability, and technical innovation—offering efficiency and coverage gains while introducing systemic and rights-based risks of unusual complexity.

Legally, obligations arising from the EU AI Act, the GDPR, SOX, and the ISAs create overlapping—and at times conflicting—compliance demands for multinational engagements, especially around data governance, retention, and evidentiary standards. Ethically, the risks of bias, opacity, and unequal burden are significant: without fairness audits and explainability obligations, certain sectors, geographies, or smaller enterprises can be disproportionately scrutinized, undermining distributive justice and trust. Operationally, explainable-AI techniques (e.g., SHAP, LIME, Model Cards) are essential but only effective when embedded in enforceable governance frameworks, supported by post-market monitoring and meaningful human oversight; advanced detection methods must also satisfy proportionality and evidentiary requirements.

The chapter therefore advocates adaptive, risk-calibrated, ethics-anchored ecosystems that couple macro-level institutional oversight with micro-level professional self-regulation, grounded in internationally recognized standards and coordinated enforcement. Looking ahead, three developments merit sustained attention: (i) continuous AI auditing with parallel oversight; (ii) self-auditing AI agents that shift human roles toward meta-assurance; and (iii) transnational regulatory alliances capable of harmonizing standards and coordinating enforcement.

A plausible 2035 horizon is one of interoperable AI auditing regimes that automate cross-border compliance verification without sacrificing rights protection or audit integrity. The integrated roadmap and evidence-based checklist presented herein bridge ambition and feasibility by translating normative demands into implementable controls for regulators and practitioners. Sustained collaboration among legal scholars, technologists, ethicists, regulators, and audit professionals is the condition for turning AI-assisted auditing into a transparent, equitable, and accountable infrastructure of global financial governance.

NOTES

1 Michael G Alles, "Drivers of the Use and Facilitators and Obstacles of the Evolution of Big Data by the Audit Profession" (2015) 29 *Accounting Horizons* 439.

2 Muh. Ardiansyah Syam, Syahril Djaddang, Hasnawati, Mohammad Roziq, and Harnovinsah, "The Digital Transformation of Auditing: Navigating the Challenges and Opportunities" (2025) 8 *Economics and Business Quarterly Reviews* 2, 49–66. https://doi.org/10.31014/aior.1992.08.02.662.

3 EU COM, "Laying Down Harmonised Rules on Artificial Intelligence (Artificial Intelligence Act) and Amending Certain Union Legislative Acts" [2021] Proposal for a regulation of the European Parliament and of the Council.

4 Protection Regulation, "General Data Protection Regulation" (2018) 25 *Intouch* 1.
5 Ahmed Eltweri, Alessio Faccia, and Scott Foster, "International Standards on Auditing (ISAs) Adoption: An Institutional Perspective" (2022) 12 *Administrative Sciences* 119.
6 Brandon Schweitzer, "Artificial Intelligence (AI) Ethics in Accounting" (2024) 25 *Journal of Accounting, Ethics & Public Policy, JAEPP* 67.
7 Barros Vale, S., & Zanfir-Fortuna, G. (2022). Automated decision-making under the GDPR: Practical cases from courts and Data Protection Authorities. Future of Privacy Forum. Retrieved from https://fpf.org/resource/fpf-report-automated-decision-making-under-the-gdpr-a-comprehensive-case-law-analysis/
8 Martin Ebers, "The European Commission's Proposal for an Artificial Intelligence Act," *Research Handbook on EU Internet Law* (Edward Elgar Publishing 2023).
9 Article 29 Data Protection Working Party, *Guidelines on Automated Individual Decision-Making and Profiling for the Purposes of Regulation 2016/679*, WP251 rev.01 (2018).
10 *PCAOB Updates Its Standards To Clarify Auditor Responsibilities When Using Technology-Assisted Analysis*, PCAOB Release (12 June 2024).
11 IAASB, *ISA 315 (Revised 2019)—Identifying and Assessing the Risks of Material Misstatement* (effective 15 December 2021).
12 IAASB, *Exploring the Growing Use of Technology in the Audit, with a Focus on Data Analytics* (Request for Input, September 2016); IAASB, *Feedback Statement—Exploring the Growing Use of Technology in the Audit, with a Focus on Data Analytics* (January 2018).
13 OCDE, *Cross-border Data Flows: Taking Stock of Key Policies and Initiatives* (OECD Digital Economy Papers No 328, 12 October 2022).
14 EDPB, *Records Management Decision*, 20 September 2023.
15 Data Protection Network, *Data Retention Guidance*, June 2022.
16 EDPB, *Recommendations 1/2022 on the Application for Approval and on the Elements and Principles to Be Found in Controller Binding Corporate Rules (Art. 47 GDPR)* (adopted 20 June 2023) <EDPB document>.
17 British Standards Institution, *BS ISO/IEC 42006:2025 Information technology—Artificial intelligence—Requirements for bodies providing audit and certification of AI management systems* (BSI, 24 July 2025). https://www.bsigroup.com/en-GB/insights-and-media/media-centre/press-releases/2025/july/bsi-publishes-standard-to-ensure-quality-among-growing-ai-audit-market/ accessed 4 September 2025.
18 Wilberforce Murikah, Jeff Kimanga Nthenge, and Faith Mueni Musyoka, "Bias and Ethics of AI Systems Applied in Auditing—A Systematic Review" (2024) 25 *Scientific African* e02281 https://doi.org/10.1016/j.sciaf.2024.e02281
19 I Munoko, HL Brown-Liburd, and M Vasarhelyi, "The Ethical Implications of Using Artificial Intelligence in Auditing" (2020) 167 *Journal of Business Ethics* 209 https://doi.org/10.1007/s10551-019-04407-1
20 Parameswaran Kamalaruban et al., "Evaluating Fairness in Transaction Fraud Models: Fairness Metrics, Bias Audits, and Challenges" (2024) https://arxiv.org/abs/2409.04373 accessed 4 September 2025.
21 Roy Wedge, James Max Kanter, Santiago Moral Rubio et al., "Solving the 'False Positives' Problem in Fraud Prediction" (2017) https://arxiv.org/abs/1710.07709 accessed 4 September 2025.
22 ISO/IEC, *Information technology—Artificial intelligence (AI)—Bias in AI Systems and AI Aided Decision Making* (ISO/IEC 24027:2021, International Organization for Standardization 2021).

23 Commission nationale de l'informatique et des libertés (CNIL), *Sanction of €20 million on Clearview AI* (19 October 2022) — breach of Articles 6, 12, 15, 17, and 31 GDPR, available via European Data Protection Board https://www.edpb.europa.eu/news/national-news/2022/french-sa-fines-clearview-ai-eur-20-million_en accessed 4 September 2025.
24 Supreme People's Court, *Provisions on Several Issues Related to the Trial of Cases by the Internet Courts* (法释 2018 16号), 7 September 2018, English trans. at China Law Translate: https://www.chinalawtranslate.com/en/the-supreme-peoples-courts-provisions-on-several-issues-related-to-trial-of-cases-by-the-internet-courts/
25 Zou, L., and Chen, D. "Using Blockchain Evidence in China's Digital Copyright Legislation to Enhance the Sustainability of Legal Systems" (2024) 12(9) *Systems* 356. https://doi.org/10.3390/systems12090356
26 Regulation (EU) 2024/1689 of the European Parliament and of the Council of 13 June 2024 Laying Down Harmonised Rules on Artificial Intelligence (Artificial Intelligence Act) (2024) OJ L, 1689/1. Available at: https://eur-lex.europa.eu/eli/reg/2024/1689/oj
27 Jon Kleinberg, Sendhil Mullainathan, and Manish Raghavan, "Inherent Trade-Offs in the Fair Determination of Risk Scores" (2017) 67 *Leibniz International Proceedings in Informatics (LIPIcs), Innovations in Theoretical Computer Science (ITCS 2017)* 43:1. https://doi.org/10.4230/LIPIcs.ITCS.2017.43
28 International Organization for Standardization (ISO) and International Electrotechnical Commission (IEC), *ISO/IEC 23894:2023 Information Technology—Artificial Intelligence—Guidance on Risk Management* (ISO/IEC 2023).
29 European Commission, *Proposal for a Regulation of the European Parliament and of the Council Laying Down Harmonised Rules on Artificial Intelligence (Artificial Intelligence Act) COM(2021) 206 final* (21 April 2021), Art 61.
30 Cynthia Rudin, "Stop Explaining Black Box Machine Learning Models for High Stakes Decisions and Use Interpretable Models Instead," *Nature Machine Intelligence*, vol 1 (Nature Publishing Group UK, London 2019), 206–215
31 Regulation (EU) 2016/679 of the European Parliament and of the Council of 27 April 2016 on the protection of natural persons with regard to the processing of personal data and on the free movement of such data (General Data Protection Regulation) (2016) OJ L 119/1.
32 European Commission, *Proposal for a Regulation of the European Parliament and of the Council Laying Down Harmonised Rules on Artificial Intelligence (Artificial Intelligence Act)* COM(2021) 206 final (21 April 2021).
33 Scott M Lundberg and Su-In Lee, "A Unified Approach to Interpreting Model Predictions" in Isabelle Guyon and others (eds), *Advances in Neural Information Processing Systems 30 (NIPS 2017)* (Curran Associates Inc., 2017) 4765.
34 Marco Tulio Ribeiro, Sameer Singh, and Carlos Guestrin, "'Why Should I Trust You?' Explaining the Predictions of Any Classifier," *Proceedings of the 22nd ACM SIGKDD International Conference on Knowledge Discovery and Data Mining* (2016).
35 International Auditing and Assurance Standards Board, *ISA 315 (Revised 2019): Identifying and Assessing the Risks of Material Misstatement* (IAASB, December 2019). https://www.iaasb.org/publications/isa-315-revised-2019-identifying-and-assessing-risks-material-misstatement
36 CFA Institute, *Explainable AI in Finance* (CFA Institute Report, 2025). https://rpc.cfainstitute.org/research/reports/2025/explainable-ai-in-finance accessed 1 September 2025.
37 UK Digital Regulation Cooperation Forum (DRCF), *Auditing Algorithms: The Existing Landscape, Role of Regulators and Future Outlook* (May 2022).

https://www.gov.uk/government/publications/findings-from-the-drcf-algorithmic-processing-workstream-spring-2022/auditing-algorithms-the-existing-landscape-role-of-regulators-and-future-outlook

38 Jakob Mokander, Maria Axente, Federico Casolari, and Luciano Floridi, "Conformity Assessments and Post-Market Monitoring: A Guide to the Role of Auditing in the Proposed European AI Regulation" (2021) *arXiv* https://arxiv.org/abs/2111.05071

39 Tianyi Chen and Charalampos E Tsourakakis, "AntiBenford Subgraphs: Unsupervised Anomaly Detection in Financial Networks" (2022) *arXiv*. https://arxiv.org/abs/2205.13426 accessed 6 September 2025.

40 Diego Vallarino, *AI-Powered Fraud Detection in Financial Services: GNN, Compliance Challenges, and Risk Mitigation* (SSRN, 7 March 2025). https://papers.ssrn.com/abstract=5170054

41 Khaleel Ibrahim Al-Daoud and Ibrahim A Abu-AlSondos, "Robust AI for Financial Fraud Detection in the GCC: A Hybrid Framework for Imbalance, Drift, and Adversarial Threats" (2025) 20 *Journal of Theoretical and Applied Electronic Commerce Research* 121. https://doi.org/10.3390/jtaer20020121

42 Sarbanes–Oxley Act of 2002, Pub L No 107–204, §404, 116 Stat 745; see also A-LIGN, *SOX 404 Explained: Demystifying Sarbanes-Oxley Act Section 404* (2025). https://www.a-lign.com/articles/sox-404-explained accessed 6 September 2025.

43 Rebecca A Delfino, "Deepfakes on Trial: A Call to Expand the Trial Judge's Gatekeeping Role to Protect Legal Proceedings from Technological Fakery" (2022) 74 Hastings LJ 293.

44 David Hartmann, José Renato Laranjeira de Pereira, Chiara Streitbörger, and Bettina Berendt, "Addressing the Regulatory Gap: Moving Towards an EU AI Audit Ecosystem Beyond the AI Act by Including Civil Society" (2025) arXiv:2403.07904. https://doi.org/10.48550/arXiv.2403.07904

45 Wilberforce Murikah, Jeff Kimanga Nthenge, and Faith Mueni Musyoka, "Bias and Ethics of AI Systems Applied in Auditing—A Systematic Review" (2024) 25 *Scientific African* e02281.

46 ISO/IEC TR 24027:2021, *Artificial intelligence (AI) — Bias in AI Systems and AI-Aided Decision Making.*

47 European Convention on Human Rights (adopted 4 November 1950, entered into force 3 September 1953) 213 UNTS 221, art 14; OECD, *OECD Guidelines for Multinational Enterprises on Responsible Business Conduct* (OECD Publishing 2023).

48 ISO/IEC 42001:2023, *Artificial Intelligence — Management System*; OECD, *Recommendation of the Council on Artificial Intelligence*, 22 May 2019, updated 2024; UNESCO, *Recommendation on the Ethics of Artificial Intelligence*, Paris, 24 November 2021.

49 European Union, *Regulation (EU) 2024/... of the European Parliament and of the Council Laying Down Harmonised Rules on Artificial Intelligence (AI Act)*, 13 March 2024; International Federation of Accountants (IFAC), *Envisioning the Future of Audit in an AI Environment*, New York, 2023.

50 ISO/IEC 42001:2023, *Artificial Intelligence—Management System (AIMS)*, International Organization for Standardization/International Electrotechnical Commission, Geneva, 2023; see also SGS, *A Guide to the ISO/IEC 42000 Series*, 2024.

51 ISO/IEC 42006 (draft 2024), *Requirements for bodies providing audit and certification of AI Management Systems (AIMS)*, ISO/IEC, Geneva; IEC, *New International Standard Sets Rules for Auditing AI Management Systems*, 2024.

52 European Data Protection Board (EDPB), *AI Auditing: Results of the Support Pool of Experts Project*, Brussels, 2023.

53 Institute of Internal Auditors (IIA), *The IIA's Artificial Intelligence Auditing Framework*, Position Paper, Orlando, 2023.
54 British Standards Institution (BSI), *AI Assurance Standard*, London, 2025; see also *Financial Times*, "BSI Publishes Standard to Ensure Quality among Growing AI Audit Market," July 2025.
55 EU AI Act, Regulation (EU) 2024 Article 6 et seq. requiring conformity assessments and documentation prior to market entry; see also OneTrust, *Conformity Assessments under the EU AI Act*, Nov. 2023.
56 Cong. Research Service, *Regulating Artificial Intelligence: U.S. and International Approaches*, 4 June 2025, noting absence of general federal AI law; see also Hickman et al., *US Relies on Existing Federal Laws and Guidelines to Regulate AI* (AI Watch Tracker, 21 July 2025).
57 OECD, *Regulatory Sandboxes in Artificial Intelligence*, July 2023 (Singapore sandbox example); Navex, *Singapore's regulatory sandbox allows businesses to experiment with AI* (Nov 2024); Japan Cabinet Secretariat, overview of Japan's regulatory sandbox (2018–2021).
58 IFRS Foundation, "What Role Does Artificial Intelligence Play in Digital Financial Reporting?" (*Digital Financial Reporting*, April 2024), highlighting AI-assisted tagging and reporting with human oversight.
59 European Commission, "EU and Japan Reinforce Tech and Digital Partnership," May 12, 2025, confirming collaboration across AI, data governance, and digital trust domains; see also reports of 2025 Digital Partnership Council meetings.
60 OECD, *Framework for the Classification of AI Systems*, 2022, providing multidimensional classification tools to inform policy and governance structures.
61 Forum of Firms, constitution and mandates via IFAC platforms, promoting consistency in transnational audit practices and quality control standards globally.

Chapter 13

The role of AI-assisted translation in enhancing audit quality in distance audit firms

Evidence from Morocco

Karima Bouziane and Abdelmounim Bouziane

13.1 INTRODUCTION

Globalization and the acceleration of digital transformation have reshaped the way audit missions are conducted worldwide. In recent years, the rise of remote auditing, particularly within multinational groups, has positioned subsidiaries in emerging markets as key players in delivering high-quality statutory audits to international clients. Moroccan subsidiaries of the Big Four, for instance, are increasingly tasked with conducting distance audits for French companies, where communication, documentation, and compliance must be guaranteed across linguistic and cultural boundaries.

The COVID-19 pandemic amplified this reliance on remote auditing, revealing both its potential and its limitations. Studies have shown that while remote audits improve efficiency and flexibility, they often generate concerns about communication quality, reduced professional skepticism, and increased psychological distance between auditors and clients (Li et al., 2024; Thompson, 2022). In such contexts, language accuracy becomes not only a practical necessity but also a determinant of audit quality, particularly in cross-border engagements where audit evidence and reports must comply with international standards.

At the same time, artificial intelligence (AI) has emerged as a transformative force in auditing. From fraud detection to automated data analysis, AI tools are redefining audit practices by enhancing efficiency and reliability (Saad-Allah & Elouidani, 2025; Wijaya et al., 2025). Among these tools, AI-assisted translation systems such as ChatGPT are being adopted to bridge linguistic gaps in multilingual audit environments. Prior research has demonstrated that neural machine translation can improve productivity in financial and legal texts (Läubli et al., 2019; Pielka et al., 2025), and recent work in Morocco has highlighted auditors' positive perceptions of ChatGPT as a translation aid for legal audit tasks (Bouziane & Bouziane, 2024). Yet, concerns remain regarding contextual accuracy, domain-specific nuances, and the risk of over-reliance on AI-generated outputs (Moneus & Sahari, 2024).

Despite this growing body of work, the intersection of remote auditing, audit quality, and AI-assisted translation remains underexplored. Existing

DOI: 10.1201/9781003650713-14

studies have largely examined AI in auditing from the perspective of automation or fraud detection, while the specific role of translation in supporting audit missions across linguistic frontiers has received little empirical attention. For Moroccan subsidiaries working with French headquarters, this gap is especially salient: translation is not a peripheral activity but a central mechanism ensuring the reliability of audit communication and documentation.

This raises a fundamental research problem:

To what extent can the translation of audit elements via ChatGPT impact the quality of audit missions conducted by offshore audit firms in Morocco?

13.2 LITERATURE REVIEW

13.2.1 Audit quality in remote auditing contexts

The shift to remote auditing, accelerated by the COVID-19 pandemic, has reshaped the audit profession and introduced new determinants of audit quality. Li et al. (2024) found that remote audits increased efficiency but also raised concerns about communication quality, professional skepticism, and auditor fatigue. While technology adoption was higher, the rigid monitoring environment and reduced client interaction posed potential risks to audit quality. Alma'aitah et al. (2024) further identified that technology readiness, particularly on the client side, significantly strengthens the positive impact of remote auditing on audit quality, whereas the audit firm's own readiness had a lesser effect.

Similarly, Hsieh et al. (2025) observed that workforce technology competency mitigated audit quality deterioration during remote work, underlining the importance of technological human capital. Palmarozzo et al. (2025) found that remote audits tend to report fewer violations, particularly when compliance checks depend on direct observation rather than document review. However, prior in-person exposure to the audited site helped offset quality losses. Thompson (2022) highlighted the role of psychological distance, noting that auditors under time pressure in remote contexts were more likely to engage in reduced audit quality (RAQ) behavior.

These studies collectively show that while remote auditing offers operational flexibility, audit quality remains sensitive to communication barriers, technological capacity, and the nature of audit procedures. This has direct implications for multilingual audit environments, where linguistic accuracy becomes an additional factor influencing quality.

13.2.2 Artificial intelligence in auditing

AI has increasingly been integrated into auditing practices to enhance efficiency, accuracy, and fraud detection.

In the Moroccan context, Saad-Allah and Elouidani (2025) observed that AI adoption is transforming audit processes by automating repetitive tasks and improving efficiency, but it also demands new technical skills and continuous auditor training. Wijaya et al. (2025), in a review of 325 Scopus-indexed articles, found AI applications particularly valuable for real-time data analysis and risk assessment, though challenges remain in auditor readiness, ethical considerations, and uneven global adoption.

Ethical frameworks for AI auditing, as reviewed by Laine et al. (2024), stress the need for transparency, fairness, and accountability to maintain public trust. Gu et al. (2024) introduced the concept of AI co-piloted auditing, where auditors and foundation models collaborate, enhancing efficiency and accuracy through structured prompting. Collins et al. (2021) further emphasized the importance of aligning AI innovations with both strategic business goals and ethical demands.

Although the literature on AI in auditing has grown rapidly, little attention has been paid to AI's role in overcoming language barriers in multinational or multilingual audit settings, a gap that AI-assisted translation directly addresses.

13.2.3 AI-assisted translation in professional and financial contexts

AI-assisted translation tools such as DeepL, Google Translate, and GPT-based systems are increasingly applied in professional contexts, including legal and financial auditing. Moneus and Sahari (2024) demonstrated that while AI translation quality in legal texts is improving, differences with human translation remain, especially in domain-specific nuance. Peng et al. (2023) found that domain-specific prompting improves GPT-based translation performance, suggesting that customized inputs are critical in specialized fields such as audit documentation.

In the financial sector, Pielka et al. (2025) introduced an automated translation-checking tool for German–English financial reports, combining heuristic algorithms with transformer-based error detection. They found that smaller models fine-tuned for the domain outperformed large general-purpose models like GPT-4 in this task. Similarly, Läubli et al. (2019) showed that neural machine translation (NMT) improved post-editing productivity for financial texts, achieving time savings without sacrificing quality.

In the Moroccan audit sector, Bouziane and Bouziane (2024) empirically tested ChatGPT as a translation tool for legal audit tasks in the Big Four. They found that perceived utility of the tool correlated strongly with perceived improvements in audit quality, particularly for tasks in languages unfamiliar to auditors. Another study by the same authors (Bouziane and Bouziane 2025) in the travel industry confirmed that user satisfaction with AI translation depends on ease of use and output quality, though these factors alone do not fully explain perceptions, indicating the influence of contextual variables.

13.2.4 Synthesis and research gap

The reviewed literature suggests that remote auditing faces quality risks due to communication barriers and reduced direct observation, but that these can be mitigated by technology readiness and workforce competency. AI tools have shown promise in improving efficiency, accuracy, and fraud detection, but the intersection of AI translation and audit quality in remote contexts remains underexplored.

Given the multilingual nature of Moroccan audit engagements, particularly for firms serving international clients, language accuracy in audit documentation and client communication is critical to audit quality. While AI-assisted translation has been tested in legal and financial domains, its targeted role in distance audit firms has not been empirically examined. This represents a clear opportunity to investigate how AI translation tools can support remote auditors in delivering high-quality, compliant, and contextually accurate audits.

13.3 METHOD

This study is based on an analysis of the impact of AI-based translation tools, particularly ChatGPT, on the quality of legal audit work within outsourced audit firms. The research was conducted in Morocco, focusing on the Big Four firms' subsidiaries in Morocco working with French companies.

13.3.1 Research population and sample

The target population consisted of external auditors employed in the Moroccan subsidiaries of the four major French audit firms in Morocco: Deloitte, PwC, KPMG, and Mazars. A structured questionnaire was distributed to all auditors working in these firms.

Total population: 102 auditors
Number of responses received: 64
Response rate: 62.7%

This response rate is considered satisfactory for survey-based research in the field of management sciences, ensuring sufficient representativeness for statistical analysis.

13.3.2 Data collection tool

The questionnaire was designed based on two complementary sources:

Previous empirical studies on AI adoption and audit quality.

The Technology Acceptance Model (TAM), which provides a theoretical framework for analyzing the determinants of technology adoption and its perceived impact.

The survey included items measuring both demographic/professional background (e.g., years of audit experience, specialization) and perceptions of AI-assisted translation in the audit context.

Key variables investigated include:

Experience using ChatGPT in translation;
Use of ChatGPT for translating audit reports and other regulated financial documents;
Perceived ease of use of ChatGPT;
Perceived usefulness of ChatGPT.

13.3.3 Data analysis

Data collected were processed and analyzed using SPSS software. To test the research model and determine the relationships between the independent variables (AI-related factors) and the dependent variable (audit quality), a multiple linear regression analysis was performed.

This approach allowed us to identify which elements of AI-assisted translation—such as perceived ease of use, perceived usefulness, or actual experience with ChatGPT—have the most significant effect on the quality of statutory audits.

13.4 RESULTS

The results of those preliminary tests were as follows (Table 13.1):

The correlation coefficient (R = 0.89) reveals a strong and significant relationship between the quality of statutory audit mission performed by the audit firms and the AI-related research variables. In addition, the robustness of the model is confirmed by the F-statistic, which is significant at the 5% level, thereby reinforcing the model's validity in explaining the observed relationships. Moreover, the Durbin–Watson statistic (DW ≈ 1.89) suggests a very low level of autocorrelation in the residuals, further enhancing confidence in the reliability and overall significance of the model.

Given the thorough assessment of our statistical model, it is important to provide an overview of the correlation matrix. This table illustrates the

Table 13.1 Validation tests

R	*R²*	*Test of Fisher*	*DW*
0.899	0.890	0.001	1.89

complex relationships between audit quality and the set of explanatory variables included in our framework. The findings presented in Table 13.2 highlight the strength of association between each explanatory variable and the dependent variable, thereby deepening our understanding of the determinants that shape audit quality.

Table 13.2 Regression model

Model	*Coefficient (A)*	*Interpretation*
Audit quality		
Age	–0.033	A small, negative, almost negligible effect. Older auditors show slightly lower perceived audit quality in relation to AI use.
Gender	–0.058	Also a very small and negative effect → gender differences are not meaningful in this model.
Being comfortable with ICT	–0.214	Surprisingly, higher ICT comfort is linked to a slight decrease in audit quality perception. This might reflect overconfidence, where reliance on general ICT skills does not directly improve audit outcomes with ChatGPT.
Experience using ChatGPT	–0.298	Negative effect → more "experience" does not automatically translate into higher audit quality, possibly because frequent users are more critical of its limitations or misuse it in non-value-added ways.
Using ChatGPT translation of audit reports	0.766	Strong positive effect → when auditors use ChatGPT to translate full audit reports, audit quality improves significantly. This supports the idea that accurate, domain-specific translation helps reduce errors and miscommunication.
Using ChatGPT in preparing email in another language to send to	–0.229	Small negative effect → occasional use for email may not substantially improve audit quality. Possibly because emails are less formal and not central to audit rigor.
Using ChatGPT in preparing email in another language to send to	–0.657	Larger negative effect → heavy reliance on ChatGPT for multilingual email drafting may reduce audit quality, maybe due to tone/context errors in client communication.
Using ChatGPT to translate instructions from international offices	–0.804	Strong negative effect → indicates risks when auditors depend on ChatGPT for translating instructions from headquarters. Misinterpretation or loss of nuance here directly undermines audit execution.
The perceived ease of ChatGPT	0.084	Slight positive effect → ease of use alone doesn't strongly drive quality, but contributes modestly.
The perceived usefulness of ChatGPT	0.945	The strongest positive predictor. When auditors believe ChatGPT is useful, audit quality significantly improves. This suggests perception and acceptance are more critical than ease of use.

13.5 DISCUSSION

The empirical findings provide important insights into how AI-assisted tools, particularly ChatGPT, influence audit quality in remote and multilingual contexts. Overall, the model confirms a strong explanatory power ($R^2 = 0.890$), showing that AI-related factors play a central role in shaping the quality of statutory audit missions. However, the results reveal a nuanced picture: while some applications of ChatGPT significantly improve audit outcomes, others appear to undermine them.

First, the positive and significant role of **perceived usefulness** ($\beta = 0.945$) aligns with the technology acceptance perspective highlighted by Saad-Allah and Elouidani (2025), who argued that AI adoption in Morocco requires not only technical integration but also a clear perception of added value by auditors. This finding reinforces the notion, emphasized by Wijaya et al. (2025), that AI's potential in auditing is best realized when users see it as instrumental to their professional tasks. In contrast, **perceived ease of use** exerted only a marginal effect, suggesting that efficiency gains alone are insufficient to drive quality improvements unless auditors are convinced of the strategic relevance of AI tools (Collins et al., 2021).

Second, the strong positive effect of **using ChatGPT for translating audit reports** ($\beta = 0.766$) provides empirical support for prior work on AI translation in professional settings. Bouziane and Bouziane (2024) found that auditors in Morocco perceive ChatGPT-based translation as improving audit quality, particularly when working in languages outside their area of expertise. This is consistent with Läubli et al. (2019), who showed that neural machine translation enhances productivity in financial texts without reducing quality. Together, these findings underscore that AI translation can add substantial value when applied to **formal, high-stakes audit documentation**, where linguistic precision directly impacts audit compliance and credibility.

Conversely, the negative coefficients associated with **ChatGPT use in email communication** ($\beta = -0.657; -0.229$) and in **translating instructions from international offices** ($\beta = -0.804$) highlight potential risks of over-reliance on AI tools for less formal or context-sensitive communication. These results resonate with Moneus and Sahari (2024), who cautioned that AI translation systems still struggle with nuance and domain-specific interpretation. In remote auditing contexts, where communication already suffers from barriers and psychological distance (Thompson, 2022), inaccurate translations may amplify misunderstandings and weaken professional skepticism, leading to reduced audit quality.

The negative effect of **ChatGPT experience** ($\beta = -0.298$) and **ICT comfort** ($\beta = -0.214$) further suggests that familiarity with digital tools does not automatically enhance audit outcomes. This observation echoes Hsieh et al. (2025), who emphasized that technological competency mitigates risks only when aligned with specific audit tasks and procedures. Our results indicate that general ICT skills or frequent ChatGPT use may create overconfidence or superficial reliance, rather than genuine quality improvements, particularly in complex audit engagements.

Finally, demographic factors such as **age** and **gender** had negligible effects, implying that the impact of AI-assisted translation on audit quality is not shaped by personal characteristics but rather by how and where the tool is applied. This finding complements Alma'aitah et al. (2024), who stressed that technology readiness on the client side matters more than individual auditor traits in shaping remote audit outcomes.

In sum, our results reinforce the literature's consensus that while AI offers transformative opportunities in auditing, its benefits are contingent on contextual application and professional judgment. AI translation appears most valuable when deployed in structured, documentation-heavy tasks (e.g., audit reports), but less so in unstructured or relational communication (e.g., emails, instructions). This asymmetry highlights the need for clear organizational policies and training programs to guide auditors on the effective and safe use of ChatGPT in multilingual audit environments.

13.6 RECOMMENDATIONS

The findings of this study highlight both the opportunities and risks of integrating ChatGPT and similar AI-assisted translation tools into remote auditing practices. To maximize the benefits while minimizing drawbacks, the following recommendations are proposed:

- *Strategic Use of AI for High-Value Tasks*
  Audit firms should encourage the use of ChatGPT for formal and complex documentation (e.g., audit reports, legal appendices, financial notes), where accuracy and linguistic precision are critical. Our results show that AI translation in these contexts strongly enhances audit quality, consistent with earlier studies on domain-specific NMT performance (Läubli et al., 2019; Bouziane & Bouziane, 2024).
- *Cautious Use in Informal Communication*
  Given the negative effects observed when ChatGPT was used for translating emails and managerial instructions, auditors should exercise caution in such contexts. Firms should establish clear guidelines on acceptable AI use in client communication and cross-office correspondence to avoid misinterpretation or tone-related errors that may damage professional credibility.
- *Continuous Training and Capacity Building*
  The negative association between ICT comfort and audit quality suggests that digital familiarity alone is insufficient. Firms should provide specialized training programs that focus not just on technical use of AI tools, but also on critical assessment of outputs, domain-specific prompting strategies, and awareness of AI limitations (Wijaya et al., 2025).

- *Embedding AI into Audit Methodologies*
  To ensure consistency, AI-assisted translation should be integrated into audit methodologies with clear review and validation protocols. Post-editing by auditors or bilingual staff should be systematically required to safeguard against errors, as recommended by Moneus and Sahari (2024).
- *Enhancing Ethical and Professional Safeguards*
  As highlighted by Laine et al. (2024), ethical frameworks are critical for maintaining public trust in AI-assisted auditing. Firms should adopt policies that ensure transparency, accountability, and confidentiality when using AI tools, particularly in handling sensitive audit data.
- *Strengthening Organizational Support*
  Audit firms should foster a culture where auditors perceive ChatGPT as genuinely useful rather than merely easy to use. This can be achieved through pilot projects, success stories, and the integration of AI outcomes into quality reviews, thereby reinforcing auditors' confidence in the value of these tools.
- *Regulatory and Professional Oversight*
  Regulators and professional bodies should issue guidance on AI translation in auditing, setting minimum standards for accuracy, documentation, and auditor accountability. This would help harmonize practices across firms and reduce the risks of inconsistent adoption.

13.7 CONCLUSION

This study examined the impact of ChatGPT-assisted translation on the quality of statutory audit missions in the Moroccan context, with a particular focus on remote and multilingual audit environments. Building on prior literature that highlighted both the opportunities and challenges of remote auditing (Li et al., 2024; Thompson, 2022) and AI adoption in auditing (Saad-Allah & Elouidani, 2025; Wijaya et al., 2025), our findings provide empirical evidence on the nuanced role of AI-assisted translation in shaping audit quality.

The statistical results revealed that audit quality is most strongly enhanced when ChatGPT is used for formal documentation tasks, such as translating audit reports, and when auditors perceive the tool as genuinely useful. In contrast, reliance on ChatGPT for informal or relational communication, such as emails or the translation of managerial instructions, was associated with reductions in audit quality. These results confirm earlier research emphasizing the importance of contextual application (Moneus & Sahari, 2024; Bouziane & Bouziane, 2024) and extend the literature by showing how the same AI tool can both enhance and undermine audit outcomes depending on its use.

From a practical perspective, the study highlights the need for strategic integration of AI tools into audit methodologies, coupled with appropriate training, ethical safeguards, and regulatory oversight. For audit firms, the key lies not in widespread reliance on AI but in targeted, high-value deployment that complements professional judgment rather than replacing it.

Overall, this research underscores that ChatGPT and similar AI-assisted translation tools hold substantial promises for improving audit quality in multilingual and remote contexts, but their benefits are contingent upon careful application, auditor training, and organizational support. Future research should extend this inquiry to larger samples and diverse professional settings, while also exploring the long-term implications of AI adoption for auditor independence, professional skepticism, and public trust.

REFERENCES

Alma'aitah, R. T., Al-Hajaya, K., Sawan, N., & Alzeban, A. (2024). The impact of remote auditing on audit quality: The moderating role of technology readiness. *Managerial Auditing Journal*, *39*(6), 624–647. https://doi.org/10.1108/MAJ-02-2024-4210

Bouziane, K., & Bouziane, A. (2024). AI translation's impact on legal audit quality in Morocco's Big Four. *Polissema—Revista de Letras do ISCAP*, *2*(24), 45–66. https://doi.org/10.34630/polissema.v24i2.6073

Bouziane, K., & Bouziane, A. (2025). Facilitating cross-cultural translation with ChatGPT in Moroccan travel agencies: A user satisfaction study. *EDPACS*, 1–19.

Collins, C., Dennehy, D., Conboy, K., & Mikalef, P. (2021). Artificial intelligence in information systems research: A systematic literature review and research agenda. *International Journal of Information Management*, *60*, 102383. https://doi.org/10.1016/j.ijinfomgt.2021.102383

Gu, H., Schreyer, M., Moffitt, K., & Vasarhelyi, M. (2024). Artificial intelligence co-piloted auditing. *International Journal of Accounting Information Systems*, *54*, 100698. https://doi.org/10.1016/j.accinf.2024.100698

Hsieh, T.-S., Tang, Z., Wang, Z., & Yoon, K. (2025). Audit quality under remote working arrangement: The role of technology competency. *Journal of Information Systems*, *39*(2), 21–40. https://doi.org/10.2308/ISYS-2023-065

Laine, J., Minkkinen, M., & Mäntymäki, M. (2024). Ethics-based AI auditing: A systematic literature review on conceptualizations of ethical principles and knowledge contributions to stakeholders. *Information & Management*, *61*(5), 103969. https://doi.org/10.1016/j.im.2024.103969

Läubli, S., Amrhein, C., Düggelin, P., Gonzalez, B., Zwahlen, A., & Volk, M. (2019). Post-editing productivity with neural machine translation: An empirical assessment of speed and quality in the banking and finance domain [Preprint]. *SSRN*. https://doi.org/10.48550/arXiv.1906.01685

Li, Y., Goel, S., & Williams, K. J. (2024). Remote audit quality, audit efficiency, and auditors' job satisfaction: Implications for audit firms and external auditors. *Current Issues in Auditing*, *18*(2), P20–P28. https://doi.org/10.2308/CIIA-2023-033

Moneus, A. M., & Sahari, Y. (2024). Artificial intelligence and human translation: A contrastive study based on legal texts. *Heliyon*, *10*(6), e28106. https://doi.org/10.1016/j.heliyon.2024.e28106

Palmarozzo, A., Toffel, M. W., & Ouellet, M. (2025). Managing remote work quality: Evidence from auditing management systems standards (Harvard Business School Working Paper No. 24-002, July 2023; revised February 2025). Harvard Business School.

Peng, K., Ding, L., Zhong, Q., Shen, L., Liu, X., Zhang, M., Ouyang, Y., & Tao, D. (2023). Towards making the most of ChatGPT for machine translation. In *Conference on Empirical Methods in Natural Language Processing*. https://api.semanticscholar.org/CorpusID:257704711

Pielka, M., Hahnbück, M., Deußer, T., et al. (2025). Automating translation checks of financial documents using large language models. *Language Resources & Evaluation*. https://doi.org/10.1007/s10579-025-09862-z

Saad-Allah, I., & Elouidani, A. (2025). Artificial intelligence and financial auditing in Morocco: Towards a redefinition of practices and skills. *African Scientific Journal*, *3*(28), 27. https://doi.org/10.5281/zenodo.14785104

Thompson, K. (2022). *Out of office: Examining how remote auditing can affect audit quality* (Doctoral dissertation). University of South Carolina. https://scholarcommons.sc.edu/etd/6846

Wijaya, J. R. T., Prasetyo, I., Rahmatika, D. N., & Indriasih, D. (2025). Artificial intelligence and audit quality: An empirical literature review from Scopus database. *Fokus Ekonomi: Jurnal Ilmiah Ekonomi*, *20*(1), 61–76. https://doi.org/10.34152/fe.20.1.61-76

Chapter 14

What role does explainable AI play in advancing transparency and compliance in financial fraud detection?

A literature review

Issam Benhayoun and Ahmad Alqatan

14.1 INTRODUCTION

Financial fraud remains a persistent and costly problem, undermining stakeholder trust, distorting capital allocation, and exposing vulnerabilities in corporate governance (Benhayoun et al., 2025). Despite significant advancements in data analytics and machine learning (ML), the complexity and adaptability of fraudulent behavior continue to outpace traditional detection systems. A major barrier to progress lies in the lack of transparency within advanced AI-based fraud detection tools. While these systems can detect anomalies with impressive accuracy, they often function as opaque "black boxes," offering limited insights into their decision-making processes. This lack of interpretability complicates the auditing process, hampers regulatory scrutiny, and raises ethical concerns around accountability and fairness.

The relevance of this problem is both theoretical and practical. Regulators, auditors, and financial institutions increasingly rely on automated systems to detect fraud in real time. However, stakeholders demand justifications for flagged transactions or decisions, especially when these decisions carry reputational or financial consequences. Regulatory frameworks such as the EU's GDPR or the U.S. SEC's reporting requirements implicitly or explicitly require a degree of explainability in automated decision systems. In response, the field of explainable artificial intelligence (XAI) has emerged to bridge this gap, offering tools and methods that make AI-driven decisions more interpretable without compromising performance.

Scholars have attempted to address this problem by integrating rule-based systems, decision trees, and feature attribution techniques like Local Interpretable Model-agnostic Explanations (LIME) and SHapley Additive exPlanations (SHAP) into fraud detection pipelines (Adadi & Berrada, 2018; Slack et al., 2020). Research has also explored hybrid models combining

DOI: 10.1201/9781003650713-15

symbolic reasoning with neural networks to balance accuracy and interpretability (Arrieta et al., 2020). These efforts have laid an important foundation, but limitations persist in model fidelity, generalizability, and domain-specific applications.

The problem persists for several reasons. First, existing XAI tools are often developed for general-purpose tasks and are not tailored to the specific needs of financial fraud detection. Second, explanations generated by current methods may be inconsistent, overly technical, or difficult for non-experts to interpret (Doshi-Velez & Kim, 2018). Third, there is a lack of consensus on how to evaluate the effectiveness of explanations, especially in regulated environments. Furthermore, organizational inertia, a lack of technical expertise among auditors, and the absence of standardized frameworks for integrating XAI into legacy systems act as additional barriers to adoption.

If these challenges remain unaddressed, the consequences will be significant. The continued reliance on opaque AI models in high-stakes financial contexts will erode stakeholder confidence, limit regulatory oversight, and increase the risk of undetected fraud. Moreover, ethical and legal implications—such as algorithmic bias, data misuse, and accountability gaps—could undermine the legitimacy of both corporate reporting and AI governance frameworks. In the worst-case scenario, failure to integrate explainable models could result in systemic risks and loss of public trust in financial institutions.

This chapter responds to these challenges by conducting a comprehensive literature review on the intersection of XAI and financial fraud detection. It synthesizes findings from academic research, regulatory reports, and industry white papers to evaluate the current state, limitations, and future directions of XAI in this domain. The review draws on both qualitative thematic analysis and quantitative bibliometric mapping to trace the evolution of techniques, applications, and theoretical frameworks. Special attention is given to model-specific vs model-agnostic approaches, regulatory alignment, and human-AI collaboration in audit settings.

The key findings suggest that XAI significantly enhances transparency, compliance, and trust in fraud detection systems by enabling interpretable decision-making. Model-agnostic tools like SHAP and LIME, while widely used, face robustness issues; interpretable-by-design models offer more reliable alternatives in high-stakes environments (Rudin, 2019). Furthermore, hybrid AI systems show promise in balancing predictive power and explanation clarity. The chapter contributes to the literature by identifying six critical research avenues: improving model fidelity, developing domain-aware explanations, aligning with regulatory standards, enhancing auditor-AI interaction, addressing ethical concerns, and ensuring adaptability to evolving fraud strategies.

In doing so, this work advances the discourse on responsible AI in financial auditing and offers actionable insights for researchers, practitioners, and regulators aiming to make fraud detection not only more accurate but also more transparent and accountable.

14.2 CONCEPTUAL FOUNDATIONS

14.2.1 Financial fraud in accounting: Definitions and typologies

Financial fraud in accounting denotes intentional acts of deception that distort financial statements or involve the misappropriation of assets, thereby compromising the credibility and integrity of financial reporting (Rezaee, 2005). The Association of Certified Fraud Examiners (ACFE, 2022) categorizes financial fraud into three primary forms: asset misappropriation, fraudulent financial reporting, and corruption. Asset misappropriation, though the most frequent, typically results in lower financial losses, whereas fraudulent financial reporting—often involving earnings manipulation—has more severe consequences due to its potential to mislead investors and regulators. Corruption, including bribery and conflicts of interest, further undermines the ethical climate of organizations.

Typologically, fraudulent financial reporting is often associated with accrual-based manipulations that artificially inflate revenue or defer expenses to meet performance targets. Skousen, Smith, and Wright (2009) examine how accruals are exploited in earnings management, making detection particularly difficult in complex accounting environments. These practices are often facilitated by managerial discretion and opaque financial instruments. Meanwhile, governance mechanisms also influence fraud likelihood. Beasley (1996) found that firms with weaker board oversight—particularly boards lacking independence and financial expertise—are more vulnerable to fraudulent activities.

Understanding these typologies is not only critical for auditors but also essential for the development of AI-driven fraud detection systems. By encoding fraud patterns derived from historical data into ML models, such systems can detect anomalies or red flags that human auditors may overlook. This underscores the importance of integrating behavioral, organizational, and accounting dimensions into technological solutions aimed at enhancing financial transparency.

14.2.2 Regulatory compliance and the transparency imperative

In response to major accounting scandals and increasing public demand for corporate accountability (Benarbi & Benhayoun, 2026), the global regulatory environment has evolved to prioritize transparency and compliance in financial reporting. Landmark frameworks such as the U.S. Sarbanes-Oxley Act (SOX) of 2002 introduced rigorous internal control requirements, external audit oversight, and executive accountability, aiming to restore investor confidence and deter financial misstatements. In parallel, the European Union's General Data Protection Regulation (GDPR) enforces stringent rules not only on data privacy but also on the traceability and accountability of automated decision-making systems, including those employed in fraud detection and risk assessment. Collectively, these frameworks underscore that transparency is not merely the availability of information, but also its intelligibility and verifiability by relevant stakeholders (Power, 2007).

The increasing integration of ML models into accounting and auditing processes introduces new challenges to this regulatory landscape. While these models offer unprecedented capacities to detect subtle, non-linear patterns of fraud, they frequently operate as opaque "black boxes," lacking transparency in their decision-making processes (Doshi-Velez & Kim, 2017). This opacity creates a fundamental tension between algorithmic efficiency and regulatory compliance. Specifically, if a model's outputs cannot be adequately explained, auditors and organizations may struggle to justify decisions to regulators or courts—particularly in jurisdictions where algorithmic accountability is legally mandated (Wachter, Mittelstadt, & Floridi, 2017).

Consequently, the interpretability of ML systems becomes not only a technical concern but a regulatory imperative. There is a growing consensus that the adoption of AI in auditing must be accompanied by robust explainability mechanisms, such as model-agnostic interpretation tools, simplified surrogate models, or inherently interpretable architectures. These mechanisms are essential to bridge the gap between computational complexity and regulatory demands. Without them, organizations risk failing to meet evolving standards of transparency and due diligence, ultimately undermining the legitimacy and admissibility of AI-based evidence in both corporate governance and legal proceedings.

14.2.3 Explainable AI: Definitions, methods, and relevance in finance

XAI encompasses a suite of methods and techniques designed to render AI model outputs and decision-making processes intelligible to human users (Gunning & Aha, 2019). Unlike conventional ML models, which often trade interpretability for predictive accuracy, XAI aims to bridge this trade-off by making complex models more transparent without significantly sacrificing performance. In high-stakes domains such as financial fraud detection, this interpretability is not merely a technical feature but a critical requirement for auditability, trust, and compliance.

XAI approaches are generally categorized into two classes: model-specific and model-agnostic. Model-specific techniques are tailored to particular algorithms. For example, attention maps in neural networks highlight which inputs were most influential in classification tasks, while decision path tracing can explain outputs in tree-based models (Molnar, 2022). Conversely, model-agnostic methods—such as LIME and SHAP—can be applied post hoc to any predictive model. These tools offer local and global interpretability by approximating complex decision boundaries or attributing importance scores to features (Ribeiro, Singh, & Guestrin, 2016; Lundberg & Lee, 2017).

In financial fraud detection, the utility of XAI lies in its ability not only to detect anomalies but to contextualize them in a manner accessible to auditors, forensic accountants, and compliance officers (Barredo Arrieta et al., 2020). For instance, SHAP values can quantify the influence of specific financial ratios or transaction attributes on a model's prediction, enabling targeted investigations (Kokina et al., 2025). This capacity enhances both operational effectiveness and regulatory defensibility.

Nevertheless, XAI deployment in financial institutions remains limited. Many organizations still rely on either simplistic rule-based systems or complex black-box models that lack interpretability. A growing body of research advocates for hybrid systems that combine rule-based logic with interpretable ML models, offering a balance between accuracy and explainability (Bussmann, Giudici, & Marinelli, 2021).

In summary, XAI represents a critical nexus of technological innovation, regulatory compliance, and ethical accountability. Its integration into fraud detection systems is essential for fostering trust, ensuring transparency, and achieving robust governance in contemporary financial ecosystems.

14.3 MACHINE LEARNING AND AI TECHNIQUES IN FINANCIAL FRAUD DETECTION

The increasing complexity and scale of financial transactions have made traditional fraud detection methods—such as manual audits and rule-based systems—increasingly inadequate. To address this, a growing body of research has turned to ML and artificial intelligence (AI) to detect anomalies indicative of financial fraud. This section reviews the primary ML and AI techniques used in the literature, categorized into traditional models, deep learning approaches, and hybrid systems, and evaluates their relevance and limitations for fraud detection.

14.3.1 Traditional machine learning techniques

Traditional ML models have been widely used in detecting fraud due to their ability to classify transactions based on learned patterns. Among the most commonly employed are logistic regression, decision trees, random forests, support vector machines (SVMs), and k-nearest neighbors (KNN).

Logistic regression, despite its simplicity, has served as a baseline model for fraud prediction tasks because of its interpretability and ability to handle binary classification (Ngai et al., 2011). Decision trees and random forests offer the advantage of transparency through hierarchical decision rules, making them easier to interpret—a property increasingly valued in regulated environments (Lenka et al., 2024). However, these models may be prone to overfitting, especially when applied to high-dimensional datasets.

SVMs are particularly effective in handling imbalanced data—a common characteristic in fraud detection where fraudulent cases represent a minority. Nonetheless, their "black-box" nature and reliance on kernel functions pose challenges for interpretability (West, 2000). Additionally, KNN and other instance-based methods are computationally intensive and sensitive to feature scaling, making them less scalable for large financial datasets.

14.3.2 Deep learning approaches

More recently, deep learning methods have been adopted for financial fraud detection due to their superior performance in capturing complex, non-linear relationships. Popular architectures include convolutional neural networks (CNNs), recurrent neural networks (RNNs), autoencoders, and generative adversarial networks (GANs).

RNNs, and their variant long short-term memory (LSTM) networks, are particularly suited for sequential data, such as transaction histories, allowing them to detect temporal anomalies (Jurgovsky et al., 2018). RNNs, though originally developed for image recognition, have been adapted to detect fraud in structured financial datasets by identifying local patterns (Oguntimilehin et al., 2024). Autoencoders are often used in unsupervised settings to identify anomalous transactions by reconstructing inputs and flagging large deviations as potential fraud (Deng & Hooi, 2021).

Despite their accuracy, deep learning models are generally less interpretable than traditional methods. Their multi-layered structure obscures the rationale behind predictions, raising concerns regarding accountability and trustworthiness in audit settings (Burrell, 2016). Additionally, training deep networks requires large labeled datasets and high computational power—resources not always available to firms, particularly in emerging markets (Benhayoun & Zejjari, 2024, 2025).

14.3.3 Hybrid and ensemble models

In response to the limitations of individual models, hybrid and ensemble approaches have gained prominence. These methods combine multiple algorithms to optimize predictive performance and, in some cases, improve interpretability.

Ensemble techniques, such as boosting (e.g., XGBoost) and bagging (e.g., Random Forests), aggregate predictions from weak learners to achieve higher accuracy (Chen & Guestrin, 2016). These models have been shown to outperform single classifiers in multiple fraud detection tasks, particularly when tuned on imbalanced datasets (Carcillo et al., 2021). However, they often remain opaque and require post-hoc explanation methods such as SHAP for transparency.

Hybrid systems that integrate rule-based logic with ML algorithms offer an effective compromise. For example, Aleskerov, Freisleben, and Rao (1997) pioneered a neuro-fuzzy system that combines neural networks with fuzzy logic to preserve interpretability. More recently, systems have been developed that allow domain experts to input heuristics while leveraging ML models for pattern recognition, thereby enhancing both explainability and adaptability (Kou et al., 2021).

Furthermore, the advent of cost-sensitive learning has allowed hybrid models to prioritize fraud cases with higher monetary impact, aligning predictive analytics with financial materiality (Bahnsen et al., 2016). These techniques are particularly important in domains where false positives carry reputational or financial costs, such as audit risk assessment and forensic investigations.

14.3.4 Evaluation metrics and practical considerations

A critical component of fraud detection model assessment is the use of appropriate evaluation metrics. Due to the high class imbalance, traditional accuracy scores can be misleading. Precision, recall, F1-score, and area under the ROC curve (AUC-ROC) are commonly used to evaluate model performance (Dal Pozzolo et al., 2015). More sophisticated applications also rely on precision-recall curves, which provide more informative evaluations in skewed datasets.

Another concern is data privacy and regulatory compliance, particularly under laws like GDPR, which require explainability and data minimization. Thus, model deployment in real-world fraud detection must not only optimize for accuracy but also satisfy constraints related to transparency, auditability, and legal accountability.

In summary, while ML and deep learning techniques have markedly improved the effectiveness of fraud detection systems, their lack of transparency remains a central limitation. Hybrid models and the incorporation of XAI techniques present a promising way forward, balancing performance with interpretability in high-stakes financial environments.

14.4 THE ROLE OF XAI IN ENHANCING TRANSPARENCY AND COMPLIANCE

As AI becomes integral to financial fraud detection, concerns about the interpretability and accountability of these models have intensified. Regulatory bodies and stakeholders increasingly demand transparent decision-making processes that can be understood, audited, and contested. This section explores how XAI can address these demands by improving model transparency, enhancing regulatory compliance, and fostering stakeholder trust in AI-driven fraud detection systems.

14.4.1 The transparency gap in AI-driven fraud detection

Traditional fraud detection systems have long depended on deterministic, rule-based algorithms that prioritize transparency over sophistication. These systems, while easy to interpret and audit, often fail to adapt to evolving fraud patterns, particularly in the face of increasingly complex financial manipulations. In contrast, ML and deep learning approaches offer enhanced predictive accuracy by identifying hidden patterns in high-dimensional datasets. However, they frequently function as "black boxes," meaning their internal reasoning remains opaque to users, including auditors, compliance officers, and regulators (Burrell, 2016). This opacity raises substantial concerns in the accounting domain, where accountability and the ability to justify decisions are non-negotiable.

The issue extends beyond the realm of technical interpretability. Transparency in AI-driven fraud detection is a socio-technical imperative, encompassing explainability, traceability, and auditability across the entire model lifecycle (Anjomshoae et al., 2019). Explainability refers to the capacity to make model decisions understandable to human stakeholders. Traceability ensures that model development, training data, and decision pathways can be reconstructed, while auditability implies that decisions made by the system can be independently verified and scrutinized. Together, these dimensions form the basis of what might be termed operational trustworthiness.

The integration of XAI methodologies serves to bridge this transparency gap. By offering post-hoc interpretability through tools like SHAP or LIME, or by designing inherently interpretable models, XAI enables stakeholders to comprehend not just the outcome of an AI system but the rationale behind it. This understanding is particularly critical in fraud detection, where alerts must be defensible under regulatory scrutiny and subject to expert interpretation.

Ultimately, the legitimacy of AI-driven systems in financial contexts hinges on their transparency. Without it, organizations risk deploying technically powerful yet socially and legally fragile systems. The challenge lies not only in making AI accurate but in making it accountable.

14.4.2 Regulatory pressures and the need for explainability

The evolving regulatory environment increasingly challenges the deployment of opaque AI systems, especially in high-stakes domains like financial fraud detection. The European Union's GDPR explicitly introduces a "right to explanation," which requires organizations to provide meaningful clarifications to individuals impacted by algorithmic decisions (Wachter, Mittelstadt, & Floridi, 2017). This provision reflects broader societal concerns about fairness, accountability, and transparency in automated decision-making. Parallel regulatory bodies in the financial sector, such as the U.S. Securities and

Exchange Commission (SEC) and the European Banking Authority (EBA), have also prioritized robust model governance, rigorous validation processes, and transparency standards for AI-driven tools (EBA, 2021).

In fraud detection, these regulatory imperatives translate into a mandate that models not only identify anomalous or suspicious transactions but do so with a degree of explainability sufficient to withstand scrutiny from auditors, regulators, and legal authorities. This requirement extends beyond technical accuracy to encompass the ability to produce human-understandable justifications for alerts. XAI plays a critical role here by generating interpretable rationales, which can be embedded in audit trails, compliance documentation, and regulatory filings. Such explainability is essential for ensuring that AI systems remain accountable and that their outputs can be reliably interpreted and challenged when necessary.

For example, in an audit context, if an AI model flags unusual revenue recognition, it must also clearly identify the key drivers behind this decision—such as atypical transaction timing, unusual patterns in related-party dealings, or discrepancies in financial ratios—and describe their relative impact on the model's output. This granular insight enables auditors to investigate effectively and regulators to assess the model's validity. Without such transparency, institutions risk non-compliance, reputational damage, and potential legal penalties.

Thus, regulatory pressure is not merely pushing for AI adoption but demanding responsible AI deployment. Explainability is no longer optional but a regulatory necessity that ensures AI technologies contribute to trustworthy and transparent financial governance.

14.4.3 XAI techniques for enhancing interpretability in practice

A variety of XAI techniques have been proposed and applied to financial fraud detection systems. These techniques can be grouped into intrinsic interpretability and post-hoc explainability.

Intrinsic interpretability is found in models that are inherently transparent. Examples include decision trees, logistic regression, and rule-based classifiers. These models are often preferred in regulated environments because their logic can be directly examined and validated (Doshi-Velez & Kim, 2017). However, their accuracy may be limited in capturing complex patterns associated with sophisticated fraud.

Post-hoc explainability, on the other hand, applies to black-box models and seeks to make their outputs interpretable after the fact. The two most prominent techniques in this category are:

- **LIME (Local Interpretable Model-agnostic Explanations)**: This technique approximates the behavior of complex models locally around a specific prediction by using interpretable surrogate models (Ribeiro,

Singh, & Guestrin, 2016). It helps financial analysts understand why a particular transaction was classified as fraudulent.
- **SHAP (SHapley Additive exPlanations)**: Based on cooperative game theory, SHAP assigns each feature a contribution score toward the prediction, offering global and local interpretability (Lundberg & Lee, 2017). For instance, SHAP can reveal that a sudden spike in accounts receivable was the most significant factor influencing a fraud alert.

These tools have been increasingly adopted in audit and fraud analytics dashboards to generate explanations accessible to both technical teams and financial auditors (Kokina et al., 2025). By integrating these tools into decision-making systems, organizations can meet both internal governance needs and external compliance demands.

14.4.4 Benefits of XAI for financial fraud ecosystems

The integration of XAI into fraud detection frameworks offers multiple strategic advantages that address both technical and organizational challenges in financial auditing.

First, improved auditability is a fundamental benefit. Models equipped with explanation capabilities allow auditors to trace the provenance of flagged anomalies and assess the rationale behind decisions more effectively (Bussmann et al., 2021). This traceability enhances the robustness of external audits by providing transparent evidence trails, which are critical in regulatory investigations and legal contexts.

Second, enhanced trust and adoption of AI systems arise from their interpretability. Users, including auditors and accountants, tend to trust AI outputs when the decision-making processes are intelligible and justifiable. This trust is especially crucial in financial settings where professionals bear legal and ethical responsibilities for their judgments and must explain these to regulators and stakeholders (Arrieta et al., 2020). Explainable models thus bridge the gap between automated predictions and human accountability.

Third, XAI contributes to ethical AI deployment by exposing and mitigating algorithmic biases inherent in financial data or model design. For example, if a fraud detection system disproportionately flags transactions associated with specific demographics or geographic regions, methods like SHAP can highlight these biases, enabling corrective actions to ensure fairness and regulatory compliance (Kleinberg et al., 2018). This transparency is essential for maintaining ethical standards and avoiding discriminatory practices.

Finally, XAI supports facilitated training and human-AI collaboration. Explanation outputs serve as educational tools for human decision-makers, improving their understanding of complex patterns and enhancing organizational learning. This collaborative synergy improves fraud investigations by integrating human expertise with AI insights, leading to more accurate and informed outcomes (Anjomshoae et al., 2019).

In sum, the adoption of XAI not only enhances technical performance but also fosters audit transparency, user trust, ethical responsibility, and effective human-machine cooperation in financial fraud detection.

14.5 CHALLENGES AND LIMITATIONS

While XAI holds significant theoretical promise, its real-world impact in financial auditing depends on effective integration. Empirical studies highlight its use in fraud detection, audit support, and enhancing decision transparency, employing tools like LIME and SHAP. However, these explanation methods are approximations and may not fully reflect complex model internals (Slack et al., 2020). Moreover, technically accurate explanations can be challenging for non-experts to interpret, illustrating the interpretability-accuracy trade-off. XAI techniques are also vulnerable to manipulation through adversarial examples, and regulatory standards for "sufficient explanations" remain unclear and inconsistent across sectors.

14.5.1 XAI in automated fraud detection systems

Transactional fraud detection has been one of the earliest and most impactful domains for the adoption of XAI within accounting and financial auditing. Early research by Ribeiro et al. (2016) pioneered the use of the LIME technique to demystify decisions made by black-box classifiers designed to identify anomalous banking transactions. Their study revealed that domain experts were significantly more inclined to trust and act upon AI-generated alerts when these were accompanied by clear, feature-based explanations. LIME, by generating local surrogate models, could highlight the key attributes driving a model's prediction. For instance, it might show that a flagged transaction was suspicious due to an unusually high frequency of vendor interactions or because it occurred during atypical late-night hours, rather than being a random output of an inscrutable model. This level of interpretability was essential in financial contexts where auditors and compliance officers require concrete evidence to justify further investigation or regulatory reporting.

Extending this work, Lundberg et al. (2020) demonstrated the application of SHAP in financial transaction monitoring, using real banking datasets to provide deeper insights into model behavior. SHAP values quantify the marginal contribution of each feature—such as transaction amount, customer risk scores, or geographic location—to the overall prediction of fraud risk. This granular attribution allowed auditors to understand which variables most strongly influenced a flagged alert, facilitating faster and more targeted investigations. Moreover, by incorporating SHAP-based explanations into compliance documentation, organizations improved transparency and met regulatory expectations for model governance and accountability. The ability to generate interpretable rationales thus not only increased operational efficiency but also enhanced regulatory trust.

Together, these foundational studies highlight several key advantages of integrating XAI in fraud detection systems. First, they improve human-AI collaboration by providing auditors with intelligible insights that support informed decision-making rather than mere black-box outputs. Second, they strengthen the defensibility of AI-based decisions in legal and regulatory contexts, addressing concerns about the "black box" nature of advanced ML models. Third, they foster organizational learning by making fraud patterns and detection logic more accessible to human experts, which can lead to improved rule design and refinement of detection strategies.

These early applications have set a precedent for the broader financial sector, illustrating how XAI can reconcile the need for high predictive accuracy with the imperative of transparency and accountability. As financial institutions increasingly rely on AI-driven systems to manage fraud risk, the adoption of interpretable models will be crucial in maintaining stakeholder trust, ensuring regulatory compliance, and ultimately safeguarding the integrity of financial markets.

14.5.2 Use of XAI in auditing and financial statement analysis

Kokina et al. (2025) investigate the current landscape of AI adoption in auditing within large public accounting firms, revealing a notable gap between the prevalent use of simple AI tools and the limited integration of more complex, advanced systems. Their qualitative study, based on 22 in-depth interviews with auditing professionals, uncovers critical challenges impeding the broader adoption of sophisticated AI applications. Among these challenges, explainability stands out as a primary concern; auditors require clear, interpretable reasoning from AI models to justify decisions and comply with regulatory standards. Additionally, AI bias and data privacy issues present significant ethical and operational hurdles. For instance, biased algorithms may unfairly flag certain clients or transactions, while stringent privacy regulations restrict access to comprehensive datasets necessary for effective model training. Kokina et al. (2025) emphasize the need for cross-disciplinary solutions that combine technical innovation with organizational change management to foster successful AI implementation in auditing.

Complementing these insights, Lou, Caruana, and Gehrke (2012) contribute to the field by demonstrating the practical viability of interpretable surrogate models in auditing contexts. Their work centers on Generalized Additive Models (GAMs), which balance transparency and predictive accuracy by modeling the effect of each variable additively, thereby making the decision process more understandable to human users. Through empirical evaluations, they show that GAMs can achieve competitive accuracy relative to deep learning techniques, which are often criticized for their opacity. In a corporate auditing case study, GAMs enabled compliance teams to directly validate risk classification logic against established accounting policies, ensuring that AI-driven classifications aligned with regulatory and internal control frameworks. This approach not only supports auditability but also strengthens trust and acceptance among practitioners, regulators, and clients.

Together, these studies highlight the dual imperative of advancing AI capabilities while preserving interpretability in auditing. The findings by Kokina et al. (2025) underscore organizational and ethical challenges, while Lou, Caruana, and Gehrke (2012) demonstrate that interpretable models can meet performance expectations without sacrificing transparency. Addressing these challenges will require ongoing research and collaboration across AI development, auditing practice, and regulatory oversight to realize AI's full potential as a trustworthy decision-support tool in financial auditing.

14.5.3 Challenges in practical implementation

Despite significant advances in XAI applications within accounting and auditing, implementing these techniques in real-world accounting environments presents substantial challenges. One core issue arises from the inherent contextual ambiguity of accounting data. Accounting concepts such as "accrued expenses" or "deferred revenue" are not universally fixed but often vary in meaning and treatment across different industries, firms, or even departments within the same organization (Binns et al., 2018). This variability complicates the development of explanation tools because generic explanations may misrepresent domain-specific semantics, leading to misunderstandings or misclassifications. Consequently, effective XAI implementations must be fine-tuned and calibrated to the precise semantic and procedural norms of the relevant accounting context, ensuring that explanations resonate accurately with domain experts.

Another significant challenge concerns user misinterpretation of explanations. Research by Slack et al. (2020) reveals that users—particularly those with limited AI literacy—may overtrust explanation outputs or mistakenly attribute causal significance to features that are merely correlated with outcomes. In accounting and auditing settings, where professionals often have limited formal training in ML or AI methodologies, this risk of cognitive bias is amplified. Such misinterpretations can lead to flawed audit judgments or misplaced confidence in automated alerts. To address this, many organizations have begun pairing XAI tools with dedicated training modules designed to enhance auditors' understanding of model logic and the inherent limitations of explanation techniques. These educational interventions emphasize critical scrutiny, ensuring users appreciate that explanations do not guarantee causality and should be interpreted cautiously.

A further complicating factor is regulatory opacity surrounding AI explainability requirements. While regulatory bodies increasingly advocate for transparency and accountability in AI-driven financial processes, there remains no universally accepted standard for what constitutes an "adequate" explanation within accounting and auditing contexts (Wachter, Mittelstadt, & Floridi, 2017). This lack of consensus complicates compliance efforts and creates inconsistencies across firms, jurisdictions, and regulatory regimes. Organizations often struggle to balance regulatory expectations with operational realities, particularly when vague or evolving guidelines leave room for interpretation.

The banking sector, given its stringent regulatory environment and wealth of transactional data, offers fertile ground for empirical XAI applications. Bussmann, Giudici, and Marinelli (2021) conducted a study on the deployment of XAI techniques in European banks' anti-money laundering (AML) and fraud detection systems. They found that institutions integrating SHAP- and LIME-based explanations within transaction monitoring workflows experienced improved acceptance from regulators, especially when explanations were explicitly linked to established business logic frameworks, such as Know Your Customer (KYC) compliance rules. These banks reported not only heightened regulator confidence but also operational benefits, including lower false-positive rates and reduced durations for case investigations. This empirical evidence underscores the practical value of context-aware XAI in enhancing both regulatory compliance and operational efficiency in high-stakes financial environments.

In summary, despite its transformative potential, the integration of XAI in accounting faces multifaceted challenges involving data semantics, user interpretation, and regulatory clarity. Addressing these requires a holistic approach combining technical refinement, user education, and evolving regulatory standards tailored to the complexity of financial domains.

14.6 FUTURE RESEARCH AND POLICY DIRECTIONS

Despite growing scholarly attention to XAI in financial fraud detection, substantial research gaps persist that must be addressed to unlock its full potential. This section outlines six interconnected themes critical for advancing the field: the tension between model fidelity and interpretability, the need for domain-specific explanations, regulatory harmonization, human-AI interaction in audit contexts, emerging ethical challenges, and the evaluation of longitudinal effectiveness in dynamic fraud environments.

A longstanding challenge in XAI concerns the trade-off between model accuracy (fidelity) and interpretability. Highly complex models, such as deep neural networks, often excel at detecting subtle, sophisticated fraud patterns but lack inherent transparency (Guidotti et al., 2018). Surrogate models—like decision trees designed to approximate neural network decisions—can offer post-hoc explanations but risk distorting the original decision logic, potentially misleading auditors or compliance officers (Slack et al., 2020).

Future research must focus on developing hybrid approaches that maintain strong predictive performance without compromising the fidelity of explanations. Promising directions include the integration of attention mechanisms within inherently interpretable architectures, such as explainable transformers, which can highlight key decision factors while preserving accuracy (Li et al., 2023).

Current XAI techniques are predominantly general-purpose and model-agnostic, often overlooking the unique semantic and procedural contexts of financial reporting, auditing standards, and accounting principles. Moving beyond generic feature importance rankings, future work should prioritize domain-adapted explanation frameworks tailored specifically to frameworks such as International Financial Reporting Standards (IFRS), audit assertions, and forensic accounting indicators. For example, a fraud detection model targeting earnings manipulation could present its rationale using well-understood constructs like the Beneish M-score or accrual-based indicators (Perols, 2011). Such development requires close collaboration between accounting scholars and computer scientists to embed accounting logic directly into explanation pipelines, ensuring explanations resonate meaningfully with practitioners.

As regulatory scrutiny over AI systems intensifies worldwide, harmonizing standards for explainability in financial applications emerges as a critical research priority. Existing guidelines, such as the EU's AI Act and the OECD's AI principles, remain high-level and non-specific, leaving ambiguity around what constitutes a "sufficient" explanation in regulated audit and fraud investigation settings (Wachter et al., 2017). Engaging regulators—including bodies like the Public Company Accounting Oversight Board (PCAOB) and the International Federation of Accountants (IFAC)—to co-develop audit-ready explanation templates that meet legal, ethical, and procedural criteria will be essential.

Human auditors and AI systems are often studied in isolation, yet future research must explore their interactive dynamics. Understanding how auditors interpret, negotiate, and act upon XAI-generated explanations in real-time is crucial. Key questions include how auditors reconcile discrepancies between their professional judgment and AI outputs, and under which circumstances explanations bolster or undermine trust. Experimental and ethnographic research within audit firms could uncover insights into cognitive load management, confirmation bias, and the delegation of responsibility within AI-augmented workflows (Kokina & Davenport, 2017).

While XAI promises to mitigate AI opacity, it also raises new ethical concerns. Explanation outputs can be selectively presented or manipulated, potentially perpetuating bias or discrimination (Binns et al., 2018). Moreover, disclosing sensitive financial thresholds through explanations risks enabling fraudsters to evade detection. Research should investigate the tension between transparency and security, developing differential explanation frameworks that vary in granularity depending on user roles—distinguishing, for example, between auditors and external stakeholders.

Finally, fraud evolves continually in response to detection mechanisms, regulations, and market shifts. Yet most XAI studies focus on static, historical datasets without accounting for adaptive fraud tactics. Longitudinal research is required to evaluate how explainable models perform over time, particularly in the presence of concept drift or data poisoning attacks. Simulated environments or digital twins of audit systems offer promising platforms to test and refine adaptive learning strategies in fraud detection (van Vlasselaer et al., 2016).

In conclusion, the research agenda for XAI in financial fraud detection must be both methodologically innovative and practically relevant. Success will be measured not only by advances in technical performance but also by the ability to support human decision-making, promote ethical AI use, and align with evolving accounting and auditing standards. Realizing the promise of XAI demands a multidisciplinary, policy-engaged effort to develop sustainable tools that enhance transparency, trust, and compliance within complex financial ecosystems.

14.7 CONCLUSION

This chapter has examined the pivotal role of XAI in enhancing transparency and compliance in financial fraud detection systems. The literature reveals that while ML and deep learning models have substantially improved the accuracy of fraud detection, their lack of interpretability has hindered regulatory acceptance and auditor trust. XAI addresses this shortcoming by offering insights into model decision-making, thereby promoting accountability, regulatory compliance, and user trust.

We explored the evolution of XAI tools and techniques, categorizing them into model-specific and model-agnostic approaches, each with its own merits and limitations. In reviewing empirical applications, we found that XAI enhances auditor understanding, facilitates regulatory reviews, and contributes to more defensible decisions. Furthermore, emerging hybrid systems that blend symbolic reasoning with deep learning architectures present a promising pathway to balance predictive performance with explainability.

However, the adoption of XAI is not without its challenges. Concerns about model fidelity, explanation robustness, user comprehension, and ethical risks persist. Moreover, a fragmented regulatory landscape and the absence of domain-specific explanation frameworks further impede its widespread use in financial contexts.

To address these issues, we identified six promising research avenues: (1) enhancing the fidelity of interpretable models, (2) developing domain-aware explanation systems, (3) aligning explanations with regulatory requirements, (4) improving human-AI collaboration in audit settings, (5) tackling ethical concerns in explanation generation, and (6) assessing long-term model resilience to evolving fraud strategies.

In sum, XAI has the potential to transform fraud detection by making AI systems not only smarter but also more transparent and accountable. Realizing this potential will require coordinated efforts across technical, regulatory, and organizational domains.

REFERENCES

ACFE. (2022). Report to the Nations: Global Study on Occupational Fraud and Abuse. Association of Certified Fraud Examiners.

Adadi, A., & Berrada, M. (2018). Peeking inside the black-box: A survey on Explainable Artificial Intelligence (XAI). IEEE Access, 6, 52138–52160. https://doi.org/10.1109/ACCESS.2018.2870052

Aleskerov, E., Freisleben, B., & Rao, B. (1997). CARDWATCH: A neural network-based database mining system for credit card fraud detection. Proceedings of the IEEE/IAFE 1997 Computational Intelligence for Financial Engineering, 220–226. https://www.semanticscholar.org/paper/CARDWATCH%3A-a-neural-network-based-database-mining-Aleskerov-Freisleben/a23936cb1af6ef77068c45807b534b729fcc9036

Anjomshoae, S., Najjar, A., Calvaresi, D., & Främling, K. (2019). Explainable agents and robots: Results from a systematic literature review. Proceedings of the 18th International Conference on Autonomous Agents and Multiagent Systems (AAMAS), 1078–1088. https://www.ifaamas.org/Proceedings/aamas2019/pdfs/p1078.pdf

Arrieta, A. B., Díaz-Rodríguez, N., Del Ser, J., et al. (2020). Explainable Artificial Intelligence (XAI): Concepts, taxonomies, opportunities and challenges toward responsible AI. Information Fusion, 58, 82–115. https://doi.org/10.1016/j.inffus.2019.12.012

Bahnsen, A. C., Aouada, D., Stojanovic, J., & Ottersten, B. (2016). Feature engineering strategies for credit card fraud detection. Expert Systems with Applications, 51, 134–142.

Beasley, M. S. (1996). An empirical analysis of the relation between the board of director composition and financial statement fraud. The Accounting Review, 71(4), 443–465.

Benarbi, M. A., & Benhayoun, I. (2026). Lexicometric and sentiment-based insights into risk allocation: A qualitative study of Moroccan public–private–partnership projects. Journal of Risk and Financial Management, 19(1), 30. https://doi.org/10.3390/jrfm19010030

Benhayoun, I., & Zejjari, I. (2024). Individual determinants of IFRS for SMEs adoption intention in Morocco - A SEM analysis. In A. Hamdan, & U. Braendle, Harnessing AI, Machine Learning, and IoT for Intelligent Business (Studies in Systems, Decision and Control ed., Vol. 550, pp. 67-77). London: Springer, Cham. doi:10.1007/978-3-031-66218-8_5

Benhayoun, I., & Zejjari, I. (2025). Investigating micro-level determinants of IFRS for SMEs prospective adoption in emerging economies – evidence from Morocco. Journal of Accounting in Emerging Economies, In Press. https://doi.org/10.1108/JAEE-06-2024-0283

Benhayoun, I., Bougrine, S., & Saissoui, A. (2025). Readiness for Artificial Intelligence adoption by auditors in emerging countries - A PLS-SEM analysis of Moroccan firms. Journal of Financial Reporting and Accounting, 23(4): 1486–1508. https://doi.org/10.1108/JFRA-07-2024-0448

Binns, R., Veale, M., Van Kleek, M., & Shadbolt, N. (2018). "It's reducing a human being to a percentage": Perceptions of justice in algorithmic decisions.

Proceedings of the 2018 CHI Conference on Human Factors in Computing Systems, 377:1–377:14. https://doi.org/10.1145/3173574.3173951.
Burrell, J. (2016). How the machine "thinks": Understanding opacity in machine learning algorithms. Big Data & Society, 3(1), 1–12.
Bussmann, N., Giudici, P., & Marinelli, D. (2021). Explainable AI in credit risk management. Computational Economics, 57(1), 203–216.
Carcillo, F., Dal Pozzolo, A., Le Borgne, Y. A., Caelen, O., Mazzer, Y., & Bontempi, G. (2021). Combining unsupervised and supervised learning in credit card fraud detection. Information Sciences, 557, 317–331.
Chen, T., & Guestrin, C. (2016). XGBoost: A scalable tree boosting system. In Proceedings of the 22nd ACM SIGKDD International Conference on Knowledge Discovery and Data Mining, 785–794. https://doi.org/10.1145/2939672.2939785
Dal Pozzolo, A., Boracchi, G., Caelen, O., Alippi, C., & Bontempi, G. (2015). Credit card fraud detection: A realistic modeling and a novel learning strategy. IEEE Transactions on Neural Networks and Learning Systems, 29(8), 3784–3797.
Deng, A., & Hooi, B. (2021). Graph neural network-based anomaly detection in multivariate time series. Proceedings of the 30th ACM International Conference on Information & Knowledge Management, 1195–1204. https://doi.org/10.48550/arXiv.2106.06947
Doshi-Velez, F., & Kim, B. (2017). Towards a rigorous science of interpretable machine learning. arXiv preprint arXiv:1702.08608.
Doshi-Velez, F., & Kim, B. (2018). Towards a rigorous science of interpretable machine learning. In Proceedings of the 2nd Workshop on Fairness, Accountability, and Transparency in Machine Learning (FAT/ML). https://arxiv.org/abs/1702.08608
EBA. (2021). Report on the use of machine learning in credit institutions. European Banking Authority. https://www.eba.europa.eu/sites/default/files/document_library/Publications/Reports/2023/1061483/Follow-up%20report%20on%20machine%20learning%20for%20IRB%20models.pdf
Guidotti, R., Monreale, A., Ruggieri, S., et al. (2018). A survey of methods for explaining black box models. ACM Computing Surveys, 51(5), 1–42.
Gunning, D., & Aha, D. (2019). DARPA's Explainable Artificial Intelligence (XAI) Program. AI Magazine, 40(2), 44–58.
Jurgovsky, J., Granitzer, M., Ziegler, K., Calabretto, S., Portier, P. E., He-Guelton, L., & Caelen, O. (2018). Sequence classification for credit-card fraud detection. Expert Systems with Applications, 100, 234–245.
Kleinberg, J., Mullainathan, S., & Raghavan, M. (2018). Inherent trade-offs in the fair determination of risk scores. Proceedings of the ACM Conference on Innovations in Theoretical Computer Science (ITCS), 43:1–43:23. https://doi.org/10.48550/arXiv.1609.05807
Kokina, J., & Davenport, T. H. (2017). The emergence of artificial intelligence: How automation Is changing auditing. Journal of Emerging Technologies in Accounting, 14, 115–122. https://doi.org/10.2308/jeta-51730
Kokina, J., Blanchette, S., Davenport, T. H., & Pachamanova, D. (2025). Challenges and opportunities for artificial intelligence in auditing: Evidence from the field. International Journal of Accounting Information Systems, 56, 100734. https://doi.org/10.1016/j.accinf.2025.100734
Kou, Y., Lu, C. T., Sirwongwattana, S., & Huang, Y. P. (2021). Survey of fraud detection techniques. Computer Science Review, 39, 100406.
Lenka, D. R., Dahe, S. V., Antico, O., Sahoo, P., Prescott, A. R., Muqit, M. M. K., & Kumar, A. (2024). Additional feedforward mechanism of Parkin activation via binding of phospho-UBL and RING0 in trans. eLife, 13, RP96699. https://doi.org/10.7554/eLife.96699
Li, Z., Li, S., & Yan, X. (2023). Time Series as Images: Vision Transformer for Irregularly Sampled Time Series. arXiv:2303.12799v2 [cs.LG] 30 Oct 2023.

Lou, Y., Caruana, R., & Gehrke, J. (2012). Intelligible models for classification and regression. In Proceedings of the 18th ACM SIGKDD International Conference on Knowledge Discovery and Data Mining, 150–158. https://doi.org/10.1145/2339530.2339556

Lundberg, S. M., Erion, G. G., Chen, H., et al. (2020). From local explanations to global understanding with explainable AI for trees. Nature Machine Intelligence, 2(1), 252–257.

Lundberg, S. M., & Lee, S.-I. (2017). A unified approach to interpreting model predictions. In Proceedings of the 31st Conference on Neural Information Processing Systems (NeurIPS), 4765–4774. https://doi.org/10.48550/arXiv.1705.07874

Molnar, C. (2022). Interpretable Machine Learning: A Guide for Making Black Box Models Explainable (2nd ed.). Leanpub.

Ngai, E. W. T., Hu, Y., Wong, Y. H., Chen, Y., & Sun, X. (2011). The application of data mining techniques in financial fraud detection: A classification framework and an academic review of literature. Decision Support Systems, 50(3), 559–569.

Oguntimilehin, A., Ngaikedi, F., Atachin, A. J., Toyin, O., Ogundipe, A. T., & Mebawondu, J. O. (2024). Financial fraud detection model using recurrent neural network. In 2024 IEEE 5th International Conference on Electro-Computing Technologies for Humanity (NIGERCON). IEEE. https://doi.org/10.1109/NIGERCON62786.2024.10927232

Perols, J. (2011). Financial statement fraud detection: An analysis of statistical and machine learning algorithms. Auditing: A Journal of Practice & Theory, 30(2), 19–50.

Power, M. (2007). Organized Uncertainty: Designing a World of Risk Management. Oxford University Press.

Rezaee, Z. (2005). Causes, consequences, and deterrence of financial statement fraud. Critical Perspectives on Accounting, 16(3), 277–298.

Ribeiro, M. T., Singh, S., & Guestrin, C. (2016). "Why should I trust you?": Explaining the predictions of any classifier. In Proceedings of the 22nd ACM SIGKDD International Conference on Knowledge Discovery and Data Mining, 1135–1144. https://doi.org/10.1145/2939672.2939778

Rudin, C. (2019). Stop explaining black box machine learning models for high stakes decisions and use interpretable models instead. Nature Machine Intelligence, 1(5), 206–215. https://doi.org/10.1038/s42256-019-0048-x

Skousen, C. J., Smith, K. R., & Wright, C. J. (2009). Detecting and predicting financial statement fraud: The effectiveness of the fraud triangle and SAS No. 99. Corporate Governance and Firm Performance, 13(2), 53–81.

Slack, D., Hilgard, S., Jia, E., Singh, S., & Lakkaraju, H. (2020). Fooling LIME and SHAP: Adversarial attacks on post hoc explanation methods. In Proceedings of the AAAI/ACM Conference on AI, Ethics, and Society, 180–186. https://doi.org/10.1145/3375627.3375830

van Vlasselaer, V., Eliassi-Rad, T., Akoglu, L., et al. (2016). GOTCHA! Network-based fraud detection for social security fraud. Management Science, 63(9), 3090–3110.

Wachter, S., Mittelstadt, B., & Floridi, L. (2017). Why a right to explanation of automated decision-making does not exist in the General Data Protection Regulation. International Data Privacy Law, 7(2), 76–99.

West, D. (2000). Neural network credit scoring models. Computers & Operations Research, 27(11–12), 1131–1152.

Index

Note: *Italicized* page numbers indicate figures, while **bold** page numbers indicate tables.

D

F

S

T

For Product Safety Concerns and Information please contact our EU
representative GPSR@taylorandfrancis.com
Taylor & Francis Verlag GmbH, Kaufingerstraße 24, 80331 München, Germany

www.ingramcontent.com/pod-product-compliance
Ingram Content Group UK Ltd.
Pitfield, Milton Keynes, MK11 3LW, UK
UKHW021514250926
475702UK00043B/495

* 9 7 8 1 0 4 1 0 9 5 5 9 0 *